SICK!

*Diseases and
Disorders,
Injuries and
Infections*

SICK!

Diseases and Disorders, Injuries and Infections

volume

2

D to **H**

**David Newton,
Donna Olendorf,
Christine Jeryan,
Karen Boyden,
Editors**

AN IMPRINT OF THE GALE GROUP

DETROIT · SAN FRANCISCO · LONDON
BOSTON · WOODBRIDGE, CT

Sick!

Diseases and Disorders, Injuries and Infections

David Newton, Donna Olendorf, Christine Jeryan, Karen Boyden, Editors

STAFF

Christine Slovey, *U·X·L Editor*

Carol DeKane Nagel, *U·X·L Managing Editor*

Meggin Condino, *Senior Analyst, New Product Development*

Thomas L. Romig, *U·X·L Publisher*

Shalice Shah-Caldwell, *Permissions Specialist (Pictures)*

Rita Wimberley, *Senior Buyer*

Evi Seoud, *Assistant Production Manager*

Dorothy Maki, *Manufacturing Manager*

Mary Beth Trimper, *Production Director*

Robert Duncan, *Imaging Specialist*

Michelle Di Mercurio, *Senior Art Director*

GGS Information Services, Inc., *Typesetting*

Michelle Cadoree, *Indexer*

Cover illustration by Kevin Ewing Illustrations.

Library of Congress Cataloging-in-Publication Data

Sick! diseases and disorders, injuries and infections/ David E. Newton...[et al.].

   p. cm.

Includes bibliographical references and indexes.

Summary: Presents articles describing the causes and symptoms, diagnosis, treatment (both traditional and alternative), prognosis, and prevention of various diseases, disorders, injuries, and infections.

   ISBN 0-7876-3922-2 (set)

   1. Diseases—Encyclopedias, Juvenile. [1. Health—Encyclopedias. 2.Diseases—Encyclopedias.] I.Newton, David E.

R130.5 .S53 1999

616'.003–dc21

99-044739

ISBN 0-7876-3922-2 (set)
ISBN 0-7876-3923-0 (vol. 1)
ISBN 0-7876-3924-9 (vol. 2)
ISBN 0-7876-3925-7 (vol. 3)
ISBN 0-7876-3926-5 (vol. 4)

Printed in United States of America
10 9 8 7 6 5 4 3 2

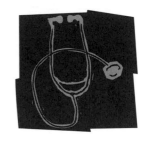

Contents

VOLUME 2: D–H

VOLUME 3: I–P

VOLUME 4: R–Z

contents

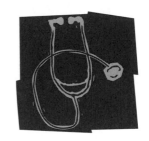

Reader's Guide

Sick! Diseases and Disorders, Injuries and Infections presents the latest information on 140 wide-ranging illnesses, disorders, and injuries. Included are entries on familiar medical problems readers might encounter in daily life, such as acne, asthma, chickenpox, cancer, and learning disorders. Some rare and fascinating illnesses are covered as well, such as smallpox, hantaviruses, and Creutzfeld Jakob disease (also known as mad cow disease).

Entries are arranged alphabetically across the four-volume set and generally range from three to eight pages in length. Each entry provides the details students need for reports and other health-related assignments under the following standard subheads: definition, description, causes, symptoms, diagnosis, treatment, prognosis, and prevention.

A "Words to Know" box included at the beginning of each entry provides definitions of words and terms used in that entry. Sidebars highlight interesting facts and individuals associated with the medical condition discussed. At the end of each entry, under the heading "For More Information," appears a list of sources for further information about the disease. The set has approximately 240 black-and-white photos. More than 80 images appear in color in an insert in each volume.

Each volume of *Sick!* begins with a comprehensive glossary collected from all the "Words to Know" boxes in the entries and a selection of research and activity ideas. Each volume ends with a general bibliography section listing comprehensive sources for studying medical conditions and a cumulative index providing access to all major terms and topics covered throughout *Sick!*

Related Reference Sources

Sick! is only one component of the three-part U•X•L Complete Health Resource. Other titles in this library include:

- *Body by Design:* This two-volume set presents the anatomy (structure) and physiology (function) of the human body in twelve chapters spread over two volumes. Each chapter is devoted to one of the eleven organ systems that make up the body. The last chapter focuses on the special senses, which allow humans to connect with the real world. Sidebar boxes present historical discoveries, recent medical advances, short biographies of scientists, and other interesting facts. More than 100 photos, many of them in color, illustrate the text.
- *Healthy Living:* This three-volume set examines fitness, nutrition, and other lifestyle issues across fifteen subject chapters. Topics covered include hygiene, mental health, preventive care, alternative medicine, and careers in health care. Sidebar boxes within entries provide information on related issues, while over 150 black-and-white illustrations help illuminate the text.

Acknowledgments

A note of appreciation is extended to U•X•L's Complete Health Resource advisors, who provided invaluable suggestions when this work was in its formative stages:

Carole Branson
Seminar Science Teacher
Wilson Middle School
San Diego, California

Bonnie L. Raasch
Media Specialist
Vernon Middle School
Marion, Iowa

Doris J. Ranke
Science Teacher
West Bloomfield High School
West Bloomfield, Michigan

Comments and Suggestions

We welcome your comments on *Sick! Diseases and Disorders, Injuries and Infections.* Please write: Editors, *Sick!,* U•X•L, 27500 Drake Rd., Farmington Hills, Michigan 48331–3535; call toll free: 1–800–877–4253; fax: 248–414–5043; or send e-mail via http://www.galegroup.com.

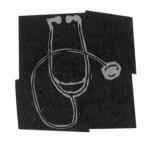

Please Read: Important Information

Sick! Diseases and Disorders, Injuries and Infections is a medical reference product designed to inform and educate readers about medical conditions. U•X•L believes this product to be comprehensive, but not necessarily definitive. While U•X•L has made substantial efforts to provide information that is accurate and up to date, U•X•L makes no representations or warranties of any kind, including without limitation, warranties of merchantability or fitness for a particular purpose, nor does it guarantee the accuracy, comprehensiveness, or timeliness of the information contained in this product.

Readers should be aware that the universe of medical knowledge is constantly growing and changing, and that differences of medical opinion exist among authorities. They are also advised to seek professional diagnosis and treatment for any medical condition, and to discuss information obtained from this book with their health care provider.

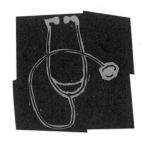

Words to Know

Diseases that are featured as main entries in *Sick!* are not covered in Words to Know.

A

Abortive: Describes an action that cuts something short or stops it.

Abscess: A pocket of infection within tissue.

Accommodation: The ability of the lens of the eye to change its shape in order to focus light waves from distant or near objects.

Acetylsalicylic acid: The chemical name for the primary compound from which aspirin is made. Shorthand terms for acetylsalicylic acid include acetylsalicylate, salicylic acid, and salicylate.

Acute: A disorder that comes on suddenly and usually does not last very long.

Acute retroviral syndrome: A group of symptoms resembling mononucleosis that are the first sign of HIV infection in 50 to 70 percent of all patients and in 45 to 90 percent of women.

Adenoid: A mass of lymph tissue located near the pharynx.

Adenoviruses: A group of viruses that usually cause infections of the lungs and ears.

African endemic Kaposi's sarcoma: A form of Kaposi's sarcoma that affects boys and men, has symptoms like those of classic Kaposi's sarcoma, and can spread rapidly and cause death.

Agoraphobia: A fear of open spaces.

AIDS dementia complex: A type of brain dysfunction caused by HIV infection that causes confusion, difficulty thinking, and loss of muscular coordination.

AIDS-related Kaposi's sarcoma: A form of Kaposi's sarcoma that occurs primarily in gay and bisexual men; it is much more dangerous than classic Kaposi's sarcoma.

Allergen: A substance that provokes an allergic response.

Allergic reaction: A series of events initiated by the immune system against substances that are normally harmless to the body.

Alveoli: Small air sacs at the ends of bronchioles through which oxygen passes from the lungs into blood.

Amalgam: A mixture of mercury, silver, and other metals used to make fillings for dental cavities.

Amenorrhea: Absence of menstrual periods.

Amnesia: Loss of memory sometimes caused by a brain injury, such as a concussion.

Amniocentesis: A medical procedure in which a sample of the fluid surrounding the fetus in a woman's womb is withdrawn and examined.

Amputation: A surgical procedure in which an arm, leg, hand, or foot is removed.

Anaphylaxis: An increased sensitivity to an allergen causing dilation (expansion) of blood vessels and tightening of muscles. Anaphylaxis can result in sharp drops in blood pressure, difficulty in breathing, and death if left untreated.

Androgen: A male sex hormone found in both males and females.

Anemia: A medical condition caused by a reduced number of red blood cells and characterized by general weakness, pale skin color, irregular heartbeat, shortness of breath, and fatigue.

Aneurysm: A weak spot in a blood vessel that may break open and lead to a stroke.

Angiography: A method for studying the structure of blood vessels by inserting a catheter into a vein or artery, injecting a dye in the blood vessel, and taking X-ray photographs of the structure.

Anti-androgen: A drug that slows down the production of androgens.

Antibiotic: A substance derived from bacteria or other organisms that fights the growth of other bacteria or organisms.

Antibody: Specific protein produced by the immune system to destroy specific invading organisms.

Anticoagulant: Describes a substance that prevents the blood from clotting.

Anticonvulsant medication: A drug used to prevent convulsions or seizures that is sometimes also effective in the treatment of bipolar disorder.

Antidepressant: A drug used to prevent or relieve depression.

Antigen: Any substance that stimulates the body to produce antibodies.

Antioxidant: A substance that prevents oxidation from taking place. Oxidation is a chemical reaction that can create heat, pain, and inflammation in the body.

Anxiety: Feeling troubled, uneasy, or worried.

Anxiety disorder: An experience of prolonged, excessive worry about the circumstances of one's life.

Aplastic: Having incomplete or faulty development.

Apnea: A temporary pause in one's breathing pattern. Sleep apnea consists of repeated episodes of temporary pauses in breathing during sleep.

Appendectomy: Surgical removal of the appendix.

Appendix: The worm-shaped pouch near the beginning of the large intestine.

Appetite suppressant: Drugs that decrease feelings of hunger and control appetite.

Aqueous humor: A watery fluid that fills the inside of the eyeball, providing nourishment to the eye and maintaining internal pressure in the eyeball.

Arteries: Blood vessels that carry blood from the heart to organs and tissues of the body.

Arteriosclerosis: Hardening of the arteries that can be caused by a variety of factors. Atherosclerosis is just one form of arteriosclerosis, but the two terms are often used interchangeably.

Artery: A blood vessel that carries blood from the heart to other parts of the body.

Arthrography: An imaging technique in which a dye is injected into a joint to make X-ray pictures of the inside of the joint easier to study.

Asperger syndrome: A type of autism that involves no problems with language.

Aspiration: Inhalation of food or saliva.

Astigmatism: A condition in which light from a single point fails to focus on a single point of the retina. The condition causes the patient to see a blurred image.

Ataxia: A condition in which balance and coordination are impaired.

Athetonia: A condition marked by slow, twisting, involuntary muscle movements.

Atopy: A condition in which people are more likely to develop allergic reactions, often because of the inflammation and airway narrowing typical of asthma.

Atrium: (plural: atria) One of the two upper chambers of the heart.

Audiometer: An instrument for testing a person's hearing.

Auditory nerve: A bunch of nerve fibers that carries sound from the inner ear to the brain.

Auditory canal: A tube that leads from the outside of the ear to the tympanic membrane.

Auricle: The external structure of the ear.

Autoimmunity: A condition in which the body's immune system produces antibodies in response to its own tissues or blood components instead of foreign particles or microorganisms.

Autonomic responses: Bodily responses that occur automatically, without the need for a person to think about it.

Autopsy: A medical examination of a dead body.

B

Bacillus Calmette-Guérin (BCG): A vaccine made from a weakened mycobacterium that infects cattle. It is used to protect humans against pulmonary tuberculosis and its complications.

Barium enema: A procedure in which a white liquid is injected into a patient's rectum in order to coat the lining of the colon so that X-ray photographs of the colon can be taken.

Becker muscular dystrophy (BMD): A type of muscular dystrophy that affects older boys and men and usually follows a milder course than Duchenne muscular dystrophy (DMD).

Benign: A growth that does not spread to other parts of the body, making recovery likely with treatment. Often used to describe noncancerous growths.

Binge: To consume large amounts of food without control in a short period of time.

Biofeedback: A technique in which a person learns to consciously control the body's response to a stimulus. Biofeedback enables a person to gain some control over involuntary body functions.

Biopsy: A procedure in which a small sample of tissue is removed and then studied under a microscope.

Blind spot: An area on the retina that is unable to respond to light rays.

Blood-brain barrier: A network of blood vessels between the neck and the brain that prevents many chemicals from passing into the brain.

Bone marrow: Soft, spongy material found in the center of bones from which blood cells are produced.

Bone marrow biopsy: A procedure by which a sample of bone marrow is removed and studied under a microscope.

Bone marrow transplantation: A process by which marrow is removed from the bones of a healthy donor and transferred to the bones of a person with some kind of blood disorder.

Bortadella pertussis: The bacterium that causes whooping cough.

Brain stem: A mass of nervous tissue that connects the forebrain and the cerebrum to the spinal cord.

Bronchi: Two large tubes that branch off the trachea and lead to the lungs; each tube is called a bronchus when referred to singularly. Also called bronchial tubes.

Bronchial tubes: Another name for bronchi. The major airways that lead to the lungs.

Bronchioles: Smaller extensions of the bronchi.

Bronchodilator: A substance that causes muscles in the respiratory system to relax, making breathing easier.

Bronchoscope: A device consisting of a long thin tube with a light and camera on the end for looking into a patient's airways and lungs.

BSA: Refers to "body surface area," a unit used in the treatment of burns to express the amount of the total body surface area covered by the burn.

C

C. botulinum: A very deadly bacteria that causes a disease known as botulism.

Calcium: An essential mineral with many important functions in the body, one of which is in the formation of bone.

Campylobacter jejuni (C. jejuni): A bacteria that is the leading cause of bacterial diarrhea in the United States. It occurs in healthy cattle, chickens, birds, and flies.

Carcinogen: Any substance capable of causing cancer.

Cardiovascular: A term that refers to the heart and blood system.

Carditis: Inflammation of the heart.

Caries: The medical term for tooth decay.

Carpal tunnel: A passageway in the wrist, created by bones and ligaments, through which the median nerve passes.

Carrier: A person whose body contains the organisms that cause a disease but who does not show symptoms of that disease.

Cartilage: Tough, elastic tissue that covers and protects the ends of bones.

Cataplexy: A sudden loss of muscular control that may cause a person to collapse.

Catatonic behavior: Behavior characterized by muscular tightness or rigidity and lack of response to the environment.

Catheter: A thin tube inserted into the patient's body, often into a vein or artery, to allow fluids to be sent into or taken out of the body.

Cavity: In dentistry, a hole or weak spot in tooth enamel caused by decay.

CD4: A type of protein molecule in human blood that is present on the surface of 65 percent of immune cells. The HIV virus infects cells that have CD4 surface proteins, and as a result, depletes the number of T cells, B cells, natural killer cells, and monocytes in the patient's blood. Most of the damage to an AIDS patient's immune system is done by the virus's destruction of CD4 lymphocytes.

Central nervous system: A system of nerve cells in the brain and the spinal cord.

Cephalosporin: A specific type of antibiotic used to treat many types of infections.

Cerebral thrombosis: Blockage of a blood vessel in the brain by a blood clot that formed in the brain itself.

Cerebral edema: Swelling of the brain caused by an accumulation of fluid.

Cerebral embolism: Blockage of a blood vessel in the brain by a blood clot that originally formed elsewhere in the body and then traveled to the brain.

Cerebrospinal fluid (CSF): Fluid made in chambers of the brain that flows over the surface of the brain and the spinal cord. CSF provides nutrients to cells of the nervous system and provides a cushion for the structures of the nervous system. It is often used to diagnose infections of the central nervous system (the brain and spinal cord).

Cerumen: Earwax.

Cervical traction: The process of using a mechanism to create a steady pull on the neck in order to keep it in the correct position while it heals.

CFTR: An abbreviation for cystic fibrosis transmembrane conductance regulator, a chemical that controls the amount of water in mucus.

Chelation therapy: Treatment with chemicals that bind to a poisonous metal and help the body quickly eliminate it.

Chemotherapy: A method of treating cancer using certain chemicals that can kill cancer cells.

Child abuse: Intentional harm done to infants and children, usually by parents or care givers.

Chlamydia: A family of microorganisms that causes several types of sexually transmitted diseases in humans.

Chloroquine: An antimalarial drug first used in the 1940s as a substitute for quinine, and still widely used in Africa because of its relatively low cost.

Cholesterol: A waxy substance produced by the body and used in a variety of ways.

Chorea: Involuntary movements that may cause the arms or legs to jerk about uncontrollably.

Chromosome: A structure located inside the nucleus (center) of a cell that carries genetic information.

Chronic: Recurring frequently or lasting a long time.

Cilia: Fine, hair-like projections that line the trachea and bronchi. Cilia wave back and forth, carrying mucus through the airways and clearing the airways of foreign materials.

Circadian rhythm: Any body pattern that follows a twenty-four-hour cycle, such as waking and sleeping.

Circumcision: The procedure in which the foreskin is removed from the penis.

Cirrhosis: A liver disorder caused by scarring of liver tissue.

Classic Kaposi's sarcoma: A form of Kaposi's sarcoma that usually affects older men of Mediterranean or eastern European background.

Clostridium tetani: The bacterium that causes tetanus.

Clonic phase: The stage of a grand mal seizure in which muscles alternately contract and relax.

Clotting factor: One of the chemicals necessary for blood clotting.

Cobb angle: A measure of the curvature of the spine, determined from measurements made on X-ray photographs.

Cognitive-behavioral therapy: A form of psychological counseling in which patients are helped to understand the nature of their disorder and reshape their environment to help them function better.

Colonoscopy: A procedure in which a long, thin tube is inserted through a patient's rectum into the colon to permit examination of the inner walls of the colon.

Colostomy: An opening created surgically that runs from the colon to the outside of the body to provide an alternative route for the evacuation of body wastes.

Comedo: A hard plug composed of sebum and dead skin cells that develops in the pores of the skin. The mildest form of acne.

Comedolytic: Drugs that break up comedos and open clogged pores.

Compulsion: A very strong urge to do or say something that usually cannot be resisted and is repeated again and again.

Computed tomography (CT) scan: A technique in which X-ray photographs of a particular part of the body are taken from different angles. The pictures are then fed into a computer that creates a single composite image of the internal (inside) part of the body. CT scans provide an important tool in the diagnosis of brain and spinal disorders, cancer, and other conditions.

Computerized axial tomography (CAT) scan: Another name for a computed tomography (CT) scan.

Condom: A thin sheath (covering) worn over the penis during sexual activity to prevent pregnancy and the spread of sexually transmitted diseases.

Conduct disorder: A behavioral and emotional disorder of childhood and adolescence. Children with a conduct disorder act inappropriately, infringe on the rights of others, and violate social rules.

Conductive hearing loss: Hearing loss that occurs in the external or middle ear.

Cone cells: Special cells in the retina responsible for color vision.

Congenital disorder: A medical condition that is present at birth.

Contact dermatitis: Inflammation of the skin caused by exposure to an allergen.

Contracture: A permanent shortening and tightening of a muscle or tendon causing a deformity.

Contrast hydrotherapy: A procedure in which a series of hot- and cold-water applications is applied to an injured area.

Contusion: A bruise.

Cornea: The transparent outer coating on the front of the eyeball.

Coronary: Referring to the heart.

Coronavirus: A type of virus that can cause the common cold.

Coxsackie virus: A virus that causes a disease known as herpangina.

Crabs: A slang term for pubic lice.

Crib death: Another name for sudden infant death syndrome.

Cryosurgery: The use of liquid nitrogen for the purpose of removing diseased tissue.

Cyanosis: A condition that develops when the body does not get enough oxygen, causing the skin to turn blue.

D

Debridement: The surgical removal of dead skin.

Decompression stops: Stops divers should make when returning to the surface to let the nitrogen in their blood dissolve safely out of their bodies. Charts developed by the U.S. Navy and other groups list the number of stops and the time to be spent at each stop.

Delusion: A fixed, false belief that is resistant to reason or factual disproof.

Dementia: Impaired intellectual function that interferes with normal social and work activities.

Densitometry: A technique for measuring the density of bone by taking photographs with low-energy X rays from a variety of angles around the bone.

Dentin: The middle layer of a tooth.

Dependence: A state in which a person requires a steady amount of a particular drug in order to avoid experiencing the symptoms of withdrawal.

Depot dosage: A form of medication that can be stored in the patient's body for several days or weeks.

Depression: A psychological condition with feelings of sadness, sleep disturbance, fatigue, and inability to concentrate.

Detoxification: The phase of treatment during which a patient gives up a substance and harmful chemicals are removed from his or her system.

Diaphragm: As a form of birth control, a thin rubber cap inserted into the vagina.

Diastolic blood pressure: Blood pressure exerted by the heart when it is resting between beats.

Digital rectal examination: A medical procedure in which a doctor inserts a lubricated gloved finger into the rectum to look for abnormal structures.

Dimercaprol (BAL): A chemical agent used in chelation therapy.

Diopter: The unit of measure used for the refractive (light bending) power of a lens.

Diplegia: Paralysis of the arm and leg on one side of the body.

Disease reservoir: A population of animals in which a virus lives without causing serious illness among the animals.

Distal muscular dystrophy (DD): A form of muscular dystrophy that usually begins in middle age or later, causing weakness in the muscles of the feet and hands.

Dominant gene: A form of a gene that predominates over a second form of the same gene.

Dopamine: A neurotransmitter that helps send signals that control movement.

DSM-IV: The *Diagnostic and Statistical Manual of Mental Disorders,* Fourth Edition, the standard reference book used for diagnosing and treating mental disorders.

Duchenne muscular dystrophy (DMD): The most severe form of muscular dystrophy, usually affecting young boys, beginning in the legs, and resulting in progressive muscle weakness.

Duodenum: The upper part of the small intestine, joined to the lower part of the stomach.

Dyslexia: Difficulty in reading, spelling, and/or writing words.

Dysthymic disorder: An ongoing, chronic depression that lasts two or more years.

Dystonia: Loss of the ability to control detailed muscle movement.

E

Echocardiogram: A test that uses sound waves to produce an image of the structure of the heart.

ECT: Electroconvulsive shock therapy, a method for using electric shocks to treat patients with mental disorders, such as bipolar disorder.

Edetate calcium disodium (EDTA calcium): A chemical agent used in chelation therapy.

Electrocardiogram: A test that measures the electrical activity of the heart to determine whether it is functioning normally.

Electroencephalogram (EEG): A test used to measure electrical activity of the brain to see if the brain is functioning normally.

Electrolytes: Salts and minerals present in the body that produce electrically charged particles (ions) in body fluids. Electrolytes control the fluid balance in the body and are important in muscle contraction, energy generation, and almost all major biochemical reactions in the body.

Electromagnetic radiation (ER): Radiation that travels as waves at the speed of light.

Electromyography: A test used to measure how well a nerve is functioning.

Enamel: The hard, outermost layer of a tooth.

Encephalopathy: A brain disorder characterized by loss of memory and other mental problems.

Endemic: The widespread occurrence of a disease over a given area that lasts for an extended period of time.

Endoscope: An instrument consisting of a long, narrow tube that can be inserted down a patient's throat to study the health of a patient's digestive system.

Enema: The injection of liquid into the intestine through the anus. This procedure is used either to induce a bowel movement or to coat the lining of the colon so that X-ray photographs can be taken of the colon.

Enzymes: Chemicals present in all cells that make possible the biological reactions needed to keep a cell alive.

Epidemic: An outbreak of a disease that spreads over a wide area in a relatively short period of time.

Epidermis: The outer layer of skin.

Epithelium: The layer of cells covering the body's outer and inner surfaces.

Epstein-Barr virus (EBV): A virus that causes mononucleosis and other diseases.

***Escherichia coli* (*E. coli*):** A bacteria that commonly causes food poisoning, most often from food products derived from cows, especially ground beef.

Estrogen: A female hormone with many functions in the body, one of which is to keep bones strong.

Eustachian tube: A passageway that connects the middle ear with the back of the throat.

Evoked potential test (EPT): A test that measures the brain's electrical response to certain kinds of stimulation, such as light in the eyes, sound in the ears, or touch on the skin.

Extrapulmonary: Outside of the lungs.

F

Facioscapulohumeral muscular dystrophy (FSH): A form of muscular dystrophy that begins in late childhood to early adulthood; affects both men and women; and causes weakness in the muscles of the face, shoulders, and upper arms.

Fecal occult blood test: A laboratory test designed to find blood in feces.

Fibrin: A thick material formed over an injured section of a blood vessel by the process of blood clotting.

Fibromyalgia: Pain, tenderness, and stiffness in muscles.

Fistula: An abnormal tubelike passage in tissue.

Flashback: A sudden memory of an event that occurred months or years earlier.

Fluoride: A chemical compound that is effective in preventing tooth decay.

Fragile X syndrome: A genetic condition involving the X chromosome that results in mental, physical, and sensory problems.

Frequency: The rate at which a wave vibrates in space.

Frostbite: A medical condition in which some part of the body has become frozen.

Fungus: A large group of organisms that includes mold, mildew, rust fungi, yeast, and mushrooms, some of which may cause disease in humans and other animals.

G

Ganglioside: A fatty substance found in brain and nerve cells.

Gangrene: Death and decay of body tissue.

Gastrointestinal system: The digestive system, consisting of the stomach and intestines.

Gel electrophoresis: A laboratory test that separates different types of molecules from each other.

Gene: A chemical unit found in all cells that carries information telling cells what functions they are to perform.

General autoimmune disorder: An autoimmune disorder that involves a number of tissues throughout the body.

Genetic disorder: A medical problem caused by one or more defective genes.

Genital: Having to do with the organs of the reproductive system.

Gingiva: The outer layer of the gums.

Ginkgo: An herb obtained from the ginkgo tree, thought by some alternative practitioners to be helpful in treating patients with Alzheimer's disease.

Glucose: A type of sugar present in the blood and in cells that is used by cells to make energy.

Gonorrhea: A sexually transmitted disease caused by the *Gonococcus* bacterium that affects the mucous membranes, particularly in the urinary tract and genital area. It can make urination painful and cause puslike discharges through the urinary tract.

Grand mal: An alternate term used for tonic-clonic epilepsy.

Granules: Small packets of reactive chemicals stored within cells.

Gray (Gy): A unit used to measure damage done to tissue by ionizing radiation.

H

Hairy leukoplakia of the tongue: A white area of diseased tissue on the tongue that may be flat or slightly raised. It is caused by the Epstein-Barr virus and is an important diagnostic sign of AIDS.

Hallucination: A perception of objects (or sounds) that have no reality. Seeing or hearing something that does not actually exist.

Helicobacter pylori: A bacterium that lives in mucous membranes and is responsible for the development of ulcers.

Hemiplegia: Paralysis of one side of the body.

Hemodialysis: A mechanical method for cleansing blood outside the body.

Hemoglobin: A molecule found in blood that gives blood its red color. Hemoglobin is responsible for transporting oxygen through the blood stream.

Hemorrhage: Heavy or uncontrollable bleeding.

Herpes virus: A group of viruses that cause many different infections in the human body, including cold sores and infections of the genital area.

Histamine: A chemical released by mast cells that activates pain receptors and causes cells to leak fluids.

Hormone replacement therapy (HRT): A method of treating osteoporosis by giving supplementary doses of estrogen and/or other female hormones.

Hormone therapy: Treatment of cancer by slowing down the production of certain hormones.

Hormones: Chemicals that occur naturally in the body and control certain body functions.

Human immunodeficiency virus (HIV): A transmissible virus that causes AIDS in humans. Two forms of HIV are now recognized: HIV-1, which causes most cases of AIDS in Europe, North and South America, and most parts of Africa; and HIV-2, which is chiefly found in West African patients. HIV-2, discovered in 1986, appears to be less virulent than HIV-1 and may also have a longer latency period.

Human papilloma virus (HPV): A family of viruses that cause hand, foot, flat, and genital warts.

Hydrocephalus: An abnormal accumulation of cerebrospinal fluid (CSF) in the brain.

Hyperbaric chamber: A sealed compartment used to treat decompression sickness, in which air pressure is first increased and then gradually decreased.

Hyperopia: Farsightedness. A condition in which vision is better for distant objects than for near ones.

Hypersomnia: The need to sleep excessively; a symptom of dysthymic and major depressive disorder.

Hyperthermia: The general name for any form of heat disorder.

Hyperventilation: Deep, heavy breathing.

Hypotonia: A condition in which muscles lack strength.

I

Iatrogenic: Caused by a medical procedure.

Iatrogenic Kaposi's sarcoma: A form of Kaposi's sarcoma that develops in people who have had organ transplants and are taking immunosuppressant drugs.

Ideal weight: Weight corresponding to the appropriate, healthy rate for individuals of a specific height, gender, and age.

Idiopathic epilepsy: A form of epilepsy for which no cause is known.

Immune system: A system of organs, tissues, cells, and chemicals that work together to fight off foreign invaders, such as bacteria and viruses.

Immunization: The process of injecting a material into a person's body that protects that person from catching a particular infectious disease.

Immunodeficient: A condition in which the body's immune response is damaged, weakened, or is not functioning properly.

Immunotherapy: Treatment of cancer by stimulating the body's immune system.

Incubation period: The time it takes for symptoms of a disease to appear after a person has been infected.

Infestation: A situation in which large numbers of organisms come together in a single area.

Inflammation: The body's response to tissue damage that includes heat, swelling, redness, and pain.

Inflammatory bowel disease: A group of disorders that affect the gastrointestinal (digestive) system.

Insomnia: Difficulty in falling asleep or in remaining asleep.

Insulin: A hormone (type of protein) produced by the pancreas that makes it possible for cells to use glucose in the production of energy.

Intestinal perforation: A hole in the lining of the intestine that allows partially digested foods to leak into the abdominal cavity.

Intracerebral hemorrhage: Bleeding that occurs within the brain.

Intraocular pressure (IOP): The pressure exerted by aqueous humor (clear liquid) inside the eyeball.

Ionizing radiation (IR): Any form of radiation that can break apart atoms and molecules and cause damage to materials.

J

Jaundice: A yellowing of the skin, often caused by a disorder of the liver.

Jet lag: A temporary disruption of the body's sleep/wake rhythm caused by high-speed air travel through different time zones.

Joint: A structure that holds two or more bones together.

K

Karyotype: The specific chromosomal makeup of a particular organism.

Ketoacidosis: A condition that results from the build-up of toxic chemicals known as ketones in the blood.

Koplik's spots: Tiny white spots on a reddish bump found inside of the mouth that are a characteristic marker for measles.

L

Lactobacillus acidophilus: A bacterium found in yogurt that changes the balance of bacteria in the intestine in a beneficial way.

Laparoscopy: A procedure in which a tube with a small light and viewing device is inserted through a small incision near the navel, allowing a surgeon to look directly into the patient's abdomen.

Laparotomy: A surgical procedure that allows a surgeon to view the inside of the abdominal cavity.

Larva: An immature form of an organism.

Larynx: The part of the airway between the pharynx and trachea, often called the voice box.

Laser: A device for producing very intense beams of light of a single color. Used in surgery to cut and/or dissolve tissues.

Latency: A period during which a disease-causing organism is inactive but not dead.

Lens: In the eye, a transparent, elastic, curved structure that helps focus light on the retina.

Lesion: Any change in the structure or appearance of a part of the body as the result of an injury or infection.

Ligament: Tough, fiber-like tissue that holds bones together at joints.

Limb-girdle muscular dystrophy (LGMD): A form of muscular dystrophy that begins in late childhood to early adulthood, affects both men and women, and causes weakness in the muscles around the hips and shoulders.

Lumbar puncture: A procedure in which a thin needle is inserted into the space between vertebrae in the spine and a sample of cerebrospinal fluid is withdrawn for study under a microscope.

Lumpectomy: A procedure in which a cancerous lump is removed from the breast.

Lymph nodes: Small round or oval bodies within the immune system. Lymph nodes provide materials that fight disease and help remove bacteria and other foreign material from the body.

Lymphocyte: A type of white blood cell that is important in the formation of antibodies and that can be measured to monitor the health of AIDS patients.

Lymphoma: A cancerous tumor in the lymphatic system that is associated with a poor prognosis in AIDS patients.

M

Macrophage: A large white blood cell, found primarily in the bloodstream and connective tissue, that helps the body fight off infections by ingesting the disease-causing organism. HIV can infect and kill macrophages.

Magnetic resonance imaging (MRI): A procedure that uses electromagnets and radio waves to produce images of a patient's internal tissue and organs. These images are not blocked by bones, and can be useful in diagnosing brain and spinal disorders and other diseases.

Malignant: Describes a tumor that can spread to other parts of the body and that poses a serious threat to a person's life.

Malnutrition: A condition in which a person is not eating enough of the right kinds of foods.

Mammogram: An X-ray photograph of the breast.

Mandible: The scientific term for the lower jaw.

Mania: A mental condition in which a person feels unusually excited, irritated, or happy.

Mantoux test: Another name for the purified protein derivative (PPD) test, which is used to determine whether a person has been infected with the tuberculosis bacterium.

Mast cells: A type of immune system cell that is found in the lining of the nasal passages and eyelids. It displays a type of antibody called immunoglobulin type E (IgE) on its cell surface and participates in the allergic response by releasing histamine from intracellular granules.

Mastectomy: Surgical removal of a breast.

Meconium ileus: A condition that appears in newborn babies with cystic fibrosis, in which the baby's first bowel movement is abnormally dark, thick, and sticky.

Median nerve: A nerve that runs through the wrist and into the hand, providing feeling and movement to the hand, thumb, and fingers.

Melanocyte: A specialized skin cell that produces melanin, a dark pigment (color) found in skin.

Melatonin: A hormone thought to control the body's natural sleep rhythms.

Meninges: The three-layer membranous covering of the brain and spinal cord.

Menopause: The end of menstruation.

Menstruation: The discharge of menses (a bloody fluid) from the uterus of women who are not pregnant that occurs approximately every four weeks from puberty to menopause.

Metabolism: A series of chemical reactions by which cells convert glucose to energy.

Metastasis: The process by which cancer cells travel from one area of the body to another.

Methadone: A chemical given to heroin addicts to help them overcome their addiction.

Miliary tuberculosis: A form of tuberculosis in which the bacillus spreads throughout the body producing many thousands of tubercular lesions.

Miscarriage: When a human fetus is expelled from the mother before it can survive outside of the womb.

MMR vaccine: A vaccine that contains separate vaccines against three diseases: measles, mumps, and rubella.

Monocyte: A large white blood cell that is formed in the bone marrow and spleen. About 4 percent of the white blood cells in normal adults are monocytes.

Mosaic: Medically, a condition in which an individual cell may contain more than one type of chromosomal composition, with forty-six chromosomes in one cell, for example, and forty-seven chromosomes in another cell, which causes relatively mild symptoms of Down's syndrome.

Motor function: A body function controlled by muscles.

Motor neuron: A nerve cell that controls a muscle.

Mucolytic: Any type of medication that breaks up mucus and makes it flow more easily.

Mucus: A mixture of water, salts, sugars, and proteins, which has the job of cleansing, lubricating, and protecting passageways in the body.

Myalgia: Muscle pain.

Myalgic encephalomyelitis: An inflammation of the brain and spinal cord.

Myelin: A layer of tissue that surrounds nerves and acts as an insulator.

Myelograph: A test in which a dye is injected into the spinal column to allow examination of the spine with X rays or a computed tomography (CT) scan.

Myocardial infarction: The technical term for heart attack.

Myopia: Nearsightedness. A condition in which far away objects appear fuzzy because light from a distance doesn't focus properly on the retina.

Myotonic dystrophy: A form of muscular dystrophy that affects both men and women and causes generalized weakness in the face, feet, and hands.

N

Narcolepsy: A sleep disorder characterized by sudden sleep attacks during the day and often accompanied by other symptoms, such as cataplexy, temporary paralysis, and hallucinations.

Narcotic: A drug that relieves pain and induces sleep.

Natural killer cells: Cells in the immune system that help fight off infections.

Necrosis: Abnormal death of body tissues.

Nervous tic: An involuntary action, continually repeated, such as the twitching of a muscle or repeated blinking.

Neural tube: A structure that forms very early in the life of a fetus and eventually develops into the central nervous system of the body.

Neurasthenia: Nervous exhaustion.

Neurofibrillary tangle: Twisted masses of peptides (fragments of protein fibers) that develop inside brain cells of people with Alzheimer's disease.

Neuron: A nerve cell.

Neurotransmitter: A chemical found in the brain that carries electrical signals from one nerve cell to another nerve cell.

Nitrogen: A tasteless, odorless gas that makes up four-fifths of Earth's atmosphere.

Nits: The eggs produced by head or pubic lice.

Nonsteroidal anti-inflammatory drugs (NSAIDs): A group of drugs, including aspirin, ibuprofen, and acetaminophen, used to treat pain and fever.

Nucleoside analogues: A medication that interferes when HIV tries reproduce by making copies of itself inside cells.

O

Obsession: A troubling thought that occurs again and again and causes severe distress in a person.

Oculopharyngeal muscular dystrophy (OPMD): A form of muscular dystrophy that affects adults of both sexes and causes weakness in the muscles of the eyes and throat.

Opiate blockers: Drugs that interfere with the action of natural opiates, substances that cause sleepiness and numbness.

Opportunistic infection: An infection by organisms that usually don't cause infection in people whose immune systems are working normally.

Optic nerve: A nerve at the back of the eyeball that carries messages from the retina to the brain.

Organ specific disorder: An autoimmune disorder in which only one type of organ is affected.

Ossicles: Tiny bones located within the middle ear responsible for transmitting sound vibrations from the outer ear to the inner ear.

Osteoarthritis: A type of arthritis that weakens the joint cartilage. It is most common among the elderly.

Otosclerosis: A disorder in which the bones of the middle ear become joined to each other.

P

Pancreas: A gland located behind the stomach that produces insulin.

Paralysis: The inability to move one's muscles.

Paranoia: Excessive or irrational suspicion or distrust of others.

Penicillin: A specific type of antibiotic used to treat many types of infections.

Peptic ulcer: A general name referring to ulcers in any part of the digestive system.

Pericardium: The membrane surrounding the heart.

Peristalsis: Periodic waves of muscular contractions that move food through the digestive system.

Peritonitis: Inflammation of the membranes that line the abdominal wall.

Persistent generalized lymphadenopathy (PGL): A condition in which HIV continues to produce chronic painless swellings in the lymph nodes during the latency period.

Petit mal: An alternative term for absence epilepsy.

Pharynx: The part of the throat that lies between the mouth and the larynx, or voice box. It connects the nose and mouth with the upper part of the digestive system.

Phenylketonuria (PKU): A genetic disorder in which a person's body is unable to break down the amino acid phenylalanine, causing damage to the brain.

Physiological dependence: A condition in which a person's body requires the intake of some substance, without which it will become ill.

Plaque: Generally refers to a build-up of some substance. The fatty material and other substances that form on the lining of blood vessels are called plaque. Patches of scar tissue that form in areas where myelin tissue has been destroyed are also called plaque. Dental plaque is a thin, sticky film composed of sugars, food, and bacteria that cover teeth.

Platelet: A type of blood cell involved in the clotting of blood.

Pleural: Having to do with the membrane that surrounds the lungs.

Polyps: Small, abnormal masses of tissue that can form on the lining of an organ.

Polysomnograph: An instrument used to measure a patient's body processes during sleep.

Positron emission tomography (PET): A diagnostic technique that uses radioactive materials to study the structure and function of organs and tissues within the body.

Primary progressive: A form of multiple sclerosis in which the disease continually becomes worse.

Prion: A form of protein that can cause an infectious disease.

Process addiction: A condition in which a person is dependent on some type of behavior, such as gambling, shopping, or sexual activity.

Prodrome: A period of time during which certain symptoms signal the beginning of a disease.

Prophylactic: Referring to a treatment that prevents the symptoms of a condition from developing.

Protease inhibitors: The second major category of drug used to treat AIDS. They work by suppressing the replication of the HIV virus.

Protein: A type of chemical compound with many essential functions in the body, one of which is to build bones.

Psychological dependence: A condition in which a person requires the intake of some substance in order to maintain mental stability.

Psychosis: Extremely disordered thinking accompanied by a poor sense of reality.

Psychosocial therapy: Any means by which a trained professional holds interviews with a patient and tries to help that patient better understand himself or herself and the reasons for his or her thoughts and actions.

Psychotic disorder: A mental disorder characterized by delusions, hallucinations, and other symptoms indicating a loss of contact with the real world.

Pulmonary: Relating to the lungs.

Pulmonary function test: A test that measures the amount of air a patient can breath in and out.

Pulmonary hypertension: High blood pressure in the arteries and veins associated with the lungs.

Pulp: The soft, innermost layer of a tooth.

Purge: To rid the body of food by vomiting, the use of laxatives, or some other method.

Purified protein derivative (PPD): A substance injected beneath the skin to see whether a person presently has or has ever had the tubercle bacillus.

Q

Quadriplegia: Paralysis of both arms and both legs.

Quinine: One of the first successful treatments for malaria, derived from the bark of the cinchona tree.

R

Rad: A unit once used to measure the amount of damage done to tissue by ionizing radiation, now replaced by the gray.

Radial keratotomy (RK): A surgical procedure in which the shape of the cornea is changed in order to correct myopia.

Radiation: Energy transmitted in the form of electromagnetic waves or subatomic particles.

Radiation therapy: Treatment that uses high-energy radiation, like X rays, to treat cancer.

Radical mastectomy: Surgical removal of an entire breast along with the chest muscles around the breast and all the lymph nodes under the arm.

Radioactive isotope: A substance that gives off some form of radiation.

Radiotherapy: Treatment of a disease using some form of radiation, such as X rays.

Radon: A radioactive gas that occurs naturally and is often found in the lower levels of buildings.

Rash: A spotted pink or red skin condition that may be accompanied by itching.

Recessive gene: A form of a gene that does not operate in the presence of a dominant form of the same gene.

Reconstructive surgery: A medical procedure in which an artificial breast is created to replace the breast removed during a mastectomy.

Rectum: The lower part of the digestive system from which solid wastes are excreted.

Red blood cells: Blood cells that carry oxygen from the lungs to the rest of the body.

Reduction: The restoration of a body part to its original position after it has been displaced, such as during a fracture.

Refraction: The bending of light waves as they pass through a dense substance, such as water, glass, or plastic.

Relapse: A reoccurrence of a disease.

Relapsing-remitting: A form of multiple sclerosis in which symptoms appear for at least twenty-four hours and then disappear for a period of time.

Rem: An older unit used to measure the amount of damage done to tissue by ionizing radiation, now replaced by the sievert.

Renal: Relating to the kidneys.

Resorption: The process by which the elements of bone are removed from bone and returned to the body.

Respiratory system: The nose, tonsils, larynx, pharynx, lungs, and other structures used in the process of breathing.

Restless leg syndrome: A condition in which a patient experiences aching or other unpleasant sensations in the calves of the legs.

Retina: A thin membrane at the back of the eyeball that receives light rays that pass through the eyeball and transmits them to the optic nerve.

Rhabdovirus: The virus that causes rabies.

Rhinovirus: A type of virus that can cause the common cold.

RICE: The term stands for the program of rest, ice, compression, and elevation that is recommended for treating tendinitis.

Rickets: A condition caused by the deficiency of certain minerals, including vitamin D and calcium, causing abnormal bone growth.

S

Salmonella: A bacteria that commonly causes food poisoning, most often from poultry, eggs, meat, and milk.

Scald: A burn caused by a hot liquid or steam.

Scoliometer: A tool for measuring the amount of curvature in a person's spine.

Screening: Using a test or group of tests to look for some specific medical disorder.

Sebum: An oily material produced by sebaceous glands that keeps the skin moist.

Secondary progressive: A form of multiple sclerosis in which a period of relapses and remissions is followed by another period in which the disease becomes progressively worse without improvement.

Secondhand smoke: Smoke that someone inhales after it is exhaled by another person.

Sedative: A substance that calms a person. Sedatives can also cause a person to feel drowsy.

Seizure: A convulsion; a series of involuntary muscular movements that alternate between contraction and relaxation.

Selective serotonin reuptake inhibitors (SSRIs): A class of drugs used to reduce depression.

Semen: A white fluid produced by the male reproductive system that carries sperm.

Seminal vesicles: The organs that produce semen.

Senile plaque: Deposits that collect inside the brain cells of people with Alzheimer's disease.

Sensory hearing loss: Hearing loss that occurs in the inner ear, auditory nerve, or brain.

Serotonin: An important neurotransmitter in the brain.

Shigella: A bacterium that grows well in contaminated food and water, in crowded living conditions, and in areas with poor sanitation. It is transmitted by direct contact with an infected person or with food that has been contaminated by an infected person.

Shingles: A disease that causes a rash and a very painful nerve inflammation. An attack of chickenpox eventually gives rise to shingles in about 20 percent of the population.

Shock: A life-threatening condition that results from low blood volume due to loss of blood or other fluids.

Sickle cell: A red blood cell with an abnormal shape due to the presence of an abnormal form of hemoglobin.

Sievert (Sv): A unit used to measure the amount of damage done to tissue by ionizing radiation.

Sigmoidoscopy: A medical procedure in which a doctor looks at the rectum and lower colon through a flexible lighted instrument called a sigmoidoscope.

Silicosis: A disease of the lungs caused by inhaling fine particles of sand.

Skin graft: A surgical procedure in which dead skin is removed and replaced by healthy skin, usually taken from elsewhere on the patient's own body.

Sleep disorder: Any condition that interferes with sleep. The American Sleep Disorders Association has identified eighty-four different sleep disorders.

Somnambulism: Also called sleepwalking, it refers to a range of activities a patient performs while sleeping, from walking to carrying on a conversation.

Spasm: A contraction of the muscles that can cause paralysis and/or shaking.

Spastic: A condition in which muscles are rigid, posture may be abnormal, and control of muscles may be impaired.

Sphygmomanometer: An instrument used to measure blood pressure.

Spinal cord: A long rope-like piece of nervous tissue that runs from the brain down the back.

Spinal transection: A complete break in the spinal column.

Spirometer: An instrument that shows how much air a patient is able to exhale and hold in his or her lungs as a test to see how serious a person's asthma is and how well he or she is responding to treatment.

Spondylosis: Arthritis of the spine.

Sputum: Secretions produced inside an infected lung. When the sputum is coughed up it can be studied to determine what kinds of infection are present in the lung.

Staphylococcus aureas: A bacteria that causes food poisoning, commonly found on foods that are kept at room temperature.

Staphylococcus: A class of bacteria found on human skin and mucous membranes that can cause a variety of infectious diseases.

Streptococcus: A class of bacteria that causes a wide variety of infections.

Stem cells: Immature blood cells formed in bone marrow.

Steroids: A category of naturally occurring chemicals that are very effective in reducing inflammation and swelling.

Stimulant: A substance that makes a person feel more energetic or awake. A stimulant may increase organ activity in the body.

Stress test: An electrocardiogram taken while a patient is exercising vigorously, such as riding a stationary bicycle.

Subarachnoid hemorrhage (SAH): Loss of blood into the subarachnoid space, the fluid-filled area that surrounds brain tissue.

Subdural hematoma: An accumulation of blood in the outer part of the brain.

Substance addiction: A condition in which a person is dependent on some chemical substance, such as cocaine or heroin.

Substantia nigra: A region of the brain that controls movement.

Succimer (Chemet): A chemical agent used to remove excess lead from the body.

Symptomatic epilepsy: A form of epilepsy for which some specific cause is known.

Synovial fluid: A fluid produced by the synovial membranes in a joint that lubricates the movement of the bones in the joint.

Synovial membrane: A membrane that covers the articular capsule in a joint and produces synovial fluid.

Syphilis: A sexually transmitted disease that can cause sores and eventually lead to brain disease, paralysis, and death.

Systemic treatment: A form of treatment that affects the whole body.

Systolic blood pressure: Blood pressure exerted by the heart when it contracts (beats).

T

T-cells: Lymphocytes that originate in the thymus gland. T-cells regulate the immune system's response to infections, including HIV.

Tartar: Plaque that has become hardened and attached to the tooth surface.

Temporal bones: The bones that form the right and left sides of the skull.

Tendon: A tough, rope-like tissue that connects muscle to bone.

Tennis elbow: A form of tendinitis that occurs among tennis players and other people who engage in the same movement of the elbow over and over again.

Testosterone: A male sex hormone.

Thermal burns: Burns caused by hot objects or by fire.

Thoracentesis: A procedure for removing fluids from the pleural space by inserting a long, thin needle between the ribs.

Throat culture: A sample of tissue taken from a person's throat for analysis. The culture is often taken by swiping a cotton swab across the back of the throat.

Thrombolytic: Capable of dissolving a blood clot.

Thrombosis: The formation of a blood clot.

Thyroid: An organ that controls a number of important bodily functions.

Tic: A muscular contraction or vocal sound over which a patient has very little control.

Tinea capitis: Scalp ringworm; a fungal infection of the scalp.

Tinea corporis: Scientific name for body ringworm, a fungal infection of the skin that can affect any part of the body except the scalp, feet, and facial area.

Tinea cruris: An fungal infection that affects the groin and can spread to the buttocks, inner thighs, and external genitalia; also called "jock itch."

Tinea unguium: Ringworm of the nails; a fungal infection that usually begins at the tip of a toenail.

Tissue plasminogen activator (tPA): A substance that dissolves blood clots in the brain.

Tolerance: The ability of a body to endure a certain amount of a substance that had previously been too much for it to tolerate.

Tonic phase: The stage of a grand mal seizure in which muscles become rigid and fixed.

Tonometer: A device used to measure intraocular pressure in the eyeball.

Tonsillectomy: A surgical procedure to remove the tonsils.

Tonsils: Oval-shaped masses of lymph gland tissue located on both sides of the back of the throat.

Toxic dilation of the colon: An expansion of the colon that may be caused by inflammation due to ulcerative colitis.

Toxin: A poison.

Trachea: The windpipe, extending from the larynx (the voice box) to the lungs.

Traction: The process of placing an arm or leg bone, or group of muscles under tension by applying weights to them in order to keep them in alignment while they heal.

Tranquilizers: Drugs that help a person to calm down.

Transcutaneous electrical nerve stimulation: A procedure in which mild electrical currents are used to stimulate nerves in order to prevent the transmission of pain messages in the body.

Translocation: A condition in which a piece of one chromosome breaks off and becomes attached to another chromosome.

Tretinoin: A drug that increases the rate at which skin cells are formed and die.

Triglyceride: A type of fat.

Trimester: Three months. Often used to refer to one third of a woman's pregnancy.

Trisomy: A condition in which three identical chromosomes, rather than two, are matched with each other.

Tumor: A mass or lump of tissue made of abnormal cells.

Twelve-step program: A plan for overcoming an addiction by going through twelve stages of personal development.

Tympanic membrane: A thin piece of tissue between the external ear and the middle ear.

U

Ulcer: An open wound in the skin or mucous membrane that is usually sore and painful.

Ultrasound test: A medical procedure in which a sound wave is transmitted into a pregnant woman's womb. The reflections produced from the sound wave can be studied for the presence of abnormalities in a fetus.

Ultraviolet (UV) light: A naturally occurring part of ordinary sunlight that may, under some circumstances, have beneficial effects in curing certain medical disorders.

Urethra: The tube through which the bladder empties to the exterior of the body.

V

Vaccine: A substance that causes the body's immune system to build up resistance to a particular disease.

Varicella-zoster immune globulin (VZIG): A substance that can reduce the severity of chickenpox symptoms.

Varicella-zoster virus: The virus that causes chickenpox and shingles.

Variola: The virus that causes smallpox. The only two small samples of variola that remain on Earth are being stored in two separate research laboratories.

Varivax: A vaccine for the prevention of chickenpox.

Vasodilator: Any drug that causes a blood vessel to relax.

Vector: An animal that transmits an infectious agent, such as a virus, from one animal to another animal.

Vector-borne disease: A disease transferred from one organism to another by means of a third organism, such as an insect or tick.

Ventricle: One of the two lower chambers of the heart.

Vertebrae: Bones that make up the spinal column.

Virus: A very small organism that can live only within a cell and that can cause some form of disease.

Volume reduction surgery: A surgical procedure in which damaged portions of a patient's lung are removed to make it easier for the patient to use healthy parts of the lung to get the oxygen needed for ordinary functioning.

Voluntary muscle: A muscle under a person's conscious control.

W

Wasting Syndrome: A progressive loss of weight and muscle tissue caused by AIDS.

White blood cells: Blood cells that fight invading organisms, such as bacteria and viruses.

Withdrawal: The process by which a person adjusts to the absence of some substance or activity to which he or she has become addicted.

X

X rays: A kind of high-energy radiation that can be used to take pictures of the inside of the body, to diagnose cancer, or to kill cancer cells.

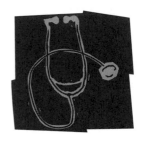

Research and Activity Ideas

The following research and activity ideas are intended to offer suggestions for complementing science and health curricula, to trigger additional ideas for enhancing learning, and to suggest cross-disciplinary projects for library and classroom use.

Disease graph: Different environments create different opportunities for diseases to spread. Obtain current data for your city or county on occurrences of a disease such as rabies or lyme disease or a condition such as asthma. Create a graph that compares the number of outbreaks in urban areas with the number in rural areas. If there are differences, brainstorm some of the environmental factors that may be causing such differences.

Public service announcement: Choose a disease or disorder and write a public service announcement that would appear on television to inform people about the condition. Your ad should include information about symptoms, warn of risk factors, mention current treatments, and dispel any myths that are associated with the disease. Record the public service announcement using a video camera or present it in class.

Geographic study: Different parts of the world often face unique challenges in controlling diseases. Choose two different countries with different cultures and environments. Find out what the top five health concerns are in each country. For each one, determine the major risk factors. Discuss what aspects of the culture or the environment may be increasing the incidences of these diseases in each country.

Disease transmission: With a group of five to eight people choose one daily activity that you will act out. This could be going to the grocery store, going through the lunch line at school, playing a game, or going out to dinner. Assign each person a role in the activity. Choose one player who will be infected with a contagious disease, such as influenza. Coat that person's hands with flour. Act out the scene as realistically as possible. At the end of the scene, note how many other players have flour on themselves and how many places the ill person left his or her germs.

Diabetic diet: Research the dietary requirements of a person with diabetes. Keep a food diary for two days, recording everything you eat. Examine how your eating habits would have to change if you had diabetes. What foods couldn't you have eaten? What might you have to eat more of?

AIDS risk factors: What are some of the myths about the transmission of AIDS? Choose five activities sometimes incorrectly thought to be risk factors for contracting AIDS. For each myth give the scientific reasons that the activity does not put one at risk of contracting AIDS.

The following Web sites offer many more research and activity ideas as well as interactive activities for students:

The American Museum of Natural History: Infection, Detection, Protection. http://www.amnh.org/explore/infection/smp_index.html

Cool Science for Curious Kids. http://www.hhmi.org/coolscience/

The Gateway to Educational Materials. http://thegateway.org/index1/SubjectIndex.html#health

Newton's Apple®. http://ericir.syr.edu/Projects/Newton/index.html

The University of Arizona. The Biology Project: An Online Interactive Resource for Learning Biology. http://www.biology.arizona.edu/

WNET School. http://www.wnet.rog/wnetschool

SICK!

*Diseases and
Disorders,
Injuries and
Infections*

DECOMPRESSION SICKNESS

DEFINITION

Decompression sickness (DCS) is a condition that occurs when divers come back to the surface too quickly after being deep under water. It is caused by the formation of nitrogen bubbles in the blood stream and, in the worst cases, can cause death

DESCRIPTION

Decompression sickness is a relatively uncommon disorder among divers. Divers Alert Network (DAN), a worldwide organization devoted to safe-diving research and promotion, estimates that less than 1 percent of all divers experience the condition. A study conducted on Okinawa (an island in the Pacific Ocean near Japan) of military personnel who make tens of thousands of dives each year, found an average of one case of decompression sickness for every 7,400 divers and one death for every 76,900 dives. Mild cases may even go unnoticed by divers.

Decompression sickness is also known by other names, such as decompression illness and caisson (pronounced KAY-son) disease. DCS was

WORDS TO KNOW

Decompression stops: Stops divers should make when returning to the surface to let the nitrogen in their blood dissolve safely out of their bodies. Charts developed by the U.S. Navy and other groups list the number of stops and the time to be spent at each stop.

Hyperbaric chamber: A sealed compartment used to treat decompression sickness, in which pressure is first increased and then gradually decreased.

Nitrogen: A tasteless, odorless gas that makes up four-fifths of Earth's atmosphere.

called caisson disease in the nineteenth century because it occurred among construction workers who worked in caissons, building the supports for bridges at the bottom of lakes and rivers.

CAUSES

Air is primarily a mixture of two gases, oxygen and nitrogen. The oxygen we breathe in is used by cells in our bodies to metabolize (burn up) food. The nitrogen has no function in our bodies. Most of it is expelled from the body when we breathe out. Some of it is absorbed into our body tissues and our bloodstream.

As a person goes underwater, pressure increases on his or her body. The deeper one goes, the greater the pressure. This increased pressure forces more and more air into the body. All gases become more soluble (dissolve better) as pressure increases. Increased pressure causes no problem with oxygen, which is used up by the body. But it can cause problems with nitrogen. Deep under water, where the pressure is high, much more nitrogen dissolves in blood than it does at the surface.

Decompression sickness occurs when a person returns to the surface after being deep under water. When that happens, pressure on the person's body decreases. Nitrogen begins to come back out of the blood. If the person comes to the surface slowly, there is no problem. The nitrogen gas can escape from the blood slowly and be exhaled.

If the person comes up too quickly, however, a problem can develop. Nitrogen begins to form tiny bubbles as it escapes from the blood. The bubbles cannot be exhaled through the lungs. Instead, they can block blood vessels, push on nerves, and cause other disturbances in the body.

The amount of risk for DCS depends on the depth to which a person has gone under water. The deeper the dive, the greater the risk. To avoid decompression problems, divers may need to stop one or more times on their way back to the surface. Charts developed by the U.S. Navy and other groups list the number of stops and the time to be spent at each stop. When these directions are followed, nitrogen has time to escape from the bloodstream normally. Bubbles do not form, and DCS does not occur.

A number of factors can increase the risk of DCS for divers. For example, people who are overweight or who have recently had alcohol to drink are at greater risk for DCS. Also, people planning to fly or travel to high-altitude locations after diving are at increased risk for DCS because they experience further decompression at higher altitudes. Experts recommend that individuals wait between twelve to twenty-four hours after a dive before flying or traveling to high altitudes.

Nitrogen bubbles can affect any of the body's tissues, including nerves, bone, blood, and muscles. For that reason, DCS can cause a wide variety of symptoms. These symptoms usually appear almost as soon as the diver surfaces. In 80 percent of all cases, they do so within eight hours of the dive.

The most common symptom of DCS is pain, often referred to by the term "bends." This pain can range from mild to severe. It usually affects the joints, but can occur anywhere. Skin problems, such as itching and rashes, are other symptoms. In more serious cases, DCS can result in paralysis, brain damage, heart attacks, and death.

decompression
sickness

A man suffering from decompression sickness is rushed to the hospital by police and emergency medical technicians. (Reproduced by permission of AP/Wide World Photos)

DIAGNOSIS

THE MOST COMMON SYMPTOM OF DCS IS PAIN, OFTEN REFERRED TO BY THE TERM "BENDS," THAT USUALLY AFFECTS THE JOINTS, BUT CAN OCCUR ANYWHERE.

Decompression sickness is usually first diagnosed by observing the diver's symptoms. If further care is necessary, a doctor may conduct a physical examination and take a medical history.

TREATMENT

Treatment of DCS involves reversing the conditions under which it first occurred. A person is placed into a hyperbaric (high pressure) chamber. Pressure is increased in the chamber, causing nitrogen gas bubbles to go back

Dr. James M. Clark is standing in front of a hyperbaric chamber treating a patient for decompression sickness. (Reproduced by permission of AP/Wide World Photos)

into the bloodstream. The pressure in the chamber is then reduced slowly. Nitrogen gas escapes from the blood again, but not in the form of bubbles.

This treatment should be used even when a person's symptoms seem to have disappeared. Nitrogen bubbles may still be present in the blood, and symptoms may reappear at a later time.

Hyperbaric chambers are now available in many locations. DAN maintains a list of such facilities and provides a twenty-four-hour hotline that provides advice on DCS and other diving emergencies.

PROGNOSIS

DCS patients who receive treatment in a hyperbaric chamber usually experience a full recovery quickly. If treatment is delayed, the prognosis is less predictable. People who have been treated even a few days later, however, may still receive benefits. A 1992 report from DAN said that half of all divers who were treated immediately after an incident experienced full recovery. Others, however, experienced numbness, tingling, and other symptoms for a few weeks, months, or even a lifetime.

PREVENTION

Decompression sickness is an entirely preventable condition. Divers who follow rules of safe diving are unlikely to experience its effects. People who are overweight, have lung or heart problems, or are otherwise in poor health should not dive. Good divers should be aware of the need for decompression stops after a dive and follow standards developed for these stops.

FOR MORE INFORMATION

Books

Martin, Lawrence. *Scuba Diving Explained: Questions and Answers on Physiology and Medical Aspects of Scuba Diving.* Flagstaff, AZ: Best Publishing, 1997. [Online] http://www.mtsinai.org/pulmonary/books/scuba/welcome.htm (accessed May 22, 1998).

Periodicals

Clenney, Timothy L., and Lorenz F. Lassen, "Recreational Scuba Diving Injuries." *American Family Physician* (April 1996): pp. 1761+.

Organizations

American College of Hyperbaric Medicine. P.O. Box 25914–130, Houston, TX 77265. (713) 528–5931. http://www.hyperbaricmedicine.org.

Divers Alert Network (DAN). The Peter B. Bennett Center, 6 West Colony Place, Durham, NC 27705. (919) 684–8111; (919) 684–4326 (diving emergencies); (919) 684–2948 (general information). http://www.dan.ycg.org.

Undersea and Hyperbaric Medical Society. 10531 Metropolitan Avenue, Kensington, MD 20895. (301) 942–2980. http://www.uhms.org.

DEPRESSIVE DISORDERS

DEFINITION

Depressive disorders are mental illnesses characterized by deep, long-lasting feelings of sadness or despair. The patient may also lose interest in things that were once pleasurable. Changes in sleep patterns, appetite, and mental processes may also accompany depressive disorders. Depressive disorders are also known simply as depression or as unipolar (one-sided) depression.

DESCRIPTION

Everyone experiences feelings of unhappiness and sadness occasionally. In some cases, however, these feelings can begin to take over a person's everyday life. They cause a person's physical and mental health to deteriorate.

Experts estimate that depressive disorders affect seventeen million Americans. One in four women is likely to experience at least one episode of depressive disorder in her lifetime. The rate is about one in eight among men. Depressive disorders can strike all age groups, from children to the elderly. The average age a first depressive episode occurs is in the middle twenties.

There are two types of depressive disorders: major depressive disorder and dysthymic (pronounced dis-THIH-mik) disorder. Major depressive disorder is defined as a depressive disorder with moderate to severe symptoms that lasts two or more weeks. The symptoms of major depressive disorder include trouble sleeping, loss of interest in once enjoyable activities, change in

WORDS TO KNOW

Dysthymic disorder: An ongoing, chronic depression that lasts two or more years.

Hypersomnia: The need to sleep excessively; a symptom of dysthymic and major depressive disorder.

Neurotransmitters: Chemicals that occur in the brain and are responsible for carrying messages in the brain.

Psychosocial therapy: Any means by which a trained professional holds interviews with a patient and tries to help that patient better understand himself or herself and the reasons for his or her thoughts and actions.

weight, difficulty in concentrating, feelings of hopelessness, and thoughts about death and suicide. In children, the main symptom of major depressive disorder is irritability (being easily upset).

Dysthymic disorder is a chronic (ongoing) form of depression that lasts at least two years (one year in children). The average period of time the disorder lasts is sixteen years. The symptoms of dysthymic disorder tend to be mild to moderate. They may be more intense at some times than at others. A person with dysthymic disorder may go for up to two months without feeling depressed. The disorder often comes on gradually. A patient may not even remember exactly when he or she started feeling depressed. Symptoms of dysthymic disorder include problems with sleeping and eating, low self-esteem (poor feelings about oneself), trouble concentrating, and feelings of hopelessness.

Depression can also occur in bipolar disorder (see bipolar disorder entry). Bipolar is a form of mental illness in which people feel wild swings of emotions. At one moment, they may feel happy and optimistic. At the next moment, they may feel sad and depressed.

CAUSES

The causes of depressive disorders are not well understood. Most experts believe that an imbalance of neurotransmitters is a major factor. Neurotransmitters are chemicals in the brain. They are responsible for carrying messages from one part of the brain to another. The presence of too many or too few neurotransmitters can cause the brain to perform abnormally.

Environmental factors are also thought to be involved in depressive disorders. It is believed that children who are abused or neglected may later develop a depressive disorder.

Heredity also seems to play a role in depressive disorders. People whose families have a history of major depression are up to three times more likely to have the disorder themselves. Many scientists now think that genetic and environmental factors work together to cause depressive disorder. Heredity may predispose (make a person more likely to have) a person to-

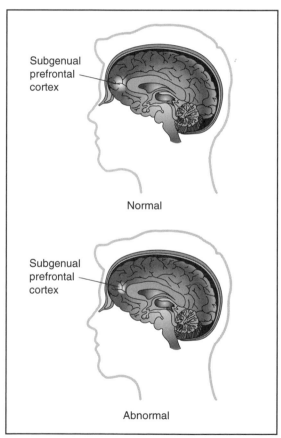

Recent scientific research indicates that the size of the subgenual prefrontal cortex (located behind the bridge of the nose) may be a determining factor in hereditary depressive disorders. (Reproduced by permission of Electronic Illustrators Group)

ward depressive disorder. But the condition develops only if the environment in which he or she grows up allows the condition to appear.

SYMPTOMS

Symptoms of depressive disorders vary depending whether the depression is caused by major depressive disorder or dysthymic disorder.

Major Depressive Episode

A person going through a major depressive episode feels depressed and/or loses interest in enjoyable activities. Children are more likely to feel irritable than depressed. In addition, five or more of the following symptoms appear on an almost daily basis for a period of at least two weeks:

• Significant change in weight
• Insomnia (inability to sleep) or hypersomnia (excessive sleep)
• Extreme tiredness or loss of energy
• Feelings of worthlessness and guilt that have no basis
• Diminished ability to think or to concentrate, or the loss of ability to make decisions
• Continuing thoughts of death or suicide and/or actual attempts at suicide

Dysthymic Disorder

The symptoms of dysthymic disorder occur along with other mental and physical symptoms. Up to 70 percent of dysthymic patients also have major depressive disorder. This condition is known as double depression. Some mental problems seen in people with dysthymic disorder include substance abuse (drug abuse), panic disorders (see panic disorders entry), and phobias (irrational fears). Physical problems that accompany dysthymia include multiple sclerosis (see multiple sclerosis entry), AIDS (see AIDS entry), chronic fatigue syndrome (see chronic fatigue syndrome entry), diabetes (see diabetes mellitus entry), and Parkinson's disease (see Parkinson's disease entry).

Scientists do not understand why dysthymic disorders are connected with these physical problems. They think the medical condition or the drugs used for treatment can affect the way a person's neurotransmitters operate in the brain.

In addition to feelings of depression, patients with dysthymic disorder also experience two or more of the following symptoms on an

SIGNS OF MENTAL DEPRESSION

Depressed mood

Lack of interest or pleasure in daily activities

Significant weight loss (without dieting) or weight gain

Difficulty sleeping or excessive sleeping

Loss of energy

Feelings of worthlessness or guilt

Difficulty in making decisions

Restlessness

Recurrent thoughts of death

(Reproduced by permission of Stanley Publishing)

If a person exhibits symptoms of depression on a daily basis for two years or more he or she may have dysthymic disorder. (© 1992 Science Photo Library. Reproduced by permission of Custom Medical Stock Photo.)

almost daily basis for a period of two or more years (one or more years in children):

• Under-eating or overeating
• Insomnia or hypersomnia

- Low energy or fatigue (extreme tiredness)
- Low self-esteem
- Poor concentration or trouble making decisions
- Feelings of hopelessness

DIAGNOSIS

The first step in diagnosing a depressive disorder is an interview with the patient. The interview is followed by one or more tests designed to find out how depressed the patient is. Examples of these tests include the Hamilton Depression Scale, Child Depression Inventory, Geriatric Depression Scale, and Beck Depression Inventory. These tests are given by a doctor, social worker, psychologist, or psychiatrist in his or her office or in a hospital.

TREATMENT

Depressive disorders are treated by one or more of three methods: drugs, psychosocial therapy, or electroconvulsive (pronounced ih-LEK-tro cun-VUL-siv) therapy (ECT). Many drugs seem to work because of changes they produce in the way neurotransmitters work in the brain. Psychosocial therapy consists of interviews between the patient and a trained specialist to find out the causes of a person's depression. ECT makes use of severe electrical shocks to treat a person's depression.

Antidepressants

One group of drugs used to treat depression is called selective serotonin re-uptake inhibitors (SSRIs). These drugs increase the amount of serotonin (pronounced sehr-uh-TOE-nun) in the brain. Serotonin is a major neurotransmitter. Some side effects of SSRIs include anxiety, diarrhea, drowsiness, headache, sweating, nausea, poor sexual functioning, and insomnia (see insomnia entry).

Another group of drug is the tricyclic antidepressants (TCAs). They are less expensive than SSRIs, but they have more side effects. These side effects include dry mouth, dizziness, and heart problems. Because of these effects, TCAs are often not recommended for elderly patients. They are also not recommended for suicidal patients since, if they are taken in large quantities, they cause death.

Monoamine oxidase inhibitors (MAO inhibitors) also act on chemicals present in the brain to relieve the symptoms of depression. One risk in using MAO inhibitors is that they react with certain foods, such as aged cheese and meats, to produce dangerous side effects.

Psychosocial Therapy

The purpose of psychosocial therapy is to discover possible causes for a person's depression. A therapist helps the patient to understand himself or herself better. This self-understanding may help the patient overcome the problems that led to depression.

One form of psychosocial therapy is called cognitive-behavioral therapy. The therapist helps the patient to recognize thought patterns (such as thinking about suicide) that lead to depression. The patient is then trained to change those negative thought patterns to positive patterns. If successful, this therapy can help relieve the symptoms of depression.

Electroconvulsive Therapy

Electroconvulsive therapy (ECT) is usually a treatment of last resort. It is tried when neither drugs nor psychosocial therapy have been very helpful with a patient. In rare cases, it is used if a patient refuses to take oral medication (drugs taken by mouth) or the patient is suicidal or out of touch with reality.

ECT consists of a series of electrical shocks administered to a patient's brain. The patient is first put to sleep with a general anesthetic and is given muscle relaxants. The muscle relaxants prevent violent responses to the electric shock that can result in broken bones. ECT is accompanied by a number of side effects, such as headache, muscle soreness, nausea, confusion, and memory loss.

No one knows how ECT works or what effects it has on the brain. In fact, some experts believe that the treatment is too dangerous to use with patients. Under the best circumstances, they say, it should be tried only in the most serious cases that do not respond to any other form of treatment.

Alternative Treatment

The herb known as St. John's wort is used throughout Europe to treat depression. Unlike prescription drugs, it has few side effects. Thus far, there is no scientific evidence about the effectiveness of this herb for the treatment of depression.

Some simple methods for increasing one's mental health include a healthy diet, proper sleep, exercise, and participation in many interesting daily activities.

PROGNOSIS

Untreated or improperly treated depression is the number one cause of suicide in the United States. Proper treatment relieves symptoms in 80 to 90 percent of all patients. The occurrence of a single episode of depression increases the chances of another such episode. After one episode, a person is 50 percent more likely to have a second episode. After a second episode, the risk rises to 70 percent for a third episode. And after a third episode, the risk reaches 90 percent for yet another episode. For this reason, patients with recurrent (repeated) episodes may require long-term treatment with drugs and/or psychosocial therapy.

PREVENTION

The basic causes of depression, such as problems with brain chemicals and heredity, may not be preventable. But anyone who has experienced the feelings of depression can do a great deal to prevent the disorder from developing. People can be taught to recognize the symptoms of depression and to know how to prevent the condition from becoming worse. In many cases, simply staying with a medication program can relieve many of the symptoms of depression. With children, the sooner treatments begin, the more likely they are to be effective.

See also: Bipolar disorder, seasonal affective disorder.

FOR MORE INFORMATION

Books

Copeland, Mary Ellen. *The Depression Workbook: A Guide for Living With Depression and Manic Depression.* Oakland, CA: New Harbinger Publications, 1992.

O'Connor, Richard. *Undoing Depression: What Therapy Doesn't Teach You and Medication Can't Give You.* Boston: Little Brown, 1997.

Thompson, Tracy. *The Beast: A Reckoning with Depression.* New York: G. P. Putnam, 1995.

Thorne, Julia. *You Are Not Alone: Words of Experience and Hope for the Journey Through Depression.* New York: Harperperennial Library, 1993.

Whybrow, Peter. *A Mood Apart.* New York: Harper Collins, 1997.

Periodicals

Miller, Sue, "A Natural Mood Booster." *Newsweek* (May 5, 1997): pp. 74–75.

Organizations

American Psychiatric Association (APA). Office of Public Affairs. 1400 K Street, NW, Washington, DC 20005. (202) 682–6119. http://www.psych.org.

American Psychological Association (APA). Office of Public Affairs. 750 First St., NE, Washington, DC 20002–4242. (202) 336–5700. http://www.apa.org.

National Alliance for the Mentally Ill (NAMI). 200 North Glebe Road, suite 1015, Arlington, VA 22203–3754. (800) 950–6264. http://www.nami.org.

National Depressive and Manic-Depressive Association (NDMDA). 730 N. Franklin St., Suite 501, Chicago, IL 60610. (800) 826–3632. http://www.ndmda.org.

National Institute of Mental Health (NIMH). 5600 Fishers Lane, Rm. 7C-02. Bethesda, MD 20857. (301) 443–4513. http://www.nimh.nih.gov/.

Web Sites

"Ask NOAH About: Mental Health." *NOAH: New York Online Access to Health.* [Online] http://www.noah.cuny.edu/mentalhealth/mental.html (accessed on October 7, 1999).

DIABETES MELLITUS

DEFINITION

Diabetes mellitus (pronounced DI-uh BEE teez MEH-luh-tuss) is a condition in which the body's cells are no longer able to utilize blood sugar. Blood sugar is the fuel that cells use to make energy. Symptoms of diabetes mellitus include excessive thirst and hunger, frequent urination, and tiredness.

DESCRIPTION

Diabetes mellitus is a chronic health disorder. Chronic means that the condition lasts for many years. Diabetes can cause serious health problems. These problems include kidney failure, heart disease, stroke (see stroke entry), and blindness. About fourteen million Americans have diabetes. As many as half of these people do not know they have the condition.

The Energy Your Body Needs

Our bodies require a constant production of energy. We use that energy to walk, talk, think, and carry on many other activities. The energy comes from the food we eat.

WORDS TO KNOW

Glucose: A type of sugar that is present in the blood and in cells, used by cells to make energy.

Insulin: A hormone (type of protein) produced by the pancreas that makes it possible for cells to use glucose in the production of energy.

Ketoacidosis: A condition that results from the build-up of toxic chemicals known as ketones in the blood.

Pancreas: A gland located behind the stomach that produces insulin.

Certain foods contain chemicals known as carbohydrates. When carbohydrates enter the body, they break down to form a simple sugar known as glucose. The glucose travels to cells throughout the body by way of the bloodstream.

To enter a cell, glucose may need the help of another chemical known as insulin. Insulin is produced in the pancreas. Insulin also travels through the bloodstream to all cells in the body. It acts like a key that opens cells so that glucose can enter.

In a healthy body, enough insulin is produced to make sure that all cells get the glucose they need. The cells can then produce enough energy to satisfy the body's needs.

In some cases, however, this system breaks down. One problem may be that the pancreas stops producing enough insulin. There is not enough insulin for all the cells that need it. Glucose cannot get into many of the body's cells. The cells cannot produce enough energy for the body's needs.

Another problem is that some cells may no longer recognize insulin. The pancreas may still produce insulin for all the body's cells, but some cells don't respond to it. Again, glucose can't get into the cells and energy is not produced to satisfy the body's needs.

Types of Diabetes Mellitus

Two types of diabetes mellitus are recognized. These two types differ in two major ways—the age at which they occur and their causes. Type I diabetes is also called juvenile diabetes. It usually begins during childhood or adolescence. In this form of diabetes, the pancreas produces little or no insulin. The condition can be treated by having a person take daily injections of insulin. For this reason, Type I diabetes is also called insulin-dependent diabetes. Type I diabetes affects about three people in one thousand in the United States.

Type II diabetes is sometimes called adult-onset diabetes. The name "adult-onset" comes from the fact that Type II diabetes usually does not appear until a person grows older. More than 90 percent of the diabetics in the United States are Type II diabetics. This form of the disorder is not caused by low levels of insulin. Instead, the body's cells do not recognize insulin in the bloodstream. They are not able to get the glucose they need to make energy.

People with Type II diabetes do not need to take insulin. Their body produces all the insulin it needs. The body just can't use it properly. As a result, Type II diabetes is sometimes called noninsulin-dependent diabetes. Type II diabetes is treated with diet, exercise, and drugs.

CAUSES

The causes of diabetes mellitus are unclear. Both heredity and environment may be involved. Studies have shown that certain genetic factors may be responsible for diabetes. Genes are chemical units found in all cells, that tell cells what functions they should perform. Genes are passed down from parents to children. If parents carry a gene for diabetes, they may pass that gene on to their children.

Some researchers believe that Type I diabetes may also be caused by a virus or some other disease-causing organism. They think the organism may attack the pancreas at an early age. The pancreas may be damaged and lose its ability to produce insulin.

Kaitlyn Bubb, age 7, watches her friend Ivan Kotunov, age 13, perform a blood sugar test. Both children have diabetes. (Reproduced by permission of AP/Wide World Photos)

A number of factors have been tied to Type II diabetes. These factors include:

- Obesity (being excessively overweight, see obesity entry)
- Having relatives with diabetes mellitus
- Belonging to certain high-risk populations, such as African Americans, Native Americans, Hispanics, or Native Hawaiians
- Having high blood pressure (see hypertension entry)
- Having an excess or deficiency of certain substances in the blood, such as cholesterol or triglycerides (a form of fat)

SYMPTOMS

The classic symptoms of diabetes include being overly tired and sick, having to urinate frequently, feeling very thirsty and hungry, and losing weight. The way these symptoms develop differs for Type I and Type II diabetes. In Type I diabetes, they usually show up slowly in children or adolescents over a period of a few days or weeks. In Type II diabetes, they develop even more slowly, over a period of years, in adults over the age of forty. Adults often do not realize they have diabetes mellitus. The condition may be discovered only during a routine physical examination for some other problem.

THE CLASSIC SYMPTOMS OF DIABETES INCLUDE BEING OVERLY TIRED AND SICK, HAVING TO URINATE FREQUENTLY, FEELING VERY THIRSTY AND HUNGRY, AND LOSING WEIGHT.

Type I diabetes is generally a more serious condition than Type II. The most dangerous effect of Type I diabetes is a condition known as ketoacidosis (pronounced KEE-toe-ASS-ih-doe-sus), which occurs when Type I diabetes is not controlled. In ketoacidosis, chemicals that are toxic (poisonous) to the body begin to collect in the blood. These chemicals can cause abdominal pain, vomiting, rapid breathing, extreme tiredness, and drowsiness. If this condition is not treated, a person may fall into a coma and die. The most characteristic symptom of ketoacidosis is sweet-smelling breath.

The symptoms of Type II diabetes usually develop more slowly and are less serious. In the worst circumstance, they include heart disease, infections of the gums and urinary tract, blurred vision, numbness in the feet and legs, and slow-healing wounds.

DIAGNOSIS

A patient with the symptoms listed above may be suspected of having diabetes. The diagnosis can be confirmed very easily and quickly with a blood and/or urine test. The amount of glucose present in the blood or urine can be measured. If the level is unusually high, it is likely the person has diabetes.

The simplest test for diabetes uses paper strips that change color when dipped into urine. The color of the strip is compared to a chart that comes with the strips. The chart shows how much glucose is present in the urine.

Blood tests can also be used to test for glucose. These tests tend to be more accurate than urine tests. A sample of blood is taken from the patient's arm. The sample is then analyzed in a laboratory. The amount of glucose present is determined. That amount is compared with the amount present in a healthy person's blood. A high level of glucose suggests the presence of diabetes.

People with diabetes often test their own blood many times a day. They use home glucose test kits that contain a small needle and a chart. They use the needle to produce a single drop of blood (often from their fingertip). The drop is then placed on a spot on the chart that contains a chemical that reacts with glucose. The color produced on the spot can be compared to the chart. It shows the level of glucose in the blood.

TREATMENT

There is currently no cure for diabetes. However, the condition can be managed well enough to allow most people to live normal lives. Treatment of diabetes focuses on two goals. The first is to keep blood glucose within a normal range, and the second is to prevent complications from developing over time.

Lifestyle Changes for Treatment of Type II Diabetes

Obesity is one of the major causes of Type II diabetes. Therefore, controlling one's weight is an important step in controlling the disorder. Type II diabetics are advised to have a well-balanced, nutritious diet and to follow a program of moderate exercise.

The goal in diet planning is to limit one's intake of calories. The term calories is used to describe the energy content of foods. If one takes in too many calories, they are not used to produce energy. They are converted into fat, which is stored in the body. The number of calories a person should take in each day depends on a number of factors, such as age, weight, and level of activity. Many professional organizations have developed diet plans for people with Type II diabetes. These plans insure that people get all necessary nourishment. They also insure that people do not eat more calories than needed for daily activities.

Oral Medications for Type II Diabetes

A number of drugs have been developed for the treatment of Type II diabetes. Most of these drugs belong to a class of compounds known as the sulfonylureas (pronounced SULL-fuh-nil-u-ree-uhz). They include tolbutamide (pronounced toll-BU-tuh-mide), tolazamide (pronounced toll-AZ-uh-mide), acetohexamide (pronounced ASS-etto-HECK-suh-mide), and chlorpropamide (pronounced klor-PRO-puh-mide). These drugs stimulate the pancreas to make more insulin.

These drugs all have side effects. For example, they may cause a person to gain weight. But weight gain is often the original cause of the problem for Type II diabetics. So the drugs may not be very useful. They are still not as satisfactory as a well-planned diet and program of exercise. The drugs are also not effective against Type I diabetes.

Insulin: Treatment for Type I Diabetes

Type I diabetes can be treated with daily injections of insulin. The injections provide the insulin that the patient's pancreas doesn't make. The amount of insulin taken depends on many factors, including the patient's age, height, weight, food intake, and level of activity.

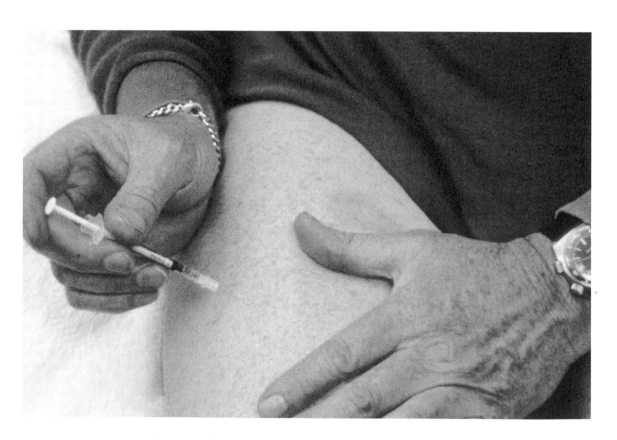

In most patients, Type I diabetes can be controlled with insulin injections. (© 1992 Science Photo Library. Reproduced by permission of Custom Medical Stock Photo.)

Insulin injections may also be needed by people with Type II diabetes. The injections are recommended when other methods of controlling the disorder do not work. The injections are given just under the skin anywhere on the body where there is loose skin.

Patients who require multiple insulin shots over the course of the day may be able to use an insulin pump. An insulin pump is a small device worn outside the body. Insulin flows from the pump through a tube connected to a needle. The needle is inserted into the abdomen. The pump is operated by a small battery. The pump can be programmed to inject a certain dose of insulin at given times of the day.

People who take insulin have to plan their injections carefully. Injections should be given to coincide with meals. If they are given at the wrong time, an insulin reaction may occur. An insulin reaction is the result of having too much insulin in the blood. A person may not have had enough to eat, or may have taken too much insulin. The patient may become cranky, confused, tired, sweaty, and shaky. Left untreated, he or she may become unconscious or have a seizure. Treatment for an insulin reaction is to give the patient food that has sugar in it. The sugar helps overcome the excess insulin in the blood.

Treatment of Last Resort: Surgery

In extreme cases, a pancreas transplant may be performed. In this procedure, the patient's own pancreas is removed and a healthy pancreas substituted. If the surgery is successful, the healthy pancreas begins producing insulin in the patient's body.

Surgery is often a treatment of last resort. Any surgical procedure has many risks involved. A doctor wants to be certain that those risks are worth the benefit the patient will gain by having a new pancreas.

Alternative Treatment

Diabetes can usually be treated successfully by the methods described above. A person should use caution in considering alternative treatments. If they are not successful, life-threatening complications can develop.

Some practitioners recommend a variety of herbal treatments for diabetes. Some of these herbs are thought to reduce glucose in the blood. They include fenugreek, bilberry, garlic, and onions. Cayenne pepper has been suggested to relieve pain in some forms of diabetes and ginkgo to prevent eye disorders related to diabetes.

Any therapy that lowers stress levels may be useful in treating diabetes. Such therapies include hypnosis, biofeedback, and meditation.

PROGNOSIS

diabetes mellitus

In most patients, diabetes can be controlled by diet, exercise, and insulin injections. If the condition is not treated, however, some serious complications may result. For example, uncontrolled diabetes is the leading cause of blindness, kidney disease, and amputations of arms and legs. It also doubles a person's risk for heart disease and increases the risk of stroke. Eye problems also occur more commonly among diabetics than in the general population.

Some other long-term effects of diabetes mellitus include the following:

- Loss of sensitivity in certain nerves, especially in the legs and feet
- Foot ulcers
- Delayed healing of wounds
- Heart and kidney disease

PREVENTION

There is currently no way to prevent Type I diabetes. The risk for Type II diabetes can be reduced, however, by maintaining an ideal weight and exercising regularly.

FOR MORE INFORMATION

Books

American Diabetes Association. *Diabetes A to Z: What You Need to Know About Diabetes : Simply Put,* 3rd edition. Alexandria, VA: American Diabetes Association, 2000.

Edelwich, Jerry, Archie Brodsky, and Ronald A. Arky. *Diabetes: Caring for Your Emotions As Well As Your Health,* Revised edition. Reading, MA: Perseus Books, 1998.

Guthrie, Diana W. *The Diabetes Sourcebook: Today's Methods and Ways to Give Yourself the Best Care,* 3rd edition. Los Angeles: Lowell House, 1997.

Milcohovich, Sue K., and Barbara Dunn-Long. *Diabetes Mellitus: A Practical Handbook,* 7th Ed edition. Palo Alto, CA: Bull Pub. Co, 1999.

Organizations

American Diabetes Association. 1660 Duke Street, Alexandria, VA 22314. (703) 549–1500. Diabetes Information and Action Line: (800) DIABETES. http://www.diabetes.org.

American Dietetic Association. 430 North Michigan Ave., Chicago, IL 60611. (312) 822–0330. http://www.eatright.org.

Juvenile Diabetes Foundation International. 120 Wall Street, New York, NY 10005–4001. (212) 785–9595; (800) JDF–CURE.

National Diabetes Information Clearinghouse. 1 Information Way, Bethesda, MD 20892–3560. (301) 654–3327.

National Institutes of Health. National Institute of Diabetes, Digestive and Kidney Diseases. 900 Rockville Pike, Bethesda, MD 20892. (301) 496–3583. http://www.niddk.nih.gov.

Web sites

"Ask NOAH About: Diabetes." *NOAH: New York Online Access to Health.* [Online] http://www.noah.cuny.edu/diabetes.diabetes.html (accessed on October 24, 1999).

Centers for Disease Control and Prevention. *Diabetes Home Page.* [Online] http://www.cdc.gov/nccdphp/ddt/ddthome.htm (accessed on October 24, 1999).

Other

Insulin-Dependent Diabetes. National Institute of Diabetes and Digestive and Kidney Diseases. National Institute of Health, NIH Publication No. 94-2098.

Noninsulin-Dependent Diabetes. National Institute of Diabetes and Digestive and Kidney Diseases. National Institute of Health, NIH Publication No. 92-241.

DOWN'S SYNDROME

DEFINITION

Down's syndrome is the most common cause of mental retardation (see mental retardation entry) and malformation in newborns. It occurs because of the presence of an extra chromosome.

DESCRIPTION

Chromosomes are structures that carry genetic information in cells. They carry the instructions that tell cells what functions they are to perform. They determine the way a person's body looks and the way it functions.

Cells normally carry two matched sets of twenty-three chromosomes for a total of forty-six chromosomes. One set of twenty-three chromosomes comes from each parent. Down's syndrome occurs when one chromosome pair is damaged. That pair is designated as chromosome #21.

CAUSES

Chromosome #21 can be damaged, for example, if one parent has two chromosomes at location 21, rather than one. A child will then get two #21 chromosomes from one parent and one #21 chromosome from the other parent, for a total of three #21 chromosomes. This form of Down's syndrome is called trisomy 21, meaning that the #21 chromosome has three units rather than two. Overall, the child has forty-seven chromosomes, rather than forty-six chromosomes. This pattern of changes occurs in more than 90 percent of all Down's patients.

Chromosome #21 can also be damaged during cell replication. Cells grow and reproduce over time. As they do so, they make copies of the original chromosomes from the parents. Sometimes, the chromosomes from the parents are normal but a problem occurs when the new cells are reproducing. Two normal chromosomes at location 21 become three chromosomes in some cells.

This condition is known as a mosaic disorder. People with this disorder have some cells containing forty-six chromosomes, and some containing forty-seven chromosomes. They may have less severe symptoms than a person whose cells all contain forty-seven chromosomes. A mosaic condition occurs rarely. Less than 2 percent of all Down's cases are caused by mosaic disorder.

Chromosome #21 can also be damaged when a normal chromosome from the parent breaks into two pieces. One piece of the chromosome becomes attached to another chromosome. This process is called translocation. Translocation occurs in about 3 to 4 percent of all Down's patients.

Down's syndrome occurs in about 1 out of every 800 to 1000 births. It affects an equal number of females and males. The most common cause of Down's syndrome is an extra #21 chromosome in the mother's egg. As a woman grows older, she faces a greater risk of having a baby with Down's syndrome. For example, a woman in her twenties faces a risk of about 1 in 4,000. By the age of thirty-five, that risk has increased to 1 in 400 and, by the age of forty-five, to 1 in 35.

WORDS TO KNOW

Chromosome: A structure located inside the nucleus (center) of a cell that carries genetic information.

Karyotype: The specific chromosomal makeup of a particular cell.

Mental retardation: A condition in which an individual has a lower-than-normal IQ.

Mosaic: Medically, a condition in which an individual cell may contain more than one type of chromosomal composition, with forty-six chromosomes in one cell, for example, and forty-seven chromosomes in another cell.

Translocation: A condition in which a piece of one chromosome breaks off and becomes attached to another chromosome.

Trisomy: A condition in which three identical chromosomes, rather than two, are matched with each other.

SYMPTOMS

Babies with Down's syndrome can often be diagnosed at birth because of some common physical characteristics. For example, they tend to be unusually quiet, less responsive, and weak. Other physical signs include:

- Flat face
- Small head
- Flat bridge of the nose
- Smaller than normal, low-set nose
- Small mouth, causing the tongue to stick out and look unusually large
- Upward slanting eyes
- Extra folds of skin at the inside corner of each eye
- Rounded cheeks
- Small, misshapened ears
- Small, wide hands
- A deep crease across the center of each palm
- A malformed fifth finger
- A wide space between the big and second toes
- Unusual creases on the soles of the feet
- Overly-flexible joints (as in people who are double-jointed)
- Shorter than normal height

Other physical defects may accompany Down's syndrome. About 30 to 50 percent of children with the disorder have heart problems. These defects often reduce the flow of blood through the body.

Gastrointestinal (digestive) tract disorders affect about 5 to 7 percent of all children with Down's syndrome. The most common problem among babies is an obstruction (narrowing or closing) of the upper part of the intestine, where digestion takes place. This obstruction can interrupt the digestion of food, and a baby may vomit after eating. As a result, the baby has trouble gaining weight appropriately.

ABOUT 30 TO 50 PERCENT OF CHILDREN WITH DOWN'S SYNDROME HAVE HEART PROBLEMS.

Other medical conditions that may accompany Down's syndrome include an increased risk for infections, especially ear infections (see earache entry) and pneumonia (see pneumonia entry); certain kidney disorders; thyroid disease; hearing loss (see hearing loss entry); vision problems (see vision disorders entry); and a greatly increased risk for leukemia (see leukemia entry).

Physical development overall takes place at a slower rate in babies with Down's syndrome than in normal babies. Down's babies tend to have weaker muscles, so they have more difficulty learning to sit up, crawl, and walk. Mild to moderate mental retardation is also common in Down's children. The range of IQs (a measure of intelligence) of Down's children varies widely. Some have normal intelligence, while others have severe mental retardation. Most fall within a range sometimes called the trainable range. That means that individuals can be taught to care for themselves and to function normally in social settings and even have simple jobs.

As people with Down's syndrome age, they face an increased risk for Alzheimer's disease (see alzheimer's disease entry). The risk of developing Alzheimer's disease in the general population is about 6 in 100. Among people with Down's syndrome, the risk is 25 in 100. Aging also increases the risk of other conditions for people with Down's syndrome, including cataracts (see cataracts entry), thyroid problems, diabetes (see diabetes mellitus entry), and seizure disorders (see epilepsy entry).

DIAGNOSIS

Diagnosis is often made at birth, when the characteristic physical signs of Down's syndrome are noted. Genetic tests can then confirm the diagnosis. These tests look for abnormal chromosomes. A blood or skin sample is taken from the child. The sample is then stained with a special chemical that makes the chromosomes visible. The pattern of chromosomes that shows up is known as a karyotype (pronounced KARR-ee-uh-tipe). The presence of an abnormal chromosome #21 stands out in the karyotype.

Two preschool children with Down's syndrome. (Photograph by Susan Woog Wagner. Reproduced by permission of Photo Researchers, Inc.)

TREATMENT

There is no cure for Down's syndrome. Many of the conditions that occur along with the disorder, however, can be treated. For example, surgery can be done to repair heart defects. Eyeglasses and hearing aids can help with vision and hearing problems.

Years ago, Down's syndrome children were placed in special institutions early in their lives. They usually spent their whole lives there. We now know that most children with Down's syndrome are able to live at home with their families. With training, most families can provide the care children with Down's syndrome need to lead relatively normal lives.

Some special community groups help families adjust to the presence of a new Down's syndrome child. They can help parents and siblings (brothers and sisters) understand the disorder and teach them how to plan for the baby's future. Schools are required by law to provide services for children with Down's syndrome. Sometimes these services are offered in special classes, and sometimes in regular classrooms. The practice of teaching children with Down's syndrome and other disabilities in regular classrooms is called mainstreaming or inclusion.

PROGNOSIS

The prognosis in Down's syndrome is quite variable. It depends on the other disorders that occur in each individual case. A child with heart defects, for example, is more likely to have serious problems in the future than one with hearing loss. About 90 percent of all Down's syndrome children with no heart problems reach their teens.

People with Down's syndrome usually go through the same physical changes of aging as other people. But those changes take place more rapidly. The average age of death for a person with Down's syndrome is about fifty to fifty-five years.

The prognosis for a baby born with Down's syndrome is better now than ever before. Antibiotics are now available to treat many kinds of infections that would once have killed a child. Community and family support allow people with Down's syndrome to live more normal lives. Down's syndrome people are often able to get an education and hold jobs.

Men with Down's syndrome appear to be uniformly sterile. That is, they are unable to have children. Women with Down's syndrome, however, are usually able to have babies. About half of these babies will also be born with Down's syndrome.

PREVENTION

The only procedure available for preventing Down's syndrome is genetic counseling. In genetic counseling, a trained professional talks with a man and a woman about the chances of their having a Down's syndrome baby. The counselor can inform a couple, for example, that the risk for Down's syndrome increases with the mother's age. Certain tests can also be performed to help with the counseling program.

One of these tests makes use of a protein known as alpha-fetoprotein (AFP, pronounced AL-fuh FEE-toe-PRO-teen). AFP occurs normally in the blood of a pregnant woman. Unusually high or low levels of AFP can, however, suggest problems with the pregnancy. An AFP test can accurately predict the presence of a Down's syndrome baby about 60 percent of the time.

Karen Gaskin and her daughter, Lydia, age twelve, leaving the elementary school where Lydia, who has Down's syndrome, is taught in a regular classroom. (Reproduced by permission of AP/Wide World Photos)

Two other tests are far more accurate. These involve the use of amniocentesis (pronounced AM-nee-oh-sen-TEE-sus) or chorionic villus sampling (CVS, pronounced kore-ee-AH-nik VI-lus). Both are correct about 98 to 99 percent of the time in predicting the presence of a Down's syndrome baby.

In amniocentesis, a long, thin needle is used to remove a sample of amniotic fluid. Amniotic fluid is the liquid that surrounds and protects the baby developing within the pregnant woman. In CVS, a tiny tube is used to remove a small sample of the placenta. The placenta is a spongy tissue that provides nourishment for the growing baby.

In both tests, the samples obtained can be used to make a karyotype of the baby's chromosomes. The karyotype can be studied to see if the chromosomes in position #21 are abnormal. If they are, there is a very strong probability that the baby will be born with Down's syndrome.

A genetic counselor can do no more than provide information to parents about the chance that their baby might be born with Down's syndrome. After that, parents have to make their own decision as to what to do with this information. Some parents decide to have the baby and give it the best possible care. Other parents decide not to continue with the pregnancy.

Once a couple has had one baby with Down's syndrome, they are often concerned about the likelihood of future offspring also being born with the disorder. In most cases, the chances of having a second Down's syndrome child are about the same as having the first. In certain forms of the disorder, however, the chance may increase. For example, if the disorder was caused in the first case by a translocation, the chance of having a second Down's syndrome child is much higher. Genetic counselors are able to calculate with some precision the risk in such cases.

FOR MORE INFORMATION

Books

Levitz, Mitchell, and Andy Bricky. *Count Us in: Growing Up With Down Syndrome*. New York: Harcourt Brace & Co., 1994.

Pueschel, Siegfried M., ed. *Parents Guide to Down Syndrome: Toward a Brighter Future*. Baltimore: Paul H. Brookes Publishing Company, 1995

Pueschel, Siegfried M., and Maria Sustrova, eds. *Adolescents With Down Syndrome: Toward a More Fulfilling Life*. Baltimore: Paul H. Brookes Publishing Company, 1997.

Selikowitz, Mark. *Down Syndrome: The Facts*. 2nd edition New York: Oxford University Press, 1997.

Stray-Gunderson, K. *Babies with Down Syndrome: A New Parents' Guide,* 2nd edition. Bethesda, MD: Woodbine House, 1995.

Tingey, C. *Down Syndrome: A Resource Handbook*. Boston: Little, Brown, Inc., 1988.

Periodicals

"Medical and Surgical Care for Children with Down Syndrome." *The Exceptional Parent* (November 1995): pp. 78+.

Roan, Shari. "Elixir of Hope?" *Los Angeles Times* (March 6, 1996): p. E1.

Organizations

National Down Syndrome Congress. 1605 Chantilly Drive, Suite 250, Atlanta, GA 30324–3269. (800) 232–6372.

National Down Syndrome Society. 666 Broadway, 8th Floor, Nw York, NY 10012–2317. (800) 221–4602. http://www.ndss.org.

Web sites

"Ask NOAH About: Mental Health." *NOAH: New York Online Access to Health.* [Online] http://www.noah.cuny.edu/mentalhealth/mental.html#Mental Retardation (accessed on October 25, 1999).

DYSLEXIA

DEFINITION

Dyslexia is a learning disability (see learning disorders entry) characterized by problems with reading, spelling, writing, speaking, or listening. In many cases, dyslexia appears to be hereditary.

DESCRIPTION

Dyslexia is not a disease. It is a condition in which a person's brain learns in a different way from that of other people. Many people with dyslexia are very intelligent and successful. The condition has nothing to do with a person's intelligence. Dyslexics are often highly talented in many areas, including art, athletics, drama, music, and engineering. These talents often require the ability to bring together sight, spatial skills (the ability to locate objects in three-dimensional space using sight and/or touch), and coordination.

The U.S. National Institutes of Health estimate that about 15 percent of the U.S. population has some form of learning disorder. Those learning disorders are usually related to the use of language and reading. Learning disorders occur in people of all ages, races, and income levels.

People with dyslexia tend to confuse certain letters and have difficulty spelling. (Photograph by Robert Huffman. Reproduced by permission of Field Mark Publications.)

CAUSES

The basic cause of dyslexia is not known. Some experts believe that the condition may be hereditary. Others suggest that it may be caused by differences in the structure of a person's brain and the way that brain functions.

SYMPTOMS

The symptoms of dyslexia are well known. Children with the disorder have trouble learning to read. They may also have problems with hearing the individual sounds in words and understanding how those sounds go together to make a word. They have a tendency to confuse certain letters, such as "b" and "d."

Often a person with dyslexia has a problem translating language into thought, as one does when listening and reading; or translating thought into language, as in writing and speaking.

Common symptoms of dyslexia include problems with:

• Identifying single words
• Understanding sounds in words, sound order, or rhymes
• Spelling
• Transposing (reversing) letters in words
• Handwriting
• Reading comprehension (understanding)
• Delayed spoken language
• Confusion with directions or handedness (right- versus left-handedness)
• Confusion with certain concepts, such as "up" and "down," "early" and "late," and so on
• Mathematics

DIAGNOSIS

A child suspected of being dyslexic should have a complete evaluation. The child's vision, hearing, and intelligence should be tested. The tests should cover all areas of learning, not just reading.

Testing is important because many dyslexic children are not identified early. Teachers and parents may attribute problems in school to factors other than dyslexia and delay treatments that can help the child.

TREATMENT

No single treatment works best with every child. Experts often disagree as to the best method to use. Treatment methods should be designed for each specific child, depending on his or her own individual problems.

TREATMENT METHODS FOR DYSLEXIA SHOULD BE DESIGNED FOR EACH SPECIFIC CHILD.

People with dyslexia often need a structured language program. Teachers need to focus on the sound of letters and the way they are put together in words. There needs to be a focus on the rules that govern written language. Emphasis should be placed on the individual phonetic (sound) units of words in speech, reading, and writing, rather than on memorizing complete words.

It is important to teach dyslexic students using all of the following functions: hearing, touching, writing, and speaking. This instruction can best be provided by teachers who have specialized training in programs for dyslexic students.

PROGNOSIS

The prognosis for dyslexics is very good. Many successful people have dyslexia. The ability to perform well in daily life depends to a large extent on the specific problems an individual has.

The prognosis is better when dyslexia is diagnosed early. Helping a person to develop a strong self-image and providing support from family, friends, and teachers are important factors. A good remedial program is essential in order to make the greatest progress possible.

PREVENTION

There is no known method for preventing dyslexia.

FOR MORE INFORMATION

Books

Davis, Ronald D., and Sheldon M. Braun. *The Gift of Dyslexia: Why Some of the Smartest People Can't Read and How They Can Learn.* New York: Perigee, 1997.

Guyer, Barbara P., and Sally E. Shaywitz. *The Pretenders: Gifted People Who Have Difficulty Learning.* Homewood, IL: High Tide Press, 1997.

Irlen, Helen. *Reading by the Colors: Overcoming Dyslexia and Other Reading Disabilities through the Irlen Method.* Garden City Park, NY: Avery Publishing Group, 1991.

Nosek, Kathleen. *Dyslexia in Adults: Taking Charge of Your Life.* Dallas: Taylor Publishing, 1997.

Nosek, Kathleen. *The Dyslexic Scholar: Helping Your Child Succeed in the School System.* Dallas: Taylor Publishing, 1995.

dyslexia

Organizations

International Dyslexia Association (formerly the Orton Dyslexia Society). 8600 LaSalle Rd., Chester Building, Suite 382, Baltimore, MD 21286. (800) ABC–D123.

Learning Disabilities Association. 4156 Library Rd., Pittsburgh, PA 15234. (412) 341–1515.

EARACHE

DEFINITION

An earache is discomfort or pain caused by an infection of the ear. The medical term for an ear infection is otitis (pronounced oh-TI-tuss).

DESCRIPTION

The ear consists of three parts: the external, middle, and interior ear. The external ear also consists of three parts—the auricle, the auditory canal, and the tympanic membrane. The auricle (pronounced OR-uh-kull) is the outermost part of the ear; the part you can see attached to the sides of your head. The auricle is connected to the interior parts of the ear by means of a narrow opening called the auditory canal. At the end of the auditory canal is the tympanic membrane, or eardrum.

Just beyond the tympanic membrane is the middle ear. The middle ear contains three bones called ossicles (pronounced AH-sih-kulls). These three bones are connected to the inner ear.

The middle ear also contains the eustachian (pronounced you-STAY-shun or you-STAY-shee-un) tube, which connects the middle ear to the pharynx (pronounced FAHR-inks). The pharynx is a passageway behind the nose through which air passes into the lungs. The eustachian tube helps maintain an equal air pressure between the middle ear and the outside world.

Sound waves enter the ear through the auricle and auditory canal. They cause the tympanic membrane to vibrate. That vibration is passed on to the ossicles in the middle ear. Those bones, in turn, pass on the sound vibrations to the inner ear. Once they reach the inner ear, the sound vibrations are sent to the brain by way of the auditory nerve. The brain then translates these vibrations into sounds.

Microorganisms that cause disease can enter the ear in one of two ways. They can enter by way of the auricle and auditory canal, or they can come in through the eustachian tube. In either case, these microorganisms can cause an infection. Infections usually occur in the outer ear or the middle ear. An infection of the outer ear is called otitis externa, and an infection of the middle ear is called otitis media.

CAUSES

Bacteria, viruses, and fungi can all cause ear infections. The way otitis externa and otitis media develop is somewhat different.

Otitis Externa

Infections of the outer ear occur most commonly in summer. People often spend time in swimming pools and lakes. Their outer ears are more likely to be filled with water than they are during the winter. The presence of water in the ear has two effects. First, it tends to wash away cerumen (pronounced seh-ROO-men) in the ear. Cerumen is ear wax. It coats the ear and protects it from microorganisms.

Second, water carries bacteria, viruses, and fungi into the external ear. The external ear is an ideal place for the growth of these microorganisms. It is warm, moist, and dark. In the absence of cerumen, these microorganisms grow rapidly and can cause an infection of the outer ear.

Otitis Media

Most cases of otitis media occur during the winter. They develop as a side effect of an upper respiratory infection (URI), such as a cold (see common cold entry) or the flu (see influenza entry). Bacteria or viruses that cause URIs travel down the Eustachian tube into the middle ear. There they grow and cause an infection of the middle ear.

Otitis media is most common among young children between the ages of three months and

WORDS TO KNOW

Adenoid: A mass of lymph tissue located near the pharynx.

Antibiotic: A substance derived from fungi or bacteria that suppresses the growth of other microorganisms. Antibiotics are used to treat infections.

Auricle: The external structure of the ear.

Cephalosporins: A specific type of antibiotic used to treat many types of infections.

Cerumen: Earwax.

Eustachian tube: A small tube that connects the middle ear to the pharynx.

Ossicles: Tiny bones located within the middle ear responsible for transmitting sound vibrations from the outer ear to the inner ear.

Penicillin: A specific types of antibiotic used to treat many types of infections.

Pharynx: The part of the airway that connects the nose and mouth with the upper part of the digestive system.

three years. During this period, the eustachian tube is still quite short. Bacteria and viruses can travel down the tube to the middle ear quite easily.

SYMPTOMS

Symptoms vary depending on the type of ear infection.

Otitis Externa

The first symptom of otitis externa is usually itching in the outer ear. As the infection develops, the ear becomes very painful. Just touching the ear can often cause severe pain.

The auditory canal may also become swollen. When this happens, it becomes narrower, making it more difficult for sounds to pass to the middle ear. The patient may find it more difficult to hear.

In severe cases of otitis externa, the outer ear may become red and swollen. A fever often develops. The lymph nodes around the ear may also become swollen and painful.

Otitis Media

Otitis media is characterized by fever, pain, and problems with hearing. Fluid may develop in the middle ear. This fluid may press on nerves, causing severe pain. Babies may have difficulty feeding because of the pressure in the middle ear.

The lymph nodes around the eustachian tubes may also become inflamed and painful. These lymph nodes are called the adenoids. Infections of the adenoids often occur along with URIs and infections of the middle ear.

DIAGNOSIS

Diagnosis of an ear infection is usually quite simple. A patient's complaint about pain in the ear is a strong hint of the problem. A simple physical examination usually confirms the diagnosis. The doctor can look into the ear with the unaided eye or with an instrument that shines light into the ear. The ear usually looks red and swollen if an infection is present.

An infection of the middle ear can usually be diagnosed by examining the tympanic membrane. The membrane itself will appear red and

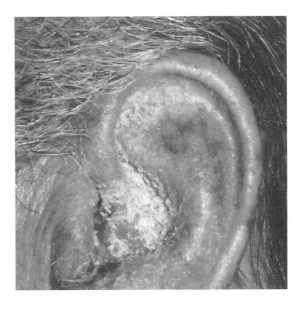

A severe case of otitis externa. (Photograph by Dr. P. Marazzi. Reproduced by permission of Custom Medical Stock Photo.)

swollen. The pattern produced by the ossicles on the membrane may also be characteristic of an infection. Under normal circumstances, this pattern has a distinctive shape called a "landmark." When the middle ear becomes infected, the landmark may no longer be visible.

The microorganism responsible for the infection can be determined by taking a culture. A clean cotton swab is wiped on the inner surface of the ear, and a small sample of tissue is removed. In the case of otitis media, fluid leaking from the middle ear can also be taken. These samples can then be incubated (kept in a warm, moist place) to encourage the growth of bacteria and viruses. After twenty-four to forty-eight hours, the samples can be studied under a microscope to determine which microorganisms are present.

TREATMENT

Most infections of the ear are treated successfully with antibiotics. The antibiotics kill any bacteria responsible for the infection. If the infection is caused by a virus, the antibiotics are of no value.

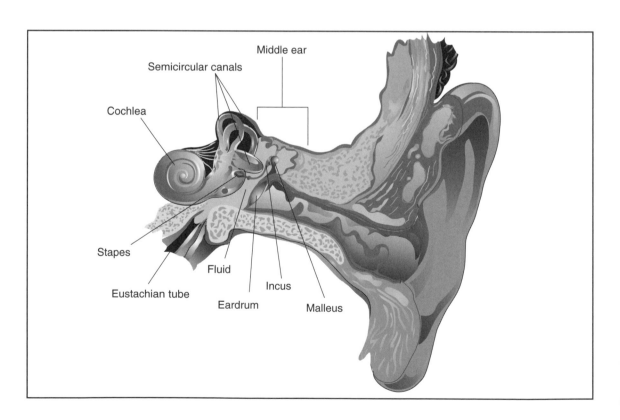

An illustration of the structures of the ear. (Reproduced by Electronic Illustrators Group)

The antibiotics can be applied directly to the outer ear in cases of otitis externa. They are often combined with steroids to help reduce inflammation and swelling.

Otitis media is usually treated with oral (taken by mouth) antibiotics. The most popular medications are penicillins and cephalosporins (pronounced seff-a-lo-SPORE-inz). They are usually given over a seven to ten day period.

Pain from an ear infection can be relieved by holding a warm compress or a water bottle filled with warm water and wrapped in a towel against the infected ear. Over-the-counter pain relievers, such as aspirin, ibuprofen, and acetaminophen, may also offer some relief from the pain. Children under the age of twelve should not take aspirin as it can cause Reye's syndrome (see Reye's syndrome entry).

PAIN FROM AN EAR INFECTION CAN BE RELIEVED BY HOLDING A WARM COMPRESS AGAINST THE INFECTED EAR.

Alternative Treatment

Some practitioners believe that food allergies (see allergies entry) increase the risk of ear infections, since allergic reactions can cause the tissues in the middle ear to swell, making it a better environment for bacteria and viruses to thrive. They recommend eliminating foods from the diet that might cause allergic reactions, such as wheat, dairy products, corn, peanuts, citrus fruits, and eggs.

Ear drops that contain herbal products are also recommended for the treatment of earache. Some herbs that have been suggested include goldenseal, mullein, St. John's wort, and echinacea (pronounced ekk-ih-NAY-shuh). Massage therapy of the skull may also be useful in relieving pressure on the ears and improving the functioning of the eustachian tube.

PROGNOSIS

With proper treatment, the prognosis for ear infections is very good. If left untreated, however, infections of the middle ear can lead to complications that may cause hearing and speech problems.

PREVENTION

Infections of the outer ear can be prevented by keeping the ear clean and dry. Adding a few

A VACCINE FOR EAR INFECTIONS

Help for ear infections may be on the way. California scientists announced in 1999 that a new vaccine for certain ear infections had been developed. The vaccine does not work on all bacteria that cause ear problems. In fact, it affects only about 7 percent of all ear problems. That may not seem like a big number, but scientists are excited about the news for two reasons.

First, eliminating even 7 percent of all ear infections could save up to $500 million a year in doctor bills. Up to two million trips to the doctor for ear problems could be eliminated.

Second, the vaccine may lead to similar treatments for other ear disorders. Other vaccines might also be developed that could totally eliminate the $5 billion a year that Americans spend on ear infections.

drops of a mixture of alcohol and acetic acid after swimming can insure that the ear dries properly.

There seems to be little chance of preventing infections of the middle ear in young children. The problem appears to be a normal part of growing up. One step that parents can take is to reduce as much as possible the young child's chance of catching a cold, the flu, or some other infection of the upper respiratory tract. In addition, the patient should receive medical attention as soon as an infection appears. Children who have had otitis media should have follow-up visits to the doctor after the infection has disappeared.

FOR MORE INFORMATION

Books

Greene, Alan R. *The Parent's Complete Guide to Ear Infections.* Allentown, PA: Peoples Medical Society, 1997.

Schmidt, Michael A., and Doris Rapp. *Healing Childhood Ear Infections: Prevention, Home Care, and Alternative Treatment,* 2nd edition. Berkeley, CA: North Atlantic Books, 1996.

Periodicals

"Keep Your Ears Dry." *Consumer Reports on Health* (July 1995): pp. 80+.

Organizations

American Academy of Otolaryngology-Head and Neck Surgery, Inc. One Prince Street, Alexandria, VA 22314–3357. (703) 836–4444.

Web sites

"Ask NOAH About: Pain." *NOAH: New York Online Access to Health.* [Online] http://www.noah.cuny.edu/pain/pain.html#E (accessed on October 25, 1999).

EMPHYSEMA

DEFINITION

Emphysema is a respiratory disorder characterized by problems in breathing. The disorder is caused by the enlargement of air sacs in the lungs.

DESCRIPTION

Emphysema is the most common cause of death from respiratory disease in the United States. It is generally caused by heavy cigarette smoking. In a small number of cases, it is caused by an inherited defect.

Emphysema is most common among people over the age of fifty. In the late 1990s, males are considered more likely to develop the disorder than females. However, that pattern is changing. The number of women who smoke is increasing rapidly. As this number continues to increase, the number of women who die of emphysema will also increase. In 1999, there were around two million people in the United States with emphysema.

CAUSES

When a person inhales, air travels into the nose and mouth. The air then moves downward into the windpipe (trachea, pronounced TRAY-kee-uh). The windpipe branches off into two large tubes called the bronchi (pronounced BRON-ki). Each bronchus, in turn, divides into many smaller tubes called bronchioles (pronounced BRON-kee-olz). Finally, the bronchioles end in many small air sacs called alveoli (pronounced al-VEE-o-lie). It is in the alveoli that oxygen from the air passes into the blood. The blood then carries the oxygen to cells.

A healthy person's lungs contain many tiny alveoli. The total surface area of these alveoli is very large. Oxygen can get through the alveoli into the blood very easily.

In people who smoke, the lungs undergo a change. The walls that separate the alveoli from each other break down. Air spaces combine with each other to make larger and larger air sacs. Although the air sacs get bigger, there are far fewer of them. Overall, the total surface area of these air sacs is much smaller than the surface area of the original alveoli. Less and less oxygen can pass through the air sacs into the blood. When this happens, the symptoms of emphysema begin to appear.

WORDS TO KNOW

Alveoli: Small air sacs at the ends of bronchioles through which oxygen passes from the lungs into blood.

Bronchi: Two large tubes that branches off the trachea and leads to the lungs; each tube is called a bronchus when referred to singularly.

Bronchioles: Smaller extensions of the bronchi.

Bronchodilators: Substances that help tissue relax and open up airways to make breathing easier.

Electrocardiogram: A test that measures the electrical activity of the heart to determine whether it is functioning normally.

Pulmonary function test: A test that measures the amount of air a patient can breath in and out.

Pulmonary hypertension: High blood pressure in the arteries and veins associated with the lungs.

Trachea: The windpipe, extending from the larynx (the voice box) to the lungs.

Volume reduction surgery: A surgical procedure in which damaged portions of a patient's lung are removed to make it easier for the patient to use healthy parts of the lung to get the oxygen needed for ordinary functioning.

emphysema

A person with emphysema has to breathe harder to take in more oxygen. He or she is often short of breath and may have to gasp for air. Patients often develop a chronic (long-lasting) mild cough and may begin to lose weight.

These conditions gradually become worse over time. At first, a person may notice shortness of breath only when exercising. Later, even a mild exertion may cause breathing problems. Eventually, the person has trouble breathing even when sitting quietly.

Emphysema often leads to other problems of the pulmonary (lung) system. These problems include pneumonia (see pneumonia entry), pulmonary

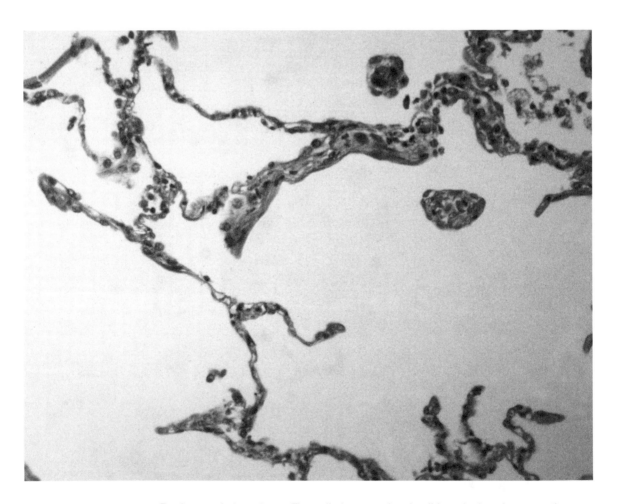

Emphysema in lung tissue. The walls between the alveoli have broken down, creating fewer alveoli. (© 1992 J.L. Carson. Reproduced by permission of Custom Medical Stock Photo.

hypertension (high blood pressure in the lungs), and chronic respiratory failure.

DIAGNOSIS

The symptoms of emphysema are obvious. However, they are similar to the symptoms of other respiratory disorders. A major goal of diagnosis is to eliminate other possible causes of the patient's symptoms.

A first step in diagnosis is a medical history. A doctor will determine if there are factors in the patient's background that might suggest emphysema. Smoking is the most obvious of these factors.

A physical examination can provide further information. A doctor may listen through a stethoscope as he or she taps on the patient's chest. A clue to the presence of emphysema is a hollow sound produced by the tapping.

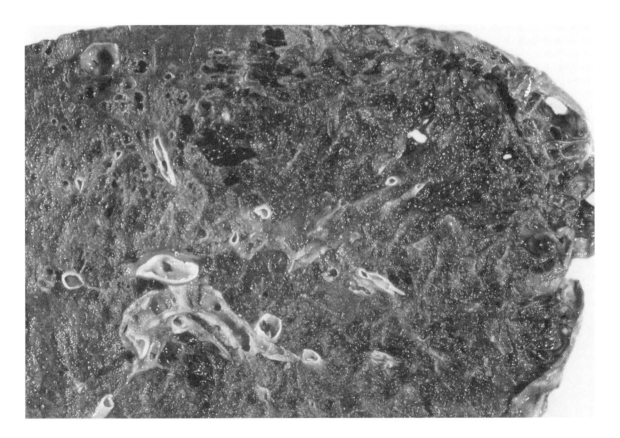

A cross section of a smoker's lung with emphysema. (Photograph by Dr. E. Walker. Reproduced by permission of the Science Photo Library/Photo Researchers, Inc.)

The hollow sound is caused by the large air sacs that develop as a result of emphysema.

A pulmonary function test may also be conducted. A pulmonary function test involves measuring the amount of air a patient can breathe in and out. That amount is measured against the amount that a healthy person can breathe. The test tells whether the person has emphysema and, if so, to what extent it has developed.

As the disease develops, an X ray can be helpful in making a diagnosis. The X ray may show expansion or stretching of the lungs. The position of the heart may change, or blisters may show up on the lungs. Muscles around the lungs may also appear larger.

Late in the disease, an electrocardiogram (pronounced ih-LEK-tro-KAR-dee-uh-gram) may show progress of the condition. An electrocardiogram measures electrical activity of the heart. As the heart is stressed by the patient's efforts to breathe, changes in electrical activity may begin to show up.

TREATMENT

Once emphysema has developed, there is no way to cure the disease or reverse the damage it has done. However, there are many steps that can be taken to slow the progress of the disease, make the patient more comfortable, and prevent the worst complications of the condition.

The first step is for the patient to stop smoking. Unless the patient makes this decision, his or her condition will only continue to get worse. Further treatment can do relatively little to relieve the symptoms of the disorder.

Special exercises may be prescribed for the patient. One objective of these exercises is to keep the lungs healthy and free of infection. Another goal is to develop the muscles used in breathing.

Bronchodilators (pronounced brong-ko-die-LATE-urs) are sometimes used to help relieve the symptoms of emphysema. Bronchodilators are substances that help tissue relax. They assist airways in opening up to allow air to travel more easily through the lungs. Antibiotics may also be used to reduce the risk of lung infections.

In later stages of the disease, oxygen therapy may be necessary. Oxygen therapy consists of providing patients with an extra supply of oxygen, usually through a nose or face mask. The additional oxygen helps the heart to work more easily and reduces the stress that can lead to heart disorders.

Volume reduction surgery is increasingly used to treat emphysema. In volume reduction surgery, damaged portions of the patient's lung are removed. The procedure makes it easier for the patient to use healthy parts of the lung to get the oxygen needed for ordinary functioning.

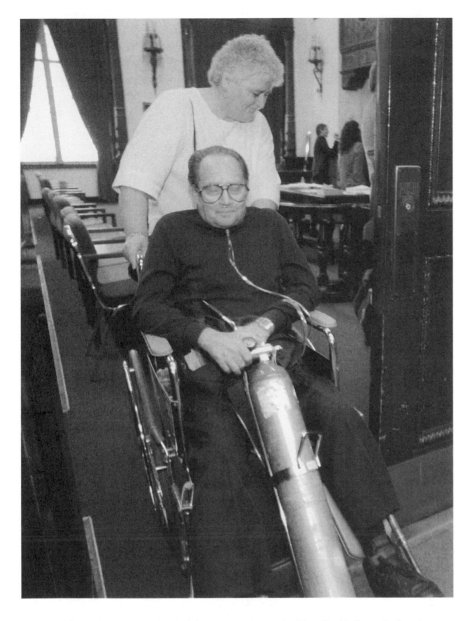

A man with emphysema is wheeled from a courtroom by his wife. He is part of a class-action lawsuit against cigarette companies. (Reproduced by permission of AP/Wide World Photos)

A treatment of last resort is a lung transplant. In a lung transplant, a healthy lung is removed from a donor and used to replace the damaged lung of an emphysema patient. The procedure is very risky. In addition, there are seldom enough lungs available for transplant to meet the needs of all patients who want them.

Alternative Treatment

Alternative treatments are most valuable when they are used in conjunction with traditional medical care. Aromatherapists may use a variety of oils to make breathing easier. These oils include eucalyptus (pronounced YOOK-ah-lip-tus), hyssop (pronounced HEYE-sop), aniseed, lavender, pine, and rosemary. The Chinese herb ephedra (pronounced EF-ed-ra; called ma huang in Chinese) is regarded as a bronchodilator, but it should not be used by patients with heart disorders or high blood pressure. Several herbs, such as elecampane (pronounced EL-i-cam-pane), may help patient's clear mucus from the lungs. Mullein (pronounced MULL-en) tea is recommended to soothe the linings of the lungs. Yoga may be helpful in improving a patient's breathing techniques.

PROGNOSIS

Emphysema is a serious and chronic disease. It cannot be cured or reversed. However, early treatment can slow the progress of the disease. It can also help to prevent its most serious complications. Overall, the survival rate of patients diagnosed with emphysema is about four years. However, that prognosis is dependent on a variety of factors. The ability of a patient to give up smoking is one of the most important factors. The availability and use of oxygen therapy is another factor.

PREVENTION

Emphysema is a condition that is relatively easy to prevent. The best way to prevent the disease is not to smoke cigarettes or, if a person already smokes, to quit. A relatively small number of cases are caused by genetic factors, over which a person has no control. But the vast majority of emphysema cases result from cigarette smoking.

Patients who have already developed emphysema can take a number of steps to slow its progress. For example, they should avoid breathing polluted air as much as possible. The pollutants in air have much the same effect on lungs as does cigarette smoke. Patients should also consider being vaccinated against diseases that affect the respiratory system, such as influenza (the flu; see influenza entry).

FOR MORE INFORMATION

Books

Adams, Francis V. *The Breathing Disorders Sourcebook*. Los Angeles: Lowell House, 1998.

Haas, Francois, and Sheila Sperber Haas. *The Chronic Bronchitis and Emphysema Handbook.* New York: John Wiley & Sons, 1990.

Ries, Andrew L., ed. *Shortness of Breath: A Guide to Better Living and Breathing,* 5th edition. St. Louis, MO: Mosby-Year Book, 1995.

Organizations

American Lung Association. (800) LUNG–USA (800–586–4872). http://www.lungusa.org.

National Heart, Lung, and Blood Institute. Building 31, Room 4A21, Bethesda, MD 20892. (301) 496–4326. http://www.nhlbi.nih.gov.

The National Lung Health Education Program and the National Emphysema Foundation. http://www.emphysemafoundation.org.

Web sites

IVI Publishing Healthnet. "Emphysema." [Online] http://www.healthnet.ivi.com/bh/cond/ailments/htm/emphysema.htm (accessed on October 25, 1999).

ENCEPHALITIS

DEFINITION

Encephalitis (pronounced in-seh-fuh-LIE-tess) is an inflammation of the brain. It may be caused by a number of different factors. One of the most common causes is direct infection of the brain by a virus or bacterium. Inflammation can also occur as a complication of some other disorder, such as mumps (see mumps entry) or herpes simplex (see herpes infections entry). About two thousand cases of encephalitis are reported in the United States each year.

DESCRIPTION

Inflammation of the brain is a reaction of the body's immune system. The immune system is a network of cells, tissues, and chemical substances designed to protect the body against invasion by foreign agents. Sometimes, a foreign agent gets directly into the brain. In the process of fighting off the foreign agent, brain tissues become swollen and inflamed. In other cases, the infection occurs elsewhere in the body, such as the throat or neck. The immune reaction to those infections can also cause inflammation of the brain.

encephalitis

There are more than a dozen viruses that can cause encephalitis. In some cases, the viruses are spread by direct contact between two people. In other cases, the viruses are transmitted by means of an animal or insect bite. Some common viruses and viral diseases that can cause encephalitis include:

- Chickenpox (see chickenpox entry)
- Measles (see measles entry)
- Mumps
- Epstein-Barr virus
- Cytomegalovirus infection (EBV)
- Human immunodeficiency virus (HIV; see AIDS entry)
- Herpes simplex virus
- Herpes zoster virus (shingles)
- Herpes B virus
- Polio (see polio entry)
- Rabies (see rabies entry)
- Viruses carried by mosquitoes (arboviruses)

Some of these viruses may infect the brain directly. In other cases, the infection spreads from another part of the body, as is usually the case with chickenpox, measles, mumps, rubella (see rubella entry), and Epstein-Barr virus. For example, a person may develop a case of chickenpox, then about five to ten days later, as an immune reaction to the chickenpox virus, the brain becomes inflamed and swollen.

Many forms of encephalitis are spread by the bites of insects or animals. Mosquitoes are common carriers of encephalitis viruses. They carry the viruses in their blood and saliva. When they bite a human, they may transfer the virus to the human's bloodstream. The virus multiplies and spreads throughout the body. When it reaches the brain, it may cause encephalitis.

Dogs, cats, mice, raccoons, squirrels, and bats are also carriers of encephalitis viruses. These animals also carry the virus in their blood and saliva. When they bite a human, they can transmit the virus to the human bloodstream.

One of the most serious forms of encephalitis is caused by the herpes simplex virus. The herpes simplex virus causes cold sores and genital herpes. Sometimes the herpes virus spreads

WORDS TO KNOW

Cerebrospinal fluid: Fluid found within the spinal column that is often used to diagnose infections of the central nervous system (the brain and spinal cord).

Electroencephalogram (EEG): A test in which electrical currents in the brain are measured to see if there has been damage to the brain.

Inflammation: A response by the immune system to invasion by a foreign body; signs of an inflammation are redness, heat, swelling, and pain.

Magnetic resonance imaging (MRI): A technique for studying the structure of internal organs by using magnetic waves.

Vaccine: A preparation containing dead or weakened viruses or bacteria to increase a person's immunity (protection) against a certain type of infection.

Virus: A very small organism that can live only within a cell and that can cause some form of disease.

directly to the brain, causing an encephalitis infection. About 10 percent of all encephalitis cases are caused by this virus. In untreated patients, the rate of death is 70 percent. The rate drops to 15 to 20 percent if patients receive treatment.

SYMPTOMS

The symptoms of encephalitis range from very mild to very severe. They include:

- Headache
- Fever
- Lethargy (sleepiness and fatigue)
- Malaise (a feeling of weakness and poor health)
- Nausea and vomiting
- Visual problems
- Tremor (shaking)
- Decreased consciousness (drowsiness and confusion)
- Stiff neck
- Seizures

Symptoms often progress rapidly. They change from being mild to severe within several days or even a few hours.

DIAGNOSIS

The first step in diagnosis may be a medical history. A doctor will try to determine if the patient has had recent contact with a virus that can cause encephalitis. The diagnosis can be confirmed with a variety of tests. These include:

- **Blood tests.** Blood tests may detect antibodies against viruses. Antibodies are chemicals produced by the body's immune system. They are manufactured when a foreign agent, such as a virus, enters the body.
- **Lumbar puncture (spinal tap).** In a lumbar puncture, a long, thin needle is inserted into the spinal column. A small amount of cerebrospinal (pronounced suh-REE-bro-spyn-al) fluid (CSF) is removed. The fluid can be tested to see if viruses or bacteria are present.
- **Electroencephalogram** (pronounced ih-LEK-tro-en-SEF-ah-lo-gram; also called an EEG). An EEG is a test in which electrical currents in the brain are measured. The test can show whether there has been damage to the brain.
- **Imaging scans.** The brain can be studied by a number of imaging techniques, such as X rays and magnetic resonance imaging (MRI). These techniques often reveal abnormal structures in the brain.

- **Biopsy.** In a biopsy, a needle is used to remove a small portion of brain tissue. The brain tissue can then be studied under a microscope. The presence of viruses or other foreign agents may be detected.

TREATMENT

The treatment used for encephalitis depends on the cause of the infection. Bacterial encephalitis can be treated with antibiotics. Antibiotics kill bacteria, but not viruses. Viral encephalitis can be treated with drugs that kill viruses. Relatively few drugs of this kind have been developed. Some antivirals that can be used are acyclovir (pronounced a-SIGH-klo-veer), ganciclovir (pronounced gan-SIGH-klo-veer), foscarnet (pronounced fos-KAHR-net), ribovarin, and azidothymidine (AZT, pronounced AZE-ih-do-thigh-mih-deen). These drugs are more effective with some forms of encephalitis than with others.

Other drugs are available for the treatment of the symptoms of encephalitis. For example, corticosteroids (pronounced kor-tih-ko-STAIR-oids) are used to reduce inflammation and swelling. Anticonvulsant drugs can be used to control seizures. Fever can be treated with aspirin or acetaminophen. Aspirin should not be given to childen due to the risk of Reye's syndrome (see Reye's syndrome entry).

PROGNOSIS

Encephalitis symptoms may last several weeks. Most cases of encephalitis are mild, however, and patients recover quickly and completely. They experience no further problems after the disease has disappeared.

About 10 percent of all encephalitis patients die from the infection. The death rate varies, depending on the kind of encephalitis. For example, there aren't any effective treatments for eastern equine encephalitis and the death rate is usually about 30 percent. Herpes encephalitis has one of the highest death rates. With treatment, 15 to 20 percent of herpes encephalitis cases result in death. Without treatment, the number of deaths jumps to 70 to 80 percent.

MOST CASES OF ENCEPHALITIS ARE MILD AND PATIENTS RECOVER QUICKLY.

Some people do experience long-term neurological damage (damage to the nervous system, including the brain) after having encephalitis. The effects include personality changes, memory loss, language difficulties, seizures, and partial paralysis.

PREVENTION

There are two major ways to avoid encephalitis. One is to reduce the risk of getting the disease from another human who has been infected. Most infections of this kind are spread hand-to-hand or mouth-to-hand. To avoid transmission of this kind, a person should remember to wash his or her hands frequently during the day.

A second way to avoid encephalitis is to reduce the chance of being bitten by mosquitoes, rats, bats, and other animals that carry the disease. One should be aware when such animals may be around. For example, mosquitoes tend to be more common in warm, moist areas. They tend to be more active at dawn and dusk. A person who has to be outdoors during these times should try not to have bare arms and legs. Mosquito repellent should be used to prevent bites.

Vaccines (treatments that enable the body to build immunity to certain viruses) are available for some viruses, such as polio, herpes B, and equine encephalitis. A person who may be at risk for these viruses should have injections of the vaccines.

FOR MORE INFORMATION

Organizations

Centers for Disease Control and Prevention. 1600 Clifton Rd., NE, Atlanta, GA 30333. (404) 639–3311. http://www.cdc.gov.

EPILEPSY

DEFINITION

Epilepsy is a seizure disorder. A seizure is an event that involves loss of consciousness and motor (muscular) control. A person with a seizure disorder often experiences repetitive muscle jerking called convulsions. The condition is caused by a sudden change in electrical activity in the brain.

DESCRIPTION

The medical profession now recognizes about twenty different kinds of epilepsy. These forms of the disorder vary on the basis of severity and the parts of the body affected by the seizure. Most patients have only one form of epilepsy. About 30 percent have two or more forms of the disorder.

Experts estimate that about 2 percent of the general population has some form of epilepsy. One in ten Americans experience at least one epileptic seizure at some time in their lives. At least 200,000 Americans have at least one seizure a month.

About 125,000 new cases of epilepsy are diagnosed in the United States each year. About a quarter of those cases are diagnosed in children younger than five years old.

The two most common types of epilepsy are called tonic-clonic seizures and absence seizures. At one time, these forms of the disorder were better known as grand mal ("great illness") and petit mal ("small illness"). About 90 percent of people with epilepsy experience tonic-clonic seizures, and 25 percent experience absence seizures. Less than 20 percent of patients experience other forms of epilepsy alone or in various combinations.

200,000 AMERICANS HAVE AT LEAST ONE SEIZURE A MONTH.

CAUSES

The brain contains a mass of neurons (nerve cells) that constantly communicate with each other. They communicate in two ways: by sending certain chemicals back and forth, and by the passage of electric currents among them. Under certain conditions, those electric currents can be disrupted. Instead of traveling smoothly between neurons, they go out of control.

When this happens, messages traveling through the brain are wildly disrupted. The brain begins to send out irregular and unpredictable messages to the rest of the body. Muscles throughout the body begin to contract and relax in random patterns. These changes bring about the symptoms of epilepsy.

Epilepsy is usually classified as symptomatic or idiopathic (pronounced ih-dee-uh-PA-thik). Symptomatic epilepsy is a form of the condition for which a cause is known. For example, a person may receive a blow to the head. The injury may cause damage that leads to the development of epilepsy. Some conditions that can cause symptomatic epilepsy include:

- Serious infections of the central nervous system
- Heat stroke (see heat disorders entry)
- An abscess (open sore) in the brain
- Rabies, tetanus, and malaria (see entries)

WORDS TO KNOW

Aura: A set of warning signals that an epileptic attack is about to begin.

Clonic phase: The stage of a grand mal attack in which muscles alternately contract and relax.

Electroencephalogram (EEG): A test used to measure electrical activity of the brain to see if the brain is functioning normally.

Grand mal: An alternative term used for tonic-clonic epilepsy.

Idiopathic epilepsy: A form of epilepsy for which no cause is known.

Neuron: A nerve cell.

Petit mal: An alternative term used for absence epilepsy.

Seizure: A convulsion; a series of involuntary muscular movements that alternate between contractions and relaxations.

Symptomatic epilepsy: A form of epilepsy for which some specific cause is known.

Tonic phase: The stage of a grand mal attack in which muscles become rigid and fixed.

- Toxic (poisonous) materials, such as lead or alcohol
- Damage to the brain or skull (see head injury entry)
- Drug allergy
- Stroke (see stroke entry)

Idiopathic epilepsy is epilepsy for which no specific cause has been identified. Some authorities believe that idiopathic epilepsy is caused by damage to a newborn baby's brain during delivery.

About 75 percent of all cases of epilepsy are idiopathic. Individuals with this condition usually experience their first seizure between the ages of two and fourteen. Symptomatic epilepsy usually does not appear until later in life, after the age of twenty-five.

SYMPTOMS

Symptoms vary depending on the type of seizure.

Tonic-clonic Seizures

A person who is about to have a tonic-clonic seizure often has a warning. That warning is called an aura. During the aura, the patient may emit a loud cry. The attack actually begins when the person loses consciousness and falls to the ground. His or her muscles become rigid for about thirty seconds. This period is known as the tonic phase of the disorder. The muscles then alternately contract and relax, causing the patient to thrash about. This phase of the attack is known as the clonic stage. The patient may also lose control of his or her bladder or bowels, or have trouble breathing.

A tonic-clonic attack usually lasts between two and five minutes. After the attack, the patient may be confused or have trouble talking. He or she may complain of headache or muscle soreness or weakness in the arms or legs. In some cases, the patient may fall into a deep sleep.

Absence Seizure

An absence seizure is a milder form of a tonic-clonic seizure. An absence seizure usually begins with a brief loss of consciousness. This phase of the attack lasts between one and ten seconds. Patients may become very quiet. They may stare blankly, roll their eyes, or move their lips. The whole attack is usually over in fewer than twenty seconds.

After an absence seizure, patients generally do not remember anything about the event. They just continue with whatever they were doing before the attack began. They may not realize that anything unusual has taken place. In cases of absence seizures that are not treated, a patient may experience as many as one hundred attacks a day. Eventually, the condition may progress to the tonic-clonic form of epilepsy.

epilepsy

The first goal of diagnosis is to eliminate other possible causes of the patient's symptoms. Other disorders of the brain, such as small strokes, fainting, and sleep disorders (see sleep disorders entry), can be confused with seizure disorders. A doctor needs to eliminate these possibilities before deciding how to treat the patient.

One goal of diagnosis is to distinguish between symptomatic and idiopathic epilepsy. In symptomatic epilepsy, it may be possible to provide treatment to cure the disorder. For example, a person may have had a severe allergic reaction to a food or drug. The allergic reaction may be responsible for the epileptic attack. This type of case can be treated by avoiding whatever

A woman with epilepsy sits hooked up to a brain wave monitor. Her dog, Ribbon, is an assistance dog that helps her get through her seizures safely. (Reproduced by permission of AP/Wide World Photos)

caused the attack in the first place. In cases of idiopathic epilepsy, where a cause is not found, other types of treatment are necessary.

The primary means of diagnosing epilepsy is the electroencephalogram (EEG, pronounced ih-LEK-tro-in-SEH-fuh-lo-gram). The EEG is a device that measures electrical activity in the brain. The results obtained from an EEG test are recorded on graph paper as a pattern of wavy lines. A doctor is able to read the lines on the paper and determine whether or not the brain is functioning normally. Seizure disorders produce characteristic patterns in an EEG test.

Doctors may try to schedule an EEG test during a seizure. They know that flashing lights (like strobe lights) or forcing the patient to breathe very deeply can trigger a seizure in patients with epilepsy. Or the patient may simply be kept in the hospital until an attack occurs. In such cases, the electrical activity of the brain during an attack can be observed and recorded.

TREATMENT

Cases of symptomatic epilepsy are treated by treating the basic cause that brought on the seizure disorder. Treatment of idiopathic epilepsy involves two steps. The first step involves protecting the patient during an attack. The second step involves the use of medications to reduce the frequency and severity of symptoms.

Patients with absence epilepsy usually require little protection. They may need help in case they lose consciousness for long enough to lose their balance and fall. Attacks of tonic-clonic epilepsy require somewhat more attention. The patient should be made comfortable during an attack by loosening clothing around the neck and providing a pillow under the head. A soft object, such as a folded handkerchief, should be placed between the teeth. The object prevents the patient from biting his or her tongue. No effort should be made to hold the tongue, however.

Several medications are now available for the treatment of epilepsy. Most of these drugs fall into the category of anticonvulsants. That is, they tend to prevent or minimize the shaking and thrashing that accompanies a seizure. Some examples of these drugs are phenobarbital (pronounced FEE-no-bar-bih-tall), primidone (pronounced PRIM-ih-doan), trimetha-

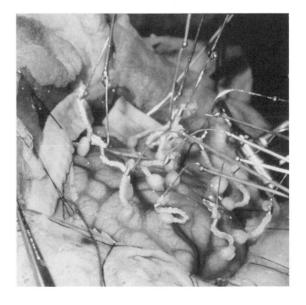

Surgery-resection of a brain mass causing epilepsy. (Reproduced by permission of Custom Medical Stock Photo)

dione (pronounced TRI-meth-uh-DIE-own), and valproate (pronounced val-PRO-ate).

No one drug is effective for all patients or for any one form of epilepsy. In fact, effective treatment of epilepsy requires finding exactly the right dose of exactly the right drug (or combination of drugs) for each individual patient. Most patients go through a period of testing in which various drugs in various combinations are tried. Eventually, the most suitable dose and combination are determined.

Medications have made it possible for most patients with epilepsy to lead relatively normal lives. However, there is one problem with drug therapy. Many drugs have side effects that can range from mild to severe for any one patient. The most common side effects are drowsiness, nausea, lethargy, and skin rash.

An important aspect of treating epilepsy is teaching the patient and his or her family how to live with the disorder. Patients are encouraged to pursue a normal life with moderate exercise and regular social activities. Families are encouraged not to become overprotective and, insofar as possible, to treat the patient as if he or she had no disorder.

Surgery

Intractable seizures are seizures that cannot be controlled without medication or without sedation or other unacceptable side effects. Surgery may be used to eliminate or control intractable seizures. This treatment is not very common as only seizures meeting very specific criteria can be controlled this way.

Alternative Treatment

Relaxation techniques can help people with epilepsy avoid some of the pressures that may bring on an attack. Yoga, meditation, hydrotherapy, aromatherapy, and acupressure may be helpful in this regard. These approaches, however, should never be substituted for the patient's regular program of medication.

For people with symptomatic epilepsy, dietary changes may be essential. Patients may need to identify the foods to which they are allergic and then eliminate those foods from their diets.

PROGNOSIS

The prognosis for most patients with epilepsy today is good. The most severe symptoms of the disorder can usually be controlled by the proper program of medications. Educating the patient about his or her condition can increase the chance that attacks will be handled properly and will not produce unnecessary emotional upsets for the patient.

In most cases, however, epilepsy is a lifelong condition. A patient has to learn to live with its symptoms while trying to lead as normal a life as possible. One important step the patient can take is to wear a medical bracelet indicating that he or she is epileptic. The bracelet should also list any medications the patient is taking.

One serious complication of tonic-clonic epilepsy is called status epilepticus (pronounced STA-tuss EP-ih-LEP-tih-kuss). Status epilepticus is a condition in which attacks of tonic-clonic seizures follow each other closely. There is no recovery period between attacks when the patient returns to consciousness and normality. The patient may have trouble breathing and his or her blood pressure may rise to dangerous levels. The condition can cause death if not treated immediately. Fortunately, status epilepticus is a rare condition.

PREVENTION

Symptomatic epilepsy can be prevented if the cause of the disorder can be identified and eliminated. There is no way to prevent idiopathic epilepsy.

The risks posed by epileptic attacks, however, can be reduced. For example, people with the condition should try to get enough sleep and exercise, and eat properly. They should avoid hyperventilating (breathing rapidly and deeply), which can bring on an attack. Individuals should make sure that they take their medications regularly, according to the prescribed pattern. If they experience an aura, they should find a safe place to lie down until the attack passes.

FOR MORE INFORMATION

Books

Carson, Mary Kay. *Epilepsy.* Hillside, NJ: Enslow Publishers, Inc., 1998.

Landau, Elaine. *Epilepsy.* New York: Twenty First Century Books, 1995.

Lechtenbert, Richard. *Epilepsy and the Family: A New Guide,* 2nd edition. Cambridge, MA: Harvard University Press, 1999.

Sander, J., and Y. Hart. *Epilepsy: Questions and Answers.* Chicago: Merit Publishing International, 1997.

Shaw, Michael, ed. *Everything You Need to Know about Diseases.* Springhouse, PA: Springhouse Corporation, 1996.

Wilner, Andrew N. *Epilepsy: 199 Answers: A Doctor Responds to His Patients' Questions.* New York: Demos Vermande, 1996.

Organizations

American Epilepsy Society. 638 Prospect Ave., Hartford, CT 06105–4298. (205) 232–4825.

Epilepsy Concern International Service Group. 1282 Wynnewood Dr., West Palm Beach, FL 33417. (407) 683–0044.

Epilepsy Foundation of America. 4251 Garden City Dr., Landover, MD 20875–2267. (800) 532–1000.

Epilepsy Information Service. (800) 642–0500.

Web sites

"Ask NOAH About: Epilepsy." *NOAH: New York Online Access to Health.* [Online] http://www.noah.cuny.edu/neuro/epilepsy.html (accessed on October 25, 1999).

Epilepsy. [Online] http://www.ninds.nih.gov/healinfo/disorder/epilepsy/epilepfs.htm (accessed February 28, 1998).

Epilepsy Facts and Figures. [Online] http://www.efa.org/what/education/FACTS.html (accessed on February 28, 1998).

FLESH-EATING DISEASE

DEFINITION

Flesh-eating disease is more properly called necrotizing fasciitis (pronounced nek-ro-TIZE-ing FASS-ee-i-tiss). The disease is caused by a rare bacterium that destroys tissues lying beneath the skin. The tissue death is called necrosis, or gangrene. It spreads very rapidly and can be fatal.

DESCRIPTION

The term flesh-eating disease is not really correct. However, it does describe what seems to happen in the disease. An infection occurs that seems to consume body tissue. Reports about flesh-eating disease increased during the 1990s. But the disease has been known for a very long time. The Greek physician Hippocrates (c. 460–c. 377b.c.) described the condition more than two thousand years ago. The disease was also common during the Civil War (1861–65).

Flesh-eating disease affects the arms and legs most often, but the infection can occur anywhere on the body.

CAUSES

In nearly every case, flesh-eating disease begins with a skin infection. Bacteria begin to grow

WORDS TO KNOW

Computed tomography (CT) scan: X rays taken of a portion of the body from various angles in order to obtain a three-dimensional picture of that region of the body.

Computerized axial tomography (CAT) scan: Another name for a computed tomography (CT) scan.

Gangrene: An extensive area of dead tissue.

Necrosis: Abnormal death of tissues.

in the infected area. They release toxins (poisons) that destroy tissue under the skin.

SYMPTOMS

Initially, the infected area appears red and swollen and feels hot. The area is extremely painful. After a few hours or days, the skin may become bluish-gray in color. Blisters filled with fluid may also form. The infected area becomes numb. An individual may go into shock and develop dangerously low blood pressure. The heart, kidneys, liver, and other organs may fail, leading to the patient's death.

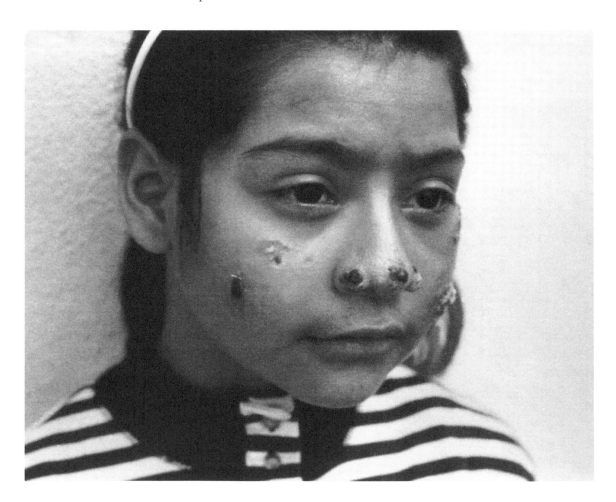

Girl affected with flesh-eating disease. (Reproduced by permission of AP/Wide World Photo)

DIAGNOSIS

Flesh-eating disease can often be diagnosed based on the way the skin looks, along with pain in the area and a fever. This diagnosis can be confirmed by a variety of tests, such as an X ray or a computed tomography (CT) scan. A CT scan is a procedure by which X rays are directed at a patient's body from various angles and the set of photographs thus obtained assembled by a computer program. This procedure is sometimes called a computerized axial tomography (CAT) scan. Samples of tissue under the skin can also be taken. Analysis of these samples will tell if the flesh-eating bacteria are present.

TREATMENT

Two treatments are used with flesh-eating disease. One is the use of antibiotics. Antibiotics such as penicillin, a family of drugs known as aminoglycosides (pronounced uh-MEE-no-gly-ko-sides), or cephalosporins (pronounced seff-a-lo-SPORE-inz) are used to kill the flesh-eating bacteria. The second method of treatment is surgery on the infected area. During surgery, dead tissue is cut away so that healthy tissue can grow back. The patient is observed carefully after surgery to make sure that the infection does not return.

PROGNOSIS

About 30 percent of those who are affected by flesh-eating disease eventually die of the infection. People with other disorders, such as diabetes (see diabetes mellitus entry), kidney disease, malnutrition, and obesity (see obesity entry), are at especially high risk for the disease. The elderly and intravenous drug users (those who inject drugs) are also at higher risk for the disease.

ABOUT 30 PERCENT OF THOSE WHO ARE AFFECTED BY FLESH-EATING DISEASE EVENTUALLY DIE OF THE INFECTION.

One consequence of the disease can be permanent scarring where the dead skin was cut away. Plastic surgery can sometimes be used to cover or reduce the amount of scarring.

PREVENTION

There is no known method of preventing flesh-eating disease.

Periodicals

Kotrappa, Kavitha S., Radhey S. Bansal, and Navin M. Amin. "Necrotizing Fasciitis." *American Family Physician* (May 1996): p. 1691.

Rth-Sahd, Lisa A., and Mary Pirrung. "The Infection that Eats Patients Alive." *RN 1997* (March 1997): p. 28.

Web sites

"The Flesh-eating Bacteria." *Microbiology Home Page: Queen Mary Hospital.* [Online] http://www.ha.org.hk/qmh/micro/strept.htm (accessed on October 19, 1999).

National Necrotizing Fasciitis Foundation Home Page. [Online] http://www.nnff.org/info.html (accessed on October 19, 1999).

Grant, Amy. "Streptococcus A–Necrotizing Fascitis." *Bacterial Infections and Mycoses.* [Online] http://www.emergency.com/strep-a.htm (accessed on October 19, 1999).

FOOD POISONING

DEFINITION

Food poisoning is a general term for health problems caused by eating contaminated food. Food may be contaminated by bacteria, viruses, toxins (poisons) from the environment, or toxins within the food itself. Symptoms of food poisoning usually include vomiting and diarrhea. Some toxins also affect the nervous system.

DESCRIPTION

Each year, millions of people suffer from bouts of vomiting and diarrhea that they blame on "something I ate." These people are usually correct. The U.S. Centers for Disease Control and Prevention (CDC) estimate that anywhere from six to thirty-three million cases of food poisoning occur in the United States each year. Many cases are mild. They pass so quickly that they are never diagnosed. On occasion, a severe outbreak affects a number of people. Newspapers, radio, and television may report on the outbreak.

Many kinds of food poisoning are caused by bacteria. The most common of these bacteria are *Salmonella* (pronounced SAL-mo-nel-uh), *Staphylococcus aureus* (pronounced STAFF-uh-lo-kock-us AW-ree-us), *Escherichia coli*

O157:H7 (pronounced ESH-ur-ick-ee-uh KO-lie), *Shigella* (pronounced shih-GEL-uh), and *Clostridium botulinum* (pronounced klos-TRID-ee-um BOTCH-u-line-um). The pattern of disease caused by each type of bacterium is slightly different. Most of them cause inflammation of the intestines and diarrhea. *Clostridium botulinum* is an exception.

Food and water can also be contaminated by other agents, such as viruses, heavy metals (such as lead, cadmium, and mercury), and poisons produced within the food itself. Mushroom and shellfish poisoning, for example, are caused by poisons produced within the food itself.

Careless food handling creates conditions for the growth of bacteria that make people sick. Food can be contaminated at many different points during its trip from farm to table. Vegetables that are eaten raw, such as lettuce, may be contaminated by bacteria in the soil in which they were grown. They can also be contaminated during washing and packing. Home canning can also lead to food poisoning. Foods may be cooked at too low a temperature or for too short a time. Bacteria may not be killed.

Raw meats carry many bacteria that can cause food poisoning. The U.S. Food and Drug Administration (FDA) estimates that at least 60 percent of all raw poultry sold to consumers carries some disease-causing bacteria. Other raw meat products and eggs are also contaminated, but to a lesser degree. Thorough cooking kills these bacteria and makes the food harmless. However, properly cooked food can become re-contaminated. It may come into contact with plates, cutting boards, counter tops, and utensils that have not been properly cleaned.

Cooked foods can also become contaminated in other ways. There are disease-causing bacteria everywhere in the environment. For example, experts estimate that half of all healthy people have the *Staphylococcus aureus* bacterium in their nasal (nose) passages and throat and on their skin and hair. These bacteria are easily transferred to food. A food handler may rub a runny nose and then touch freshly cooked food. Bacteria grow well at room temperature. They will rapidly reproduce to a level where they can

WORDS TO KNOW

C. botulinum: A very deadly bacteria that causes a disease known as botulism.

Campylobacter jejuni (C. jejuni): A bacteria that is the leading cause of bacterial diarrhea in the United States. It occurs in healthy cattle, chickens, birds, and flies.

Electrolytes: Salts and minerals present in the body that produce electrically charged particles (ions) in body fluids. Electrolytes control the fluid balance in the body and are important in muscle contraction, energy generation, and almost all major biochemical reactions in the body.

Escherichia coli (E. coli): A bacteria that commonly causes food poisoning, most often from food products derived from cows, especially ground beef.

Platelets: Blood cells needed to help blood clot.

Salmonella: A bacteria that commonly causes food poisoning, most often from poultry, eggs, meat, and milk.

Shigella: A bacterium that grows well in contaminated food and water, in crowded living conditions, and in areas with poor sanitation. It is transmitted by direct contact with an infected person or with food that has been contaminated by an infected person.

Staphylococcus aureus: A bacteria that causes food poisoning, commonly found on foods that are kept at room temperature.

make people sick. To prevent this growth, food must be kept hot or cold, but never just warm.

The food supply in the United States is probably the safest in the world. Still, anyone can get food poisoning. Serious outbreaks are rare. When they do occur, they strike some groups of people harder than others. The very young, the very old, and those with weakened immune systems are especially at risk. For example, people in these categories are twenty times more likely to become infected with the *Salmonella* bacterium than the general population.

People who travel outside the United States also have a greater chance of getting food poisoning. In many countries, less attention is paid to sanitation, water purification, and good food handling procedures. People living in institutions such as nursing homes are also more likely to get food poisoning.

CAUSES

Food poisoning is caused by toxins released by bacteria and other organisms. These toxins (except those from *Clostridium botulinum*) cause in-

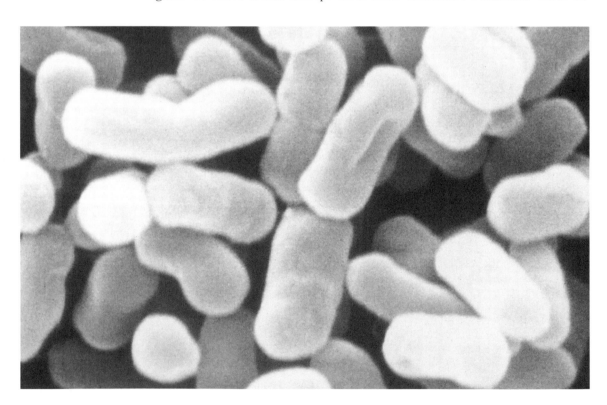

A magnified image of *Escherichia Coli* (*E. coli*). (© 1997. Reproduced by permission of Custom Medical Stock Photo.)

flammation of the stomach and intestines. The result is abdominal (stomach) muscle cramping, vomiting, diarrhea, fever, and possibly dehydration. Dehydration is the process by which the body loses water faster than it should.

Salmonella

About fifty thousand cases of *Salmonella* poisoning were reported in the United States in 1995. The CDC estimates that between two and four million cases probably went unreported. Many people who have *Salmonella* poisoning are not aware that they have it. They do not see a doctor for treatment.

The main sources of *Salmonella* poisoning are egg yolks from infected chickens, raw and undercooked poultry and other meats, dairy products, fish, and shrimp. The bacterium is also found in many other foods. Egg yolks may be the most serious problem. The CDC estimates that 1 out of every 50 Americans consumes contaminated egg yolk in a year. *Salmonella* poisoning can be avoided by thoroughly cooking any of the foods in which it occurs. The bacteria are also found in the feces of pet reptiles, such as turtles, lizards, and snakes.

About 1 out of every 1,000 people get food poisoning from *Salmonella*. Of these people, two-thirds are under the age of twenty. The majority are under the age of nine. Most cases occur during the warm months between July and October.

Staphylococcus aureus

Staphylococcus aureus occurs everywhere in the environment. It is found in dust, air, and sewage. The usual method of transmission is by food han-

FOOD IRRADIATION

Many methods for preserving food are available. These methods include freezing, drying, and canning. A method that may become more popular in the future is irradiation.

Irradiation is a process by which food is bombarded with high-energy radiation, such as X rays. This radiation kills bacteria in the food. Studies have shown that food irradiation is at least as effective as other methods of food preservation. For example, pork that is irradiated remains safe to eat for about ninety days. Pork kept under refrigeration is safe for no more than about forty days.

Today, the most common method for irradiating foods is with radioactive isotopes, such as cobalt 60 and cesium 137. Radioactive isotopes are materials that break apart and give off high-energy radiation.

Many people worry about the use of irradiation for preserving food. They fear that food may become radioactive and unsafe to eat. Or they worry that radiation may affect the taste, texture, or nutritional value of food.

Food irradiation is not a new technique. It has been used in other parts of the world for many years. The Food and Drug Administration (FDA) has given approval for the use of food irradiation in about a dozen kinds of foods. Whether that list becomes much longer remains to be seen.

dlers who use poor sanitary practices. For example, a cook may forget to wash his or her hands after using the bathroom. Bacteria can then be transferred from the cook's hands to food. Almost any kind of food can be contaminated in this way, but some foods are especially likely to be contaminated. These foods include salad dressings, milk products, cream pastries, and any food kept at room temperature.

It is difficult to estimate the number of *Staphylococcus aureus* poisoning cases that occur. Most cases are quite mild, and the patient never sees a doctor.

Escherichia coli (E. coli)

E. coli is a very common bacterium. It occurs in many different strains (forms). Some forms are beneficial. They may even be essential to the normal function of our digestive systems. The strain that causes most cases of food poisoning is *E. coli* O157:H7. Food poisoning caused by this bacterium occurs in about 3 out of every 10,000 people. The primary sources of *E. coli* are foods obtained from cows, such as dairy products and beef, especially ground beef.

Campylobacter jejuni (C. jejuni)

According to the FDA, *Campylobacter jejuni* (pronounced KAMP-puh-lo-BAK-tur jeh-JOO-ni) is the leading cause of bacterial diarrhea in the United States. Anyone can get food poisoning from *C. jejuni*. However, children under the age of five and young adults between the ages of fifteen and twenty-nine are most frequently affected.

C. jejuni occurs in healthy cattle, chickens, birds, and flies. It is also found in ponds and stream water. The bacterium is very potent (powerful). Consuming no more than a few hundred *C. jejuni* bacteria can cause a person to become ill.

Shigella

Shigella is a common cause of diarrhea in people who travel to developing countries. In these countries, sanitation practices may not be as well developed as they are in the United States. The *Shigella* bacterium grows well in contaminated food and water, in crowded living conditions, and in areas with poor sanitation. *Shigella* toxins infect the small intestine.

Clostridium botulinum (C. botulinum)

C. botulinum causes a disease known as botulism (pronounced BOTCH-u-liz-um). Two forms of botulism are known—adult and infant botulism. The *C. botulinum* bacterium is unlike any other bacterium in that it causes food poisoning in three ways.

First, *C. botulinum* is an anaerobic (pronounced AN-uh-RO-bik) bacterium. The term anaerobic means "able to live only in the absence of oxygen." That is, *C. botulinum* bacteria exposed to the air die quickly. Second, the toxins released by *C. botulinum* are neurotoxins. Neurotoxins are poisons that attack the nervous system, such as the brain and spinal cord. They may cause paralysis without producing any of the more traditional symptoms of food poisoning, such as vomiting and diarrhea. Third, botulism is a much more serious disease than other forms of food poisoning. People can die after consuming only very small amounts of the bacterium.

Adult botulism is usually caused by contaminated foods that are canned improperly at home. Less commonly, the *C. botulinum* bacterium is found in commercially canned foods. When foods are canned (at home or in a factory), they must first be heated to a high temperature. The temperature must be high enough to kill all *C. botulinum* bacteria that may be present. If the temperature is too low, some bacteria may survive. In such cases, conditions inside the can are an ideal setting for the bacteria to begin growing. No oxygen is present, and the canned food provides all the nourishment the bacteria need.

SYMPTOMS

How serious the symptoms of food poisoning are depends on many factors. These factors include the kind of bacteria, the amount consumed, and the individual's general health and sensitivity to the bacterial toxin.

Salmonella

Symptoms of *Salmonella* poisoning appear twelve to seventy-two hours after a person has eaten contaminated food. These symptoms are the tradi-

COMMON PATHOGENS CAUSING FOOD POISONING	
Pathogen	*Common Host(s)*
Campylobacter	Poultry
E.coli 0157:H7	Undercooked, contaminated ground beef
Listeria	Found in a variety of raw foods, such as uncooked meats and vegetables, and in processed foods that become contaminated after processing
Salmonella	Poultry, eggs, meat, and milk
Shigella	This bacteria is transmitted through direct contact with an infected person or from food or water that become contaminated by an infected person
Vibrio	Contaminated seafood

(Source: Food Safety and Inspection Service, U.S. Department of Agriculture. Reproduced by permission of Stanley Publishing.)

tional food poisoning symptoms, such as abdominal pain, diarrhea, vomiting, and fever. The symptoms usually last two to five days. In the most severe cases, dehydration can be a serious problem. People usually recover without being treated with antibiotics. However, they usually continue to feel tired for a week after the symptoms have passed.

Staphylococcus aureus

Symptoms of *Staphylococcus aureus* poisoning usually appear quickly, often within eight hours of eating the contaminated food. The most serious symptoms are vomiting, diarrhea, and severe abdominal cramps. These symptoms usually last three to six hours, and rarely more than twenty-four hours. Most people recover without medical assistance. Deaths are rare.

Escherichia coli (E. coli)

Symptoms of *E. coli* poisoning appear more slowly than symptoms of other kinds of food poisoning. These symptoms normally first arise one to three days after eating contaminated food. One symptom is severe abdominal cramps. Another symptom is diarrhea that is watery at first, but then becomes bloody. Both fever and vomiting are likely to be absent with *E. coli* poisoning. In most cases, the watery, bloody diarrhea disappears after one to eight days.

A possible complication of *E. coli* infection, especially in children under five and elderly people, is hemolytic uremic syndrome (HUS). This disease causes the kidneys to fail and red blood cells to be destroyed. Most people recover fully from HUS, but the disease can be fatal.

Campylobacter jejuni (C. jejuni)

The first symptoms of *C. jejuni* poisoning appear two to five days after eating contaminated food. These symptoms include fever, abdominal pain, nausea, headache, muscle pain, and diarrhea. The diarrhea can be watery or sticky. It may also contain blood. Symptoms of the infection last from seven to ten days. Relapses (reoccurrences of the infection) occur in about one-quarter of all patients. Dehydration can be a serious complication.

Shigella

Symptoms of *Shigella* poisoning appear thirty-six to seventy-two hours after eating contaminated food. These symptoms are slightly different from other forms of food poisoning. The usual watery diarrhea, nausea, vomiting, abdominal cramps, and fever are present. But up to 40 percent of children infected with the bacterium show neurological (nervous system) problems. These symptoms include seizures, confusion, headache, lethargy (listlessness), and a stiff neck.

The disease usually lasts two to three days. Dehydration is a common complication. Most people recover on their own. But they may feel exhausted for days or weeks after symptoms have disappeared. Children who are malnourished (poorly fed) or who have weakened immune systems can die of the infection.

Clostridium botulinum (C. botulinum)

Symptoms of adult botulism usually appear eighteen to thirty-six hours after the contaminated food is eaten. The first signs of botulism are a feeling of weakness and dizziness, followed by double vision. As the bacteria spread through the nervous system, paralysis begins. The patient finds it difficult to speak and swallow. Eventually, the muscles of the respiratory (breathing) system are affected. The patient may die of asphyxiation (suffocation; pronounced as-FIK-see-A-shun). People who show the symptoms of botulism require immediate medical attention.

Infant botulism was first recognized in 1976. It differs from adult botulism in both causes and symptoms. Infant botulism occurs when a child under the age of one year inhales or swallows the spores of *C. botulinum*. Spores are reproductive cells from non-flowering plants, such as mosses and ferns. *C. botulinum* spores are found in the soil. A more common source in the case of food poisoning, however, is honey.

Once inside an infant's body, *C. botulinum* spores become stuck in the baby's intestines. They begin to grow and release their neurotoxin. Symptoms begin to appear very gradually. Initially, the baby is constipated. Eventually, it loses interest in eating, begins to drool, becomes weak and lethargic, and makes a very distinctive crying sound. Eventually the baby loses its ability to control its head muscles. Beyond that point, paralysis sets in throughout the baby's body.

DIAGNOSIS

An important step in diagnosing food poisoning is studying the behavior of groups of people. Doctors try to find out if a number of people have eaten the same food and have the same symptoms. If that is the case, the food may have been contaminated. Diagnosis of food poisoning can be confirmed with a stool culture. A sample of feces is taken from the patient. The sample can then be studied to see whether the bacteria that cause food poisoning are present. Laboratory tests can also be conducted on the contaminated food. The bacteria present can be detected.

The diagnosis of botulism presents different problems. First, the characteristics of botulism are very different from those of other forms of food poisoning. Second, a rapid diagnosis is essential. A person who has botulism can become ill and die very quickly.

Many cases of food poisoning are never diagnosed. People may not even realize that they are sick. In most cases, the symptoms of food poisoning disappear quickly.

food poisoning

People with food poisoning should modify their diet during the period of illness. They should drink clear liquids frequently, but in small amounts. As their condition improves, soft, bland foods can be added to the diet. A commonly recommended diet is called the BRAT diet. The BRAT diet gets its name from the four foods it includes: banana, rice, applesauce, and toast. Milk products, spicy food, alcohol, and fresh fruit should be avoided until all symptoms disappear. These dietary changes are often the only treatment necessary for food poisoning.

In all cases of food poisoning except botulism, the major concern is dehydration. Diarrhea and vomiting both result in the loss of water and electrolytes from the body. Electrolytes are chemicals that control many important body functions. When they are lost, normal body functions may be disrupted. This problem can be especially serious in young children and elderly people.

Simple dehydration is easily treated. Over-the-counter (non-prescription) fluids that restore electrolytes can be purchased in any drug store. These fluids are usually pleasant tasting and restore lost water and electrolytes efficiently. If dehydration is serious, further treatment may be necessary. Fluids may have to be injected directly into a person's bloodstream.

In very serious cases of food poisoning, medications may be given to stop cramping and vomiting. Nothing should be done to stop diarrhea, however. Diarrhea helps remove toxins from the body.

In some cases, doctors may decide to use drugs to treat food poisoning. The most frequently prescribed antibiotics are a combination of trimethoprim and sulfamethoxazole (pronounced tri-METH-o-prim and SULL-fuh-meth-OCK-suh-zole, trade names Septra, Bactrim), ampicillin (pronounced AMP-ih-SIL-in, trade names Amcill, Polycill), or ciprofloxacin (pronounced SIP-ro-FLOK-suh-sin, trade names Ciloxan, Cipro).

The treatment of botulism is a much more difficult problem. A botulism antitoxin exists. The antitoxin counteracts the poison produced by *C. botulinum.* But it must be given within seventy-two hours after symptoms first appear. After that time, the antitoxin has no effect. The antitoxin also cannot be used on infants.

Both infants and adults who have botulism require hospital care. Patients may need to have a mechanical device to help them breathe until paralysis disappears.

Alternative Treatment

Alternative practitioners offer the same advice regarding diet modification as that described above. They also recommend taking charcoal tablets.

Charcoal has the ability to attract and soak up toxins in the body. Other recommended treatments include two bacteria found in milk products, *Lactobacillus acidophilus* (pronounced LACK-toe-buh-sill-us a-suh-DAH-fuh-luss) and *Lactobacillus bulgaricus* (pronounced LACK-toe-buh-sill-us bul-GAR-ih-kuss), and citrus seed extract.

A fluid to replace water and electrolytes can be made at home. It is made by adding one teaspoon of salt and four teaspoons of sugar to one quart of water. Two herbs that are recommended for treating forms of food poisoning other than botulism are *Arsenicum album* and *Nux vomica*.

PROGNOSIS

Except for botulism, most cases of food poisoning clear up on their own within a week without medical assistance. The patient may continue to feel tired for a few days after the symptoms disappear. As long as a person does not become dehydrated, there are usually no long-term symptoms. Deaths are rare. They tend to occur in the very young, the very old, and people with weakened immune systems.

Long-term effects are somewhat more common with *Salmonella*. Arthritis-like symptoms may occur three to four weeks after the original infection. Death from *Salmonella* is rare, but not unheard of. Most of these deaths have occurred among elderly people living in nursing homes.

Food poisoning caused by *E. coli* can also be serious, but usually in children rather than adults. The bacterium can attack platelets and red blood cells. Platelets are needed to make blood clot. In about 5 percent of the people infected with *E. coli*, this problem is so serious that their kidneys begin to fail. Kidney dialysis may be necessary. Kidney dialysis is a procedure in which a machine does the kidney's job of filtering out the body's waste products.

Botulism is the deadliest form of food poisoning. With prompt medical care, prognosis is good. Less than 10 percent of patients die. Without medical care, however, prognosis is very poor. The rate of death is very high.

PREVENTION

Food poisoning is almost entirely preventable. Good sanitation and food handling techniques are the key to avoiding the disease. The instructions to keep in mind are as follows:

- Keep hot foods hot and cold foods cold.
- Cook meat to the recommended internal temperature. Use a meat thermometer to be sure. Cook eggs until they are no longer runny.

- Refrigerate leftovers promptly. Do not let food stand at room temperature.
- Avoid contaminating surfaces and foods with the juices of uncooked meats.
- Wash fruits and vegetables before using.
- Purchase pasteurized dairy products and fruit juices. Pasteurized foods are heated to a temperature hot enough to kill the bacteria that cause food poisoning.
- Throw away bulging or leaking cans or any food that smells spoiled.
- Wash hands well before and during food preparation and after using the bathroom.
- Sanitize food preparation surfaces regularly.

Proper handling of food can help prevent food poisoning. This fast-food worker uses tongs to turn hamburger patties. (Reproduced by permission of AP/Wide World Photo)

FOR MORE INFORMATION

Books

Cody, Mildred McInnes. *Safe Food for You and Your Family*. Minneapolis: Chronimed Publishers, 1996.

Latta, Sara L. *Food Poisoning and Foodborne Diseases*. Hillside, NJ: Enslow Publishers, Inc., 1999.

Patten, Barbara J. *Food Safety*. Vero Beach, FL: The Rourke Book Company, Inc., 1997.

Scott, Elizabeth, and Paul Sockett. *How to Prevent Food Poisoning : A Practical Guide to Safe Cooking, Eating, and Food Handling*. New York: John Wiley & Sons, 1998.

Periodicals

U.S. Food and Drug Administration. "The Unwelcome Dinner Guest: Preventing Food-Borne Illness." *FDA Consumer* (December 1997).

Web sites

"Botulism (*Clostridium botulinum*)." [Online] http://www.cdc.gov/ncidod/diseases/foodborn/botu.htm (accessed on October 19, 1999).

Centers for Disease Control and Prevention. [Online] http://www.cdc.gov (accessed on October 19, 1999).

U.S. Food and Drug Administration. Center for Food Safety and Applied Nutrition. *Bad Bug Book*. [Online] http://www.cfsan.fda.gov (accessed on October 19, 1999).

FRACTURES, SPRAINS, AND STRAINS

DEFINITION

Fractures, sprains, and strains are injuries caused to bones, ligaments, joint capsules, or muscles. A joint capsule consists of all the tissues that hold a joint together. Specifically, a fracture is a complete or incomplete break in a bone. A sprain is damage or tearing of ligaments or a joint capsule. A strain is damage or tearing of a muscle.

fractures, sprains, and strains

Fractures usually result from a strong force applied to a bone. The bone and the tissue surrounding it may break apart completely, or they may be dislocated (pushed out of position).

Fractures are classified as being simple or compound. A simple fracture is one in which the skin is not broken. The area may be bruised and swollen, but it is not possible to tell simply by looking that a bone is broken. A simple fracture is also called a closed fracture. A compound fracture is one in which the skin is broken. The broken bone is actually visible to the eye. There may be damage to tissue surrounding the bone. Infection is a common complication of a compound fracture.

Fractures are also classified as complete or incomplete. A complete fracture is one in which the bone is broken all the way through. In an incomplete fracture, the break goes only part way through the bone. An incomplete fracture is also known as a greenstick fracture.

Bone breaks can also be classified as single or multiple. These terms describe the number of places in which a bone is broken. A single fracture is one in which the bone is broken in only one place. In a multiple fracture, a bone is broken in more than one place.

Fractures can also be described by other sets of terms. For example, they may be classified according to the direction of the break. A linear fracture runs in the same direction as the length of the bone. A transverse fracture is one that cuts across the width of the bone.

WORDS TO KNOW

Ligament: Tough, fiber-like tissue that holds bones together at joints.

Osteoporosis: A condition in which bones lose protein and minerals, causing them to become weak and subject to fracture.

Reduction: The restoration of a body part to its original position after it has been displaced, such as during a fracture.

Rickets: A condition caused by the deficiency of certain minerals, including vitamin D and calcium, causing abnormal bone growth.

Traction: The process of placing a bone, arm or leg, or group of muscles under tension by applying weights to them, in order to keep them in alignment while they heal.

Sprains and Strains

Bones are connected to each other in joints by ligaments. When excessive force is applied to a joint, ligaments may be torn or damaged. This type of injury is a sprain. The seriousness of a sprain depends on how badly ligaments are damaged. Sprains can occur in any joint, but they occur most commonly in the ankle, knee, and finger.

Sprains are often classified as being in one of three categories. A grade I sprain is a mild injury. The ligament is not actually torn. The joint continues to function normally. There may be some swelling and tenderness.

A grade II sprain involves a partial tear in a ligament. There is obvious swelling, extensive bruising, pain, and reduced function in the joint.

A grade III sprain occurs when a ligament is completely torn. Pain becomes severe, and use of the joint is lost. These symptoms are somewhat similar to those of a bone fracture.

Strains are tears in muscle tissue. Strains are sometimes called pulled muscles. They usually occur when a person forces a muscle to work too hard. They are often caused by using incorrect lifting techniques.

CAUSES

Fractures, sprains, and strains are all caused when excessive force is applied to some part of the body. Normally, bones, muscles, ligaments, and other body parts are very resilient. They can withstand large forces and twisting actions. But sometimes these forces and actions become too great. In such cases, bones may be broken, ligaments torn, or muscles bruised.

Risk Factors for Fractures

Anyone can fracture a bone. People who are active are more likely to break a bone, however. For example, people who participate in contact sports, like football and basketball, are at high risk for fractures. The elderly are more likely to break bones than are younger people. Bones become more brittle as one grows older.

Before the age of fifty, more men than women suffer fractures. These fractures are often caused in work-related injuries. After the age of fifty, more women than men suffer fractures. Women tend to lose bone mass more quickly than do men as they grow older.

Some diseases of the bone can increase a person's risk for fractures. Two examples are rickets and osteoporosis (pronounced OSS-tee-o-puh-RO-sis; see osteoporosis entry).

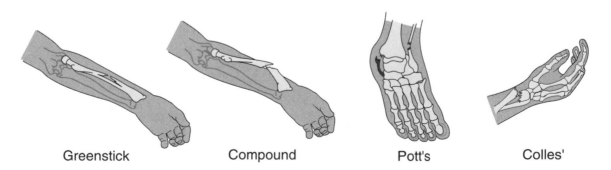

| Greenstick | Compound | Pott's | Colles' |

Common types of bone fractures. (Illustration by Electronic Illustrators Group)

Risk Factors for Sprains and Strains

Sprains and strains are common. Anyone can have them. But children under the age of eight are less likely to have sprains than older people. Their ligaments are quite tight. If too much force is placed on a joint, a bone is more likely to break than a ligament is to tear. People who are active in sports suffer more sprains and strains than less active people. Repeated sprains in the same joint can make the joint less stable and more likely to suffer sprains again in the future.

SYMPTOMS

The first symptoms of all three kinds of injuries are usually pain and swelling. The amount of discomfort depends on the extent of the injury. A serious fracture can produce other symptoms as well. There may be a loss of pulse below the fracture site. The patient may experience numbness, tingling, or even paralysis below the fracture. An open or compound fracture may also be accompanied by bleeding.

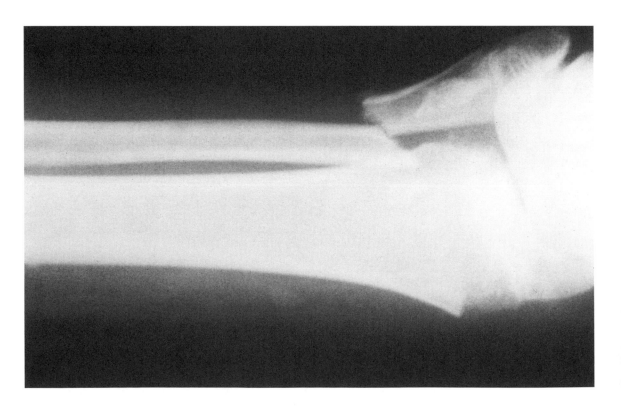

X ray of an ankle fracture. (© 1990 Custom Medical Stock. Reproduced by permission.)

DIAGNOSIS

Some types of fractures can be diagnosed easily by simply observing the damaged area. In the case of a compound fracture, for example, the broken bone can actually be seen protruding through the skin. If the fracture cannot be seen clearly, an X ray is usually the next step. Most X rays show the presence of a damaged or broken bone. In some cases, X rays can themselves be questionable. For example, a broken rib is often difficult to see on a single X ray. A series of X rays taken from different angles may be necessary to diagnose a fractured rib.

One kind of fracture that may be difficult to diagnose is a stress fracture. A stress fracture is a very small break in a bone that may not show up on an X ray. A stress fracture can sometimes be diagnosed with a tuning fork. A tuning fork is a metal instrument used in tuning musical instruments. It is placed on the skin over the bone in which a stress fracture is suspected. If the patient reports increased pain, a stress fracture may be present.

Diagnosis of Sprains and Strains

In the case of sprains and strains, patients may actually recognize their own condition due to the swelling and pain. In mild cases, they may decide not to seek medical advice. Grade II and III sprains, however, are often seen by a doctor. The usual procedure is to have an X ray taken of the injured site. The X ray can be used to distinguish between a sprain and a fracture.

TREATMENT

The treatment of fractures depends on many factors, such as the seriousness of the injury, the patient's age, and his or her general health. In the case of serious fractures, a number of actions may be necessary. For example, patients with open fractures may need to have bleeding brought under control. They may also need antibiotics to protect against infection.

The fundamental goal in treating fractures is to restore a broken bone to its original position, if necessary, and then immobilize it. Bones begin to grow back soon after they are broken so this should be done by a trained medical person as soon as possible. In many cases, immobilization is the only treatment needed for a fracture. If there is displacement, the bone is first forced into the correct position and then held in place with a splint, cast, or brace. Once restored to its original position and held in place, the bone will re-grow to its former shape.

Getting the bone into its correct position is called fracture reduction. It can be done without breaking the skin or the doctor may need to perform surgery to realign the bones. Reduction done without breaking the skin is called a closed reduction and can be performed by a doctor with the patient under anesthetic. The doctor can move the bone parts around until they are back in their correct position. Some form of immobilization can then be applied.

Realigning the bones is sometimes difficult. The fractures may be complicated or serious enough to require an open reduction, or surgery, to reset the bones. The damaged area is cut open and the bones placed in their proper alignment. Devices such as plates, nails, screws, and rods may be used to hold the bones in this alignment while they heal. When healing is complete, the physician may or may not elect to remove these devices.

Traction is sometimes used to treat fractures. Traction involves the use of heavy weights to pull on a damaged bone. It forces the broken bone to line up correctly, the way it looked before the break. The traction may be necessary until the bone has grown back in its normal and correct position.

Treatment of Sprains and Strains

Grade I sprains and mild strains can be treated at home. Basic first aid for sprains consists of a system known as RICE. This term stands for four steps:

- **R**est
- **I**ce for forty-eight hours
- **C**ompression, such as wrapping the injured area with an elastic bandage
- **E**levation, or raising the sprained area above the heart

Over-the-counter pain medication, such as aspirin, acetaminophen, or ibuprofen, can be taken to relieve pain. Children should avoid aspirin, however, as it can cause Reye's syndrome (see Reye's syndrome entry).

People with grade II and grade III sprains should also follow the steps in RICE. They usually need additional treatment, however. In the case of sprains of the ankle or knee, they may need to stay off their feet by staying in bed or using crutches. Physical therapy or home exercises may be needed to restore normal joint function.

Grade III sprains usually require immobilization in a cast. The cast must stay on until the sprain heals, usually for several weeks. In extreme cases, surgery may be needed to repair torn ligaments. Physical therapy is often required after surgery.

Alternative Treatment

Calcium supplements are often recommended to help prevent fractures. The body uses calcium to build bones. Some physical therapists may recommend electrostimulation to treat a fracture. In electrostimulation, a small electrical current is passed through needles inserted near the damaged site. The electrical current is thought to increase the speed with which bones heal.

Two homeopathic remedies recommended for fractures are *Arnica* (pronounced AHR-nih-kuh) and *Symphytum* (pronounced SIM-fih-tum). These remedies are thought by some practitioners to increase the rate at which bones heal. Hydrotherapy is also recommended for fractures in the legs and arms. Warm water may increase the rate of circulation in the area and, thereby, the rate of healing.

Alternative treatments for sprains and strains may include the use of nutritional supplements, such as vitamin C and bioflavonoids. Certain herbs are recommended to reduce inflammation in a damaged area. These herbs include bromelain, turmeric, *Arnica*, *Ruta*, and *Rhus toxicodendron*.

PROGNOSIS

Fractures usually heal well when properly immobilized. Bones tend to grow back over time, correcting any breaks that may have occurred in them.

Chauncy Billups, a guard for the Denver Nuggets, grimaces after spraining his ankle during a game. (Reproduced by permission of AP/Wide World Photos)

A key factor in healing is prompt treatment. Bones that are not immobilized within six hours of injury are much more difficult to re-align. Healing time varies considerably, depending on many factors. In older people, for example, bones re-grow more slowly.

Mild and moderate sprains usually heal in less than four weeks. Severe sprains may take much longer. At one time, a torn ligament meant the end of an athlete's career. Today, advanced surgical procedures can be used. Nearly normal function can be restored. Even then, however, the joint is never as strong as it was before the injury.

PREVENTION

An adequate level of calcium in the diet is essential to reduce the risk of fractures. People with too little calcium in their diet tend to have weak bones that break more easily. Calcium supplements may be necessary if a person does not get enough of the nutrient in his or her regular diet.

Exercise can help strengthen bones. Older people in particular can benefit from a regular program of moderate exercise.

The risk of fractures can also be reduced by making use of safety measures. For example, passengers in cars should always wear seat belts. Anyone who engages in contact sports should use protective equipment available for the sport. Women past the age of fifty should consider taking estrogen replacement medication to help reduce the chance of osteoporosis. Osteoporosis is a weakening of bones that occurs commonly in women past the age of menopause.

Sprains and strains can be prevented by following some simple guidelines, including warming up before exercise, using proper lifting techniques, wearing properly fitting shoes, and taping or bracing joints that may receive unusual stress.

FOR MORE INFORMATION

Books

American Red Cross. *Community First Aid and Safety.* St. Louis: Mosby, 1993.

Arnheim, Daniel D. *Modern Principles of Athletic Training.* St. Louis: Mosby, 1989.

Burton Goldberg Group. "Sprains," in James Strohecker, ed. *Alternative Medicine: The Definitive Guide.* Puyallup, WA: Future Medicine Publishing, 1994.

"Sprains and Strains," in *The Medical Advisor: The Complete Guide to Alternative and Conventional Treatments.* Alexandria, VA: Time-Life Books, 1996.

Periodicals

Wexler, Randall K. "The Injured Ankle." *American Family Physician* (February 1, 1998): p. 474.

Organizations

American College of Sports Medicine. P.O. Box 1440, Indianapolis, IN 46206–1440. (317) 637–9200.

FROSTBITE

DEFINITION

Frostbite is damage to the skin and other tissue caused by freezing. The term frostnip is sometimes used for a mild form of frostbite.

DESCRIPTION

Frostbite is caused by exposure to temperatures well below freezing (32°F or 0°C). Dry conditions contribute to frostbite damage. At temperatures closer to freezing, frostnip is more likely to occur. Humid air is also more likely to produce frostnip than frostbite.

In North America, frostbite occurs most frequently in Alaska, Canada, and the northernmost regions of the United States. In recent years, the number of cases of frostbite and frostnip have decreased considerably. One reason for this change is that the general public is better educated about the dangers of these two conditions. Also, warmer clothing and footwear are generally available.

The one group of people among whom frostbite and frostnip has increased are the homeless. Homeless people often have no place to go when the temperature drops. The growing popularity of outdoor sports has also increased the number of people at risk for frostbite and frostnip.

CAUSES

The human body can withstand temperatures a little below freezing for hours before freezing. However, exposure to very cold temperatures can freeze skin in minutes or even sec-

WORDS TO KNOW

Amputation: A surgical procedure in which an arm, leg, hand, or foot is removed.

Contrast hydrotherapy: A procedure in which a series of hot and cold water applications is applied to an injured area.

Narcotic: A drug that relieves pain and induces sleep.

onds. Air temperature, wind speed, and moisture all affect the rate at which the body loses heat. For example, wet clothing increases the risk for frostbite. Water absorbs heat quickly and efficiently. It causes the body to cool off very quickly.

The permanent damage done to the body depends more on how long it was exposed to cold temperatures than on how cold it got. This fact explains why so many people are injured by frostbite. The overnight temperature may not drop very low, but homeless people are forced to remain outside for hours at a time. This long exposure to even mildly cold temperatures can cause frostbite.

EXPOSURE TO VERY COLD TEMPERATURES CAN FREEZE SKIN IN MINUTES OR EVEN SECONDS.

Several factors increase a person's risk for frostbite. Alcohol use is a major risk factor for frostbite. Alcohol reduces blood circulation. It causes the body to cool off quickly. It also impairs ones judgement. A person who has been drinking may not notice how cold it is, or realize that he or she is getting frostbite, and stay outdoors even after injury has occured. In one study

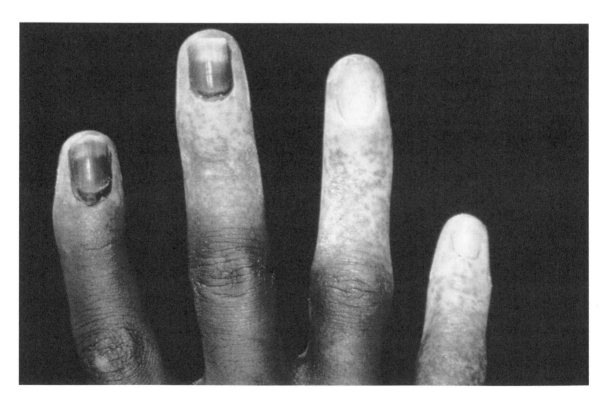

Frostbite on fingers. (Photograph by SIU. Reproduced by permission of the National Audubon Society Collection/Photo Researchers, Inc.)

of frostbite injuries, nearly half occurred among people who had been drinking. Other factors contributing to the risk for frostbite include:

- Psychiatric illness
- Inadequate clothing
- Fatigue
- Infection from a wound
- Atherosclerosis (see atherosclerosis entry)
- Diabetes (see diabetes mellitus entry)
- Previous injuries due to cold temperatures

SYMPTOMS

Most frostbite injuries affect the feet or hands. About 10 percent of all cases involve the ears, nose, cheeks, or penis. The first symptoms of frostbite are a feeling of cold and numbness in the affected body part. The skin then begins to turn white or yellowish. Many patients experience severe pain in the affected part.

Symptoms continue as the body begins to warm up. The pain returns or continues during this period. It may last for days or weeks. As the skin begins to thaw, fluids may collect, causing swelling of the affected area. In more serious cases, deep, blood-filled blisters may form. In the most severe cases of frostbite, the muscles, tendons, nerves, and bones may also be damaged by cold. In such cases, dead tissue may drop off or become infected.

The symptoms of frostnip are less severe. The skin may turn pale. Numbness and tingling are likely to occur in the affected area.

DIAGNOSIS

A first diagnosis of frostbite or frostnip can usually be made on the basis of environmental conditions. A person found unconscious in freezing weather may be presumed to be at risk for frostbite. Physical examination of the skin often confirms this diagnosis. The skin tends to be cold, hard, white, and numb if frostbite is present. As it warms, the skin becomes red, swollen, and painful. Doctors usually classify the extent of frostbite as being superficial or deep. The prognosis for all forms of frostbite is often not clear for many days.

TREATMENT

Frostbite is a potentially serious problem that requires emergency medical treatment. First aid involves replacing wet clothing with warm, dry clothing or blankets. A splint or padding can be used to protect the injured area. Observers should not attempt to warm the patient in the field. The re-warming procedure should take place under controlled conditions in the hospital.

The outcome of a frostbite injury cannot be predicted in the first few days. For that reason, the same treatment is used with all patients. Treatment involves re-warming of the affected area at a temperature of 104° to 108°F (40° to 42°C). The injury is treated with aloe vera and splinted, wrapped, and elevated.

Injections of tetanus vaccine and penicillin may be given. These injections protect the patient against infection. An anti-inflammatory drug, such as aspirin or ibuprofen, may also be given. In some cases, narcotics may be needed to treat the severe pain that occurs with deep frostbite.

In the most serious cases, frostbite may cause extensive tissue damage. Amputation (removal) of an arm, leg, hand, or foot may be necessary. A decision to take this action is usually delayed as long as possible to see if the damaged tissue will recover.

Dr. Beck Weathers who suffered severe frostbite on his face and hands after being trapped in a blizzard on Mt. Everest. (Reproduced by permission of AP/Wide World Photos)

Alternative Treatment

Alternative treatments of frostbite should not be attempted until the patient has received medical care. After that point, methods are available for shortening the recovery period. One such method is contrast hydrotherapy. In contrast hydrotherapy, a series of hot and cold water applications is used on the affected area.

Some homeopathic remedies suggested for frostbite recovery include *Hypericum* and *Arnica* (pronounced AHR-nih-kuh). Circulation may be improved by drinking hot ginger tea or taking small amounts of cayenne pepper.

PROGNOSIS

A new approach to frostbite treatment was developed in the 1980s. The major emphasis in this method is to re-warm the body as quickly as possible. This method has proved to be very successful. In one study, about two-thirds of patients with superficial frostbite recovered completely without tissue loss. The success rate using older methods was only about 35 percent (or about one-third of patients).

The most serious consequence of frostbite may be amputation. People who do not require amputation may still experience long-term symptoms. These symptoms include extreme throbbing pain, a burning sensation or tingling feelings, color changes of the skin, changes in the shape of nails or loss of nails, joint stiffness, excessive sweating, and a heightened sensitivity to cold.

PREVENTION

Frostbite typically occurs when a person is exposed to extreme weather conditions, such as very cold temperatures and high winds. Anyone who expects to encounter these conditions should prepare for them by dressing warmly and staying outside no longer than necessary. Outer garments should be wind- and water-resistant. If clothing becomes wet, it should be replaced as quickly as possible. Alcohol, drugs, and smoking should be avoided if one will be exposed to the elements for long periods of time.

Some groups of people, such as the homeless, may find it more difficult to avoid frostbite. They may not understand the need for protection from the cold or, more often, they do not have the resources to buy the clothing or shelter needed for protection. In such cases, the community may be responsible for providing the protection that homeless people are not able to provide for themselves.

See also: Hypothermia.

frostbite

Books

The Burton Goldberg Group. *Alternative Medicine: The Definitive Guide.* Puyallup, WA: Future Medicine Publishing, 1993.

McCauley, Robert L., et al., "Frostbite and Other Cold-Induced Injuries," in Paul S. Auerbach, ed. *Wilderness Medicine: Management of Wilderness and Environmental Emergencies.* St. Louis: Mosby, 1995.

Wilkerson, James A., and Cameron C. Bangs, eds. *Hypothermia, Frostbite, and Other Cold Injuries: Prevention, Recognition and Pre-Hospital Treatment.* Seattle, WA: Mountaineers Books, 1986.

Periodicals

Gill, Paul G., Jr., "Winning the Cold War." *Outdoor Life* (February 1993): pp. 62+.

GLAUCOMA

DEFINITION

Glaucoma is a disorder of the eye in which the optic nerve is damaged. The optic nerve carries light messages from the eye to the brain. Left untreated, glaucoma can result in loss of vision.

DESCRIPTION

Over two million people in the United States have glaucoma. About eighty thousand of these individuals are legally blind because of the disorder. Glaucoma is the leading cause of preventable blindness in the United States. The condition is about three times as common among African Americans as among whites. The risk for glaucoma increases rapidly with age, but the condition can affect any age group, including newborn infants and fetuses.

Glaucoma is actually a class of disorders. More than twenty different forms of the condition have been identified. They all develop in a similar way, however. The amount of aqueous (pronounced a-kwee-us) humor, a watery fluid that fills the inside of the eyeball, begins to build up. As more of this fluid collects, it places greater pressure on all parts of the eye, including the optic nerve. Eventually the excess pressure destroys the nerve.

The many forms of glaucoma are grouped into two large categories: open-angle glaucoma and closed-angle glaucoma. Open-angle glaucoma is a progressive disease. That is, it gets worse over time if not treated. At first, only a few nerve cells in the optic nerve are destroyed. Blind spots develop in areas where those nerve cells are located. Over time, more and more nerve cells are destroyed. A larger and larger area of vision is lost. Eventually, a person may lose his or her sight completely.

Closed-angle glaucoma happens very quickly. Some type of accident or change in the eye causes aqueous humor to build up very suddenly. The effects of glaucoma appear in a very short time.

CAUSES

Aqueous humor is produced by tissues in the front of the eyeball. Aqueous humor brings nourishment to the cornea and lens. It also maintains the proper pressure inside the eyeball. Proper pressure is necessary for the eyeball to maintain the correct shape. The amount of pressure produced by aqueous humor is called the intraocular ("inside the eye") pressure (IOP).

Aqueous humor drains out of the eyeball through a network of tiny tubes also located in the front of the eyeball. Glaucoma develops when the flow of aqueous humor is altered. In some cases, the fluid is produced too rapidly. In other cases, it is not removed from the eyeball fast enough. In either case, too much aqueous humor collects in the eyeball. The fluid causes pressure that pushes on blood vessels in the retina of the eye. The retina is a thin membrane at the back of the eyeball. It receives light rays that pass through the eyeball and transmits them to the optic nerve. Over time, excess pressure in the eye can damage cells in the retina and optic nerve. The cells die and the optic nerve is no longer able to carry messages to the brain. A person's vision is reduced.

WORDS TO KNOW

Aqueous humor: A watery fluid that fills the inside of the eyeball, providing nourishment to the eye and maintaining internal pressure in the eyeball.

Blind spot: An area on the retina that is unable to respond to light rays.

Cornea: The tough, transparent tissue that covers the front of the eyeball.

Intraocular pressure (IOP): The amount of pressure caused by aqueous humor inside the eyeball.

Laser: A device for producing very intense beams of light of a single color.

Optic nerve: A nerve at the back of the eyeball that carries messages from the retina to the brain.

Retina: A thin membrane at the back of the eyeball that receives light rays that pass through the eyeball and transmits them to the optic nerve.

Tonometer: A device used to measure intraocular pressure in the eyeball.

SYMPTOMS

There are usually no noticeable symptoms of open-angle glaucoma. The loss of vision occurs very slowly, often over a period of years. If only one eye is affected, the other eye takes over the task of seeing for both eyes. The person with glaucoma does not realize that vision is being affected. Eventually, however, loss of vision becomes severe. The patient becomes aware that a problem exists. By this time, the glaucoma is more difficult to treat.

The symptoms of closed-angle glaucoma are more obvious. A person may experience blurred vision, severe pain, sensitivity to light, and nausea. The cornea, the transparent tissue at the front of the eye, becomes cloudy. Closed-angle glaucoma is a medical emergency and requires immediate treatment.

DIAGNOSIS

Glaucoma is usually diagnosed during a routine visit to an eye specialist. Because of its mild symptoms, patients are less likely to visit a doctor about the condition.

The fastest test for glaucoma is a measurement of the IOP. The eye specialist first numbs the patient's eye with eye drops that have a yellow coloring. The pressure inside the eyeball is then measured with an instrument called a tonometer (pronounced toe-NAHM-etter). The test takes only a few seconds and provides a fast diagnosis of glaucoma.

If glaucoma is suspected, the eye specialist can then examine the back of the patient's eye for possible damage or changes. The specialist uses an ophthalmoscope (pronounced ahf-THAL-muh-skope) for this purpose. An ophthalmoscope is a device that shines light on the retina. The eye specialist is able to see if the retina and optic nerve are damaged in any way.

Visual tests can also be used to find blind spots in the patient's field of vision. The patient is asked to look at cards with various geometric patterns on them. Difficulty in seeing any one part of a pattern tells the eye specialist where a blind spot may be.

TREATING GLAUCOMA

An interesting footnote in the history of medicine is the role played by the study of the eye, ear, nose, and throat. These parts of the body are now regarded as important special fields of medicine. However, until the nineteenth century, they were not regarded as legitimate topics of medical study. They were left to "quacks." A quack is someone who treats human disease without having adequate medical preparation.

Thus, the first scientific discussion of glaucoma appeared around 1850. At that time, the German physician Albrecht von Graefe (1787–1840) described a surgical method for treating glaucoma.

He tells of operating on patient's whose vision was "perfectly restored in all cases."

At about the same time, drugs were being developed for treatment of the disorder. The first such drugs were actually discovered by Christian missionaries. The missionaries were introduced by native people to plants that had the effect of reducing the worst symptoms of glaucoma. Those plants were later found to contain a chemical known as *physostigmine*. Nearly a century later, the great black American chemist Percy Julian (1899–1975) discovered a way to make physostigmine synthetically in the laboratory. Physostigmine has now largely been replaced by other drugs for the treatment of glaucoma.

glaucoma

Glaucoma may be treated with either medication or surgery. Medication is usually tried first. The drugs used are substances that reduce intraocular pressure. In general, they either decrease the rate at which aqueous humor is produced in the eye, or they increase the rate at which it is drained off. All of the medications used for glaucoma have side effects. Various individual drugs and combinations of drugs may have to be tried to see which works best for any one patient.

Some patients do not respond well to medication. In such cases, surgery may be necessary. The purpose of surgery is to open up the canals through which aqueous humor drains out of the eye. The surgery is often done with lasers.

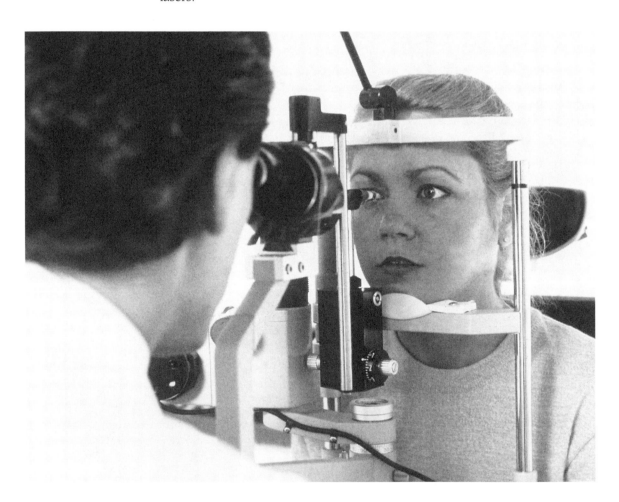

Patient receiving a glaucoma test. (© 1992. Reproduced by permission of Custom Medical Stock.)

Surgery is usually quite effective in solving glaucoma problems. However, its effects may not last very long. In many cases, surgery is required again in a year or less.

Alternative Treatment

Some vitamins and minerals are thought to reduce intraocular pressure. These include vitamins C and B$_1$ (thiamine) and chromium and zinc.

Research suggests that marijuana reduces IOP. However, there is some dispute as to whether the drug should be used for this purpose. Researchers are currently weighing the advantages of using marijuana to relieve the symptoms of glaucoma against public concerns about the drug.

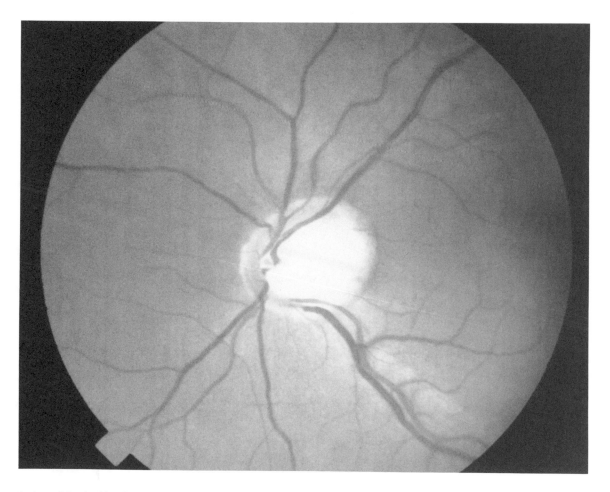

A view of the inside of the human eye. Glaucoma is a disorder caused by too much pressure from the aqueous fluid building up inside the eyeball. (© 1995 SPL, Western Ophthalmic Hospital/Science Photo Library. Reproduced by permission of Custom Medical Stock Photo.)

PROGNOSIS

About half of the people who develop glaucoma are not aware of their condition until fairly late in the course of the disorder. Many of these individuals will lose part or all of their vision. Vision loss caused by glaucoma cannot be repaired. Patients who are diagnosed with glaucoma usually respond to treatment. The prognosis for those individuals is very good.

PREVENTION

Researchers currently do not know the factors that cause glaucoma. As a result, there is no way to prevent the disorder. However, it is relatively easy to diagnose glaucoma in its early stages. The best preventive step is to have regular eye checkups. A normal part of those checkups is a tonometer test for glaucoma. Early detection of glaucoma can prevent the most serious consequences of the condition.

FOR MORE INFORMATION

Books

Marks, Edith, and Rita Montauredes. *Coping with Glaucoma.* Garden City Park, NY: Avery, 1997.

Trope, Graham E. *A Patient's Guide to the Disease.* Toronto: University of Toronto Press, 1997.

Organizations

American Academy of Ophthalmology. P.O. Box 7424, San Francisco, CA 94120–7424. (415) 561–8500. http://www.eyenet.org/aao_index.html.

Glaucoma Research Foundation. 490 Post Street, Suite 830, San Francisco, CA 94102. (415) 986–3162; (800) 826–6693. http://www.glaucoma.org.

Prevent Blindness America. 500 East Remington Rd., Schaumburg, IL 60173. (800) 331–2020. http://www.prevent-blindness.org.

Web sites

"Ask NOAH About: The Eye." *NOAH: New York Online Access to Health.* [Online] http://www.noah.cuny.edu/eye/eye.html#G (accessed on October 20, 1999).

Titcomb, Lucy. "Treatment of Glaucoma." http://www.pharmacymag.co.uk/glau.htm (accessed on April 29, 1998).

HANTAVIRUS INFECTIONS

DEFINITION

Hantavirus infections are caused by a group of viruses known as hantaviruses. These viruses cause two serious illnesses in humans. They are hemorrhagic (pronounced heh-meh-RA-jik) fever with renal syndrome (HFRS) and hantavirus pulmonary syndrome (HPS).

DESCRIPTION

Hantaviruses live in rodents, such as rats and mice, without causing any symptoms. The viruses can be transmitted (passed on to) humans by way of urine, feces, or saliva from the rodents. Five different kinds of hantaviruses have been discovered so far. Each is found in a different geographical region and in different kinds of rodents. As an example, the virus known as the hantaan virus is carried by the striped field mouse. It is found primarily in Korea, China, East Russia, and the Balkans. This virus causes HFRS. Another type of hantavirus is called the Sin Nombre virus. It is carried by the deer mouse and found primarily in southwestern United States and causes severe cases of HPS.

SYMPTOMS

The two forms of hantavirus infections each have distinctive symptoms.

Hemorrhagic Fever with Renal Syndrome (HFRS)

The three most common symptoms of HFRS are mentioned in the name of the disease. The first of those symptoms is a fever. The second symptom is malfunction of the kidneys. The term renal means "relating to the kidneys." The third symptom is a low platelet count. Platelets are blood cells that promote the clotting of blood. When the number of platelets in blood is reduced, blood clotting does not occur properly. A person tends to hemorrhage (pronounced hem-ir-idj) or bleed easily.

Patients with HFRS have pain in the head, stomach, and lower back. They may also have bloodshot eyes and blurry vision. Hemorrhaging may occur through tiny openings on the upper body and in the mouth. The patient's face, chest, abdomen, and back often appear bright red, as if sunburned.

Five days into the disease, the patient may experience a sudden drop in blood pressure. He or she may go into shock. Shock occurs when the heart does not pump enough blood through the veins and arteries. Cells do not get blood and the needed oxygen it carries. Shock can cause damage to the body's organs, especially the brain.

After about eight days, kidney damage may taken place. The kidneys are responsible for filtering toxins (poisons) out of the blood. If the kidneys do not function properly, those toxins can damage cells throughout the body. Hemorrhaging may also become more serious throughout the body. Blood may begin to appear in the urine or when a person vomits. Hemorrhaging in the brain can cause the most serious problems that can include a loss of consciousness.

These symptoms can become even more serious about eleven days into the infection. A person may become very confused, begin to have hallucinations, and go into seizures. A person who hallucinates sees and hears things that are not really there. Problems can also develop with the lungs and the ability to breathe normally.

At this point, the patient faces a turning point. He or she may continue to become more and more ill, with death as the result. Or the infection may begin to clear up. In the latter case, full recovery may take up to six weeks.

Hantavirus Pulmonary Syndrome (HPS)

The first symptoms of HPS are fever and a sudden drop in blood pressure. These symptoms may be followed by shock and loss of blood in the lungs. When this happens, fluids may collect in the lungs, leading to shortness of breath. These symptoms can occur so quickly that the

WORDS TO KNOW

Hemodialysis: A mechanical method for cleansing blood outside the body.

Hemorrhagic: Relating to a condition in which there is massive, difficult-to-control bleeding.

Platelets: Blood cells that have a role in the process of blood clotting.

Pulmonary: Relating to the lungs.

Renal: Relating to the kidneys.

Shock: A condition in which blood pressure drops suddenly and the flow of blood to cells is dramatically reduced. Because of this reduced flow, cells are not able to get the oxygen they need.

patient goes into respiratory failure in a matter of hours. Respiratory failure means that the patient has lost the ability to breathe on his or her own.

DIAGNOSIS

Blood tests are used to diagnose hantavirus infections. Blood taken from a patient is analyzed for the presence of certain hantavirus antibodies. Antibodies are substances produced by the blood when it has been infected by a foreign body, such as a bacterium or a virus. Antibodies are very specific. That is, a particular kind of antibody is produced to fight every different kind of infective agent (bacterium, fungus, virus, etc.). An analysis of a person's blood can tell whether he or she has been infected with a hantavirus and, if so, by what kind of hantavirus.

TREATMENT

There is no way to kill the hantavirus. Treatments for hantavirus infections are designed, therefore, to relieve the symptoms of the disease. For ex-

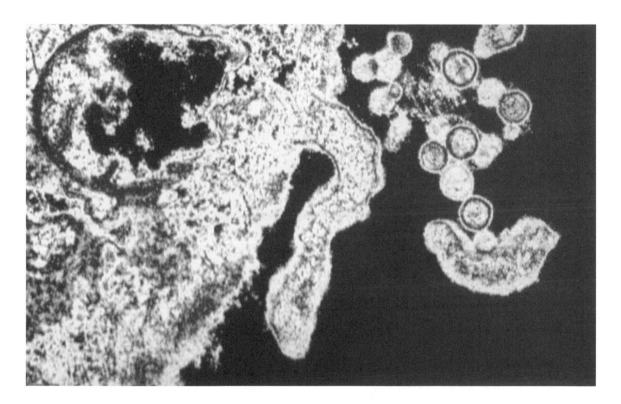

An image of the hantavirus magnified 88,000 times. (© 1995. Reproduced by permission of Custom Medical Stock Photo.)

ample, a person who has been hemorrhaging or who is in shock may require blood transfusions. Hemodialysis (pronounced HEE-mo-die-ali-sis) is used to remove toxins from the blood of a person whose kidneys have failed. Hemodialysis is a procedure by which a person's blood is passed through a machine to take out dangerous toxins (replacing the function of the kidneys).

Hantavirus infections progress very rapidly. It is important, therefore, to begin treatment as quickly as possible and to observe the patient very carefully.

An experimental drug being tested on hantavirus infections is called ribavirin (pronounced RI-buh-vih-rin). The drug has been shown to kill the hantavirus in laboratory tests. It is too soon to tell how well it will work in human beings.

PROGNOSIS

Hantavirus infections are very lethal (capable of causing death). About 6 to 15 percent of those who develop HFRS will die of the disease. The death

The deer mouse is a carrier of one type of hantavirus that caused severe cases of HPS in the southwestern United States. (© 1997 S.R. Maglione. Reproduced by permission of Photo Researchers, Inc.)

rate for those who contract (catch) HPS is about 50 percent. These numbers point out how important it is for people with symptoms of hantavirus infections to get treatment as quickly as possible.

PREVENTION

There is no way to prevent a hantavirus infection. The best way to avoid getting the disease is to reduce one's exposure to the rodents that carry the virus. That means keeping one's living quarters as clean as possible.

FOR MORE INFORMATION

Books

Cockrum, E. Lendell. *Rabies, Lyme Disease, Hanta Virus: And Other Animal-Borne Human Diseases in the United States and Canada.* Tucson, AZ: Fisher Books, 1997.

Harper, David R. and Andrea S. Meyer. *Of Mice, Men, and Microbes; Hantavirus.* New York: Academic Press Inc., 1999.

Stoffman, Phyllis. *The Family Guide to Preventing and Treating 100 Infectious Diseases.* New York: John Wiley & Sons, 1995.

Periodicals

"Outbreak of Hantavirus Is Unusual." *The New York Times* (June 17, 1997): pp. C4+.

HAY FEVER

DEFINITION

Hay fever is an inflammation of the nasal passages. It is an allergic reaction to substances present in the air. The medical name for hay fever is allergic rhinitis (pronounced ri-NI-tuss).

DESCRIPTION

Hay fever is the most common allergic condition (see allergies entry). An allergic condition is a reaction by the body to some substance that is harmless to most people. For example, most people are not bothered by dust in the air. For other people, however, inhaling dust can cause dramatic bodily changes, such as sneezing, coughing, and itchy and watery eyes.

Between 10 and 20 percent of all people in the United States have hay fever. The condition accounts for about 2 percent of all visits to doctors. The drugs used to treat hay fever make up a significant fraction of both prescription and over-the-counter drug sales each year.

There are two types of hay fever: seasonal and perennial. Seasonal hay fever occurs in the spring, summer, and early fall. During these seasons, the level of plant pollens in the air is at its highest. Perennial hay fever occurs all year. It is usually caused by substances found in the air at home or in the workplace. A person may have one or both types of hay fever. Symptoms of seasonal hay fever are worst after being outdoors. Symptoms of perennial hay fever are worst after spending time indoors. Both forms of hay fever can develop at any age. In most cases, they first appear during childhood. They may become either worse or better over time.

CAUSES

WORDS TO KNOW

Allergen: A substance that provokes an allergic response.

Anaphylaxis: Increased sensitivity caused by previous exposure to an allergen that can result in blood vessel dilation (swelling) and smooth muscle contraction. Anaphylaxis can result in sharp blood pressure drops and difficulty breathing.

Antibody: A specific protein produced by the immune system in response to a specific foreign protein or particle called an antigen.

Granules: Small packets of reactive chemicals stored within cells.

Histamine: A chemical released by mast cells that activates pain receptors and causes cells to that leak fluids.

Mast Cells: A type of immune system cell that is found in the lining of the nasal passages and eyelids. It displays a type of antibody called immunoglobulin type E (IgE) on its cell surface and participates in the allergic response by releasing histamine from intracellular granules.

Hay fever is a kind of immune reaction. The immune system consists of cells, tissues, and molecules whose job it is to fight off foreign invaders, such as bacteria and viruses. When a foreign substance enters the body, the immune system releases antibodies. Antibodies are chemicals with the ability to destroy the foreign substances.

In the case of hay fever, the immune system becomes confused. It treats dust, pollen, and other harmless substances as if they were dangerous invaders. Substances that cause this kind of reaction are known as allergens. The immune system releases antibodies against allergens the way it does against bacteria, viruses, and other dangerous substances.

The combination of antibody and allergen sets off a series of reactions designed to protect the body. These reactions cause cells and blood vessels to leak fluids. These fluids cause the familiar symptoms of hay fever, such as a runny nose, red and irritated eyes, an itchy nose, and a scratchy throat.

The number of possible allergens found in the air is enormous. Seasonal hay fever is most

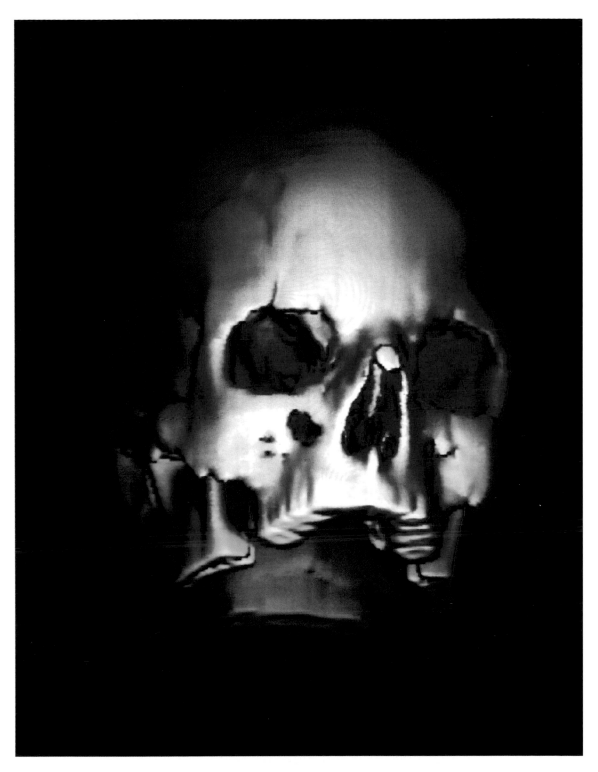

A computerized axial tomography (CAT) scan (also called a CT scan) of a human skull with a fracture above the eye (left side of image). (Reproduced by permission of Custom Medical Stock Photo.)

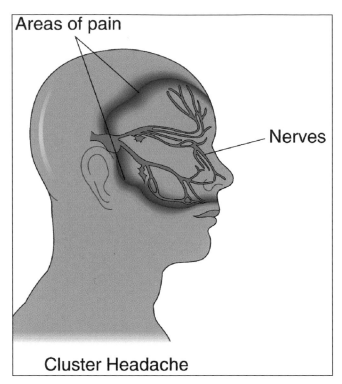

Areas of pain

Nerves

Cluster Headache

An illustration of the nerves affected by cluster headaches and typical areas of pain. (Reproduced by permission of Electronic Illustrators Group.)

Surgery-resection of a brain mass causing epilepsy. (Reproduced by permission of Custom Medical Stock Photo.)

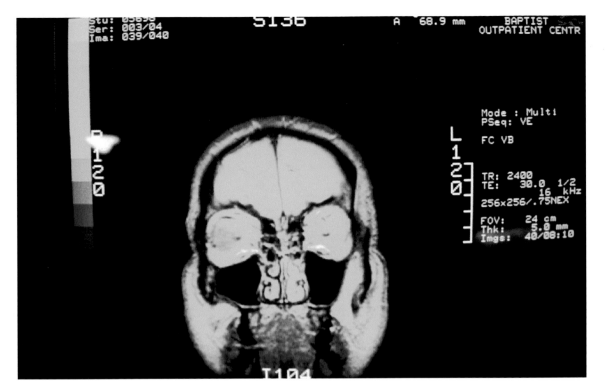

Computerized axial tomography (CAT) scans (also called CT scans) are often used to diagnose head injuries, as well as brain disorders such as Alzheimer's disease, headaches, brain aneurysms, and strokes. (© 1995 PhotoDisc.)

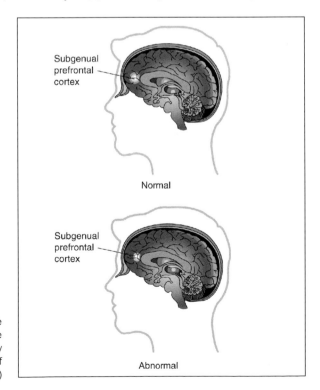

Subgenual prefrontal cortex

Normal

Subgenual prefrontal cortex

Abnormal

Recent scientific research indicates that the size of the subgenual prefrontal cortex (located behind the bridge of the nose) may be a determining factor in hereditary depressive disorders. (Reproduced by permission of Electronic Illustrators Group.)

Heat exhaustion is a common problem among athletes, firefighters, construction and factory workers, and anyone who wears heavy clothing in hot weather. (© Richard Hutchings. Reproduced by permission of Photo Researchers, Inc.)

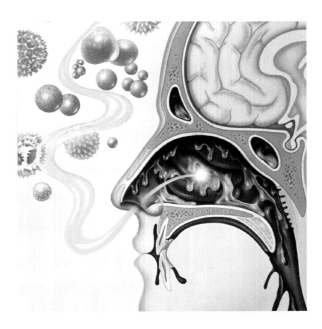

Illustration of excessive mucus production in the nose after inhalation of airborne pollen. (Reproduced by permission of Photo Researchers, Inc.)

Seasonal hay fever is most commonly caused by grass and tree pollen. Cutting grass introduces more allergens into the air and can make symptoms worse for seasonal allergy sufferers. (© 1995 PhotoDisc.)

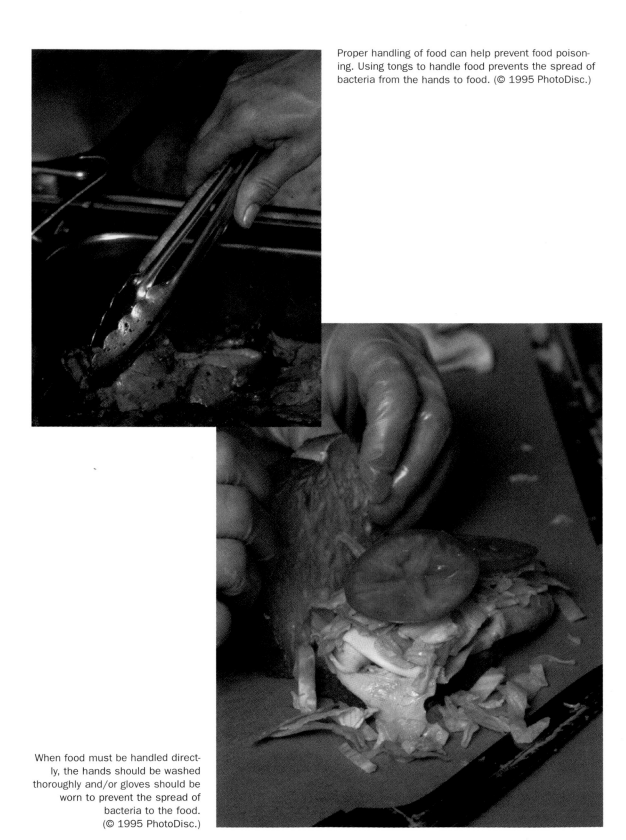

Proper handling of food can help prevent food poisoning. Using tongs to handle food prevents the spread of bacteria from the hands to food. (© 1995 PhotoDisc.)

When food must be handled directly, the hands should be washed thoroughly and/or gloves should be worn to prevent the spread of bacteria to the food. (© 1995 PhotoDisc.)

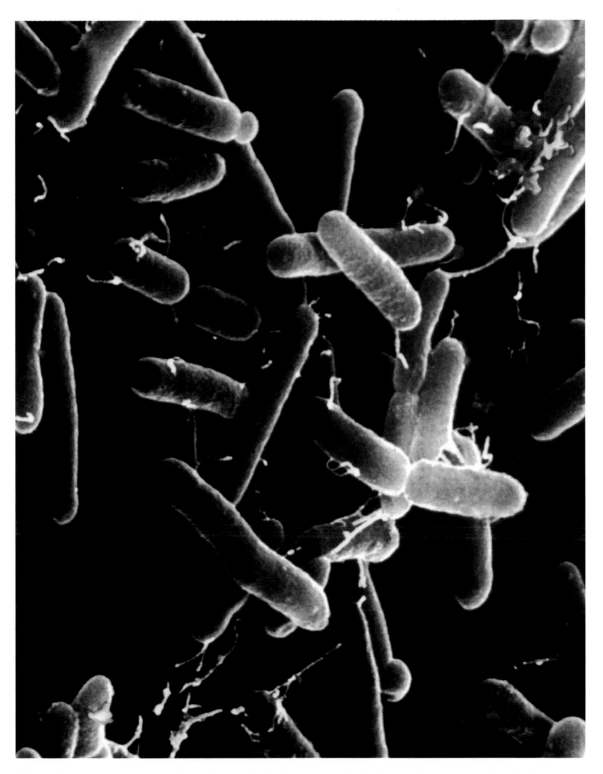

Salmonellosis are bacteria that commonly cause food poisoning, most often from poultry, eggs, meat, and milk. (Reproduced by permission of Photo Researcher, Inc.)

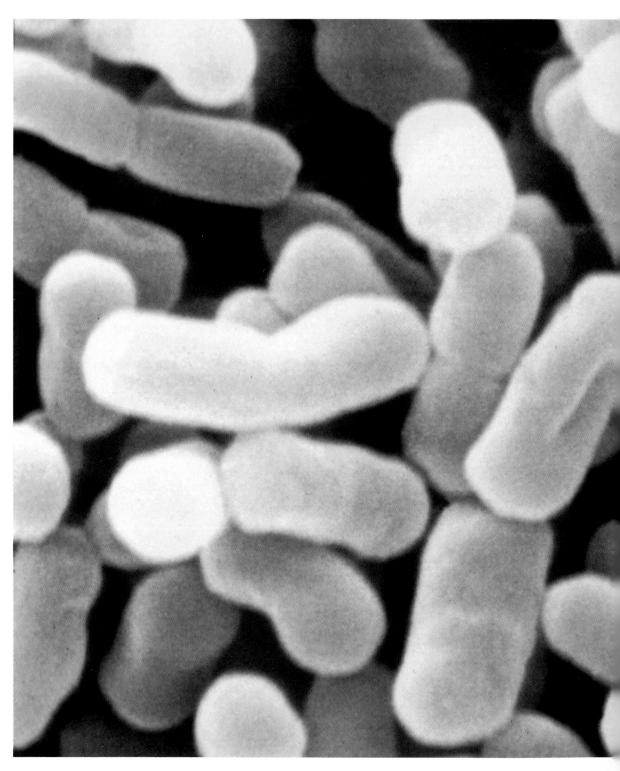

Escherichia Coli (*E. coli*) are bacteria that commonly cause food poisoning, most often from food products derived from cows, especially ground beef. (© 1997. Reproduced by permission of Custom Medical Stock Photo.)

Escherichia coli

1 μm

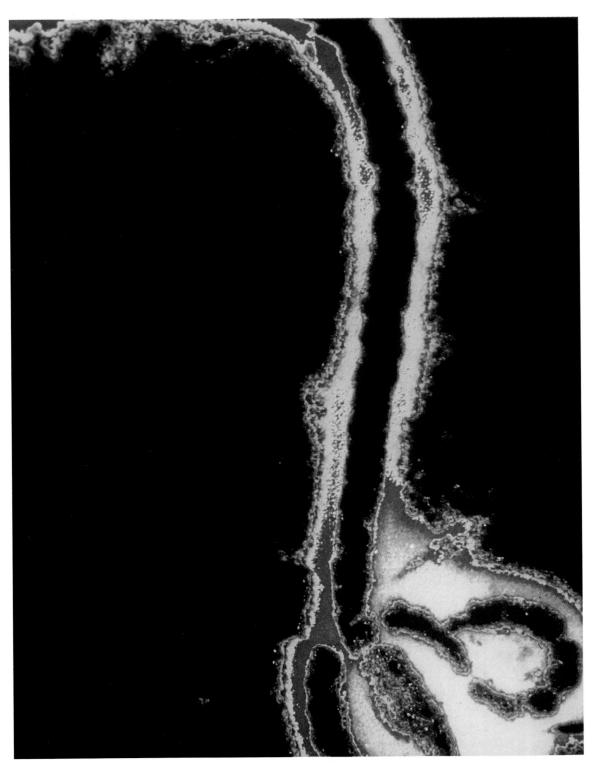

An image of an ebola virus. Infection with ebola causes severe bleeding and is fatal in 50 to 90 percent of cases. (© 1996 CDC/CMSP. Reproduced by permission of Custom Medical Stock Photo.)

The deer mouse is a carrier of one type of hantavirus that caused severe cases of infection in the Southwestern United States. (© 1997 S.R. Maglione. Reproduced by permission of Photo Researchers, Inc.)

An image of hantavirus magnified 88,000 times. (© 1995. Reproduced by permission of Custom Medical Stock Photo.)

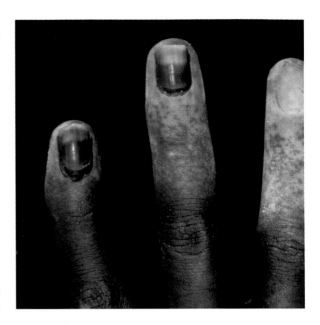

Frostbite on fingers. (Photograph by SIU. Reproduced by permission of the National Audubon Society Collection/Photo Researchers, Inc.)

An X ray of an ankle fracture. (© 1990. Reproduced by permission of Custom Medical Stock Photo.)

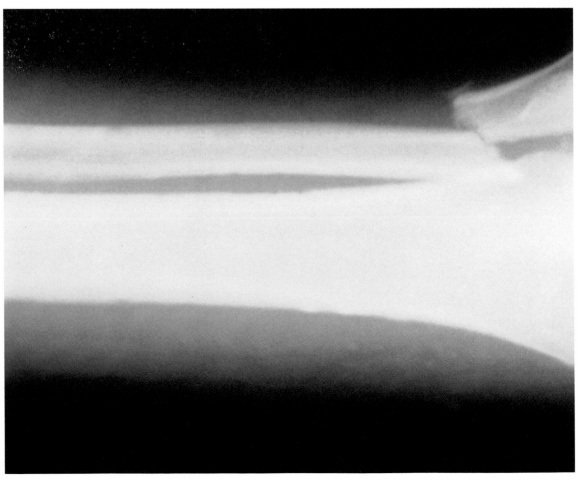

A cross section of a smoker's lung with emphysema. (Photograph by Dr. E. Walker. Reproduced by permission of the Science Photo Library/Photo Researchers, Inc.)

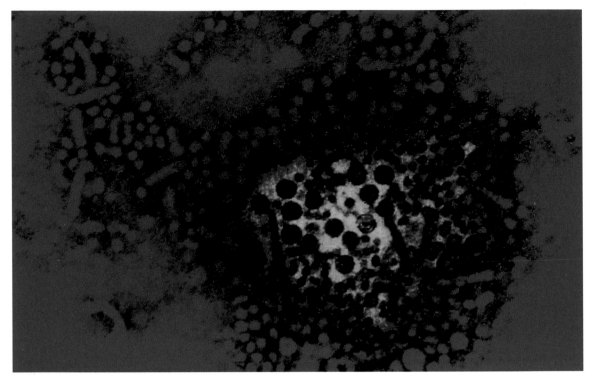

A digitized, magnified image of a hepatitis B virus. (© 1994. Reproduced by permission of Custom Medical Stock Photo.)

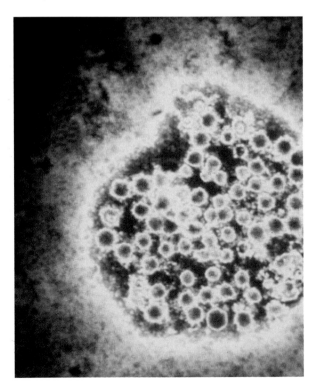

An image of a hepatitis A virus magnified 225,000 times. (© 1990. Reproduced by permission of Custom Medical Stock Photo.)

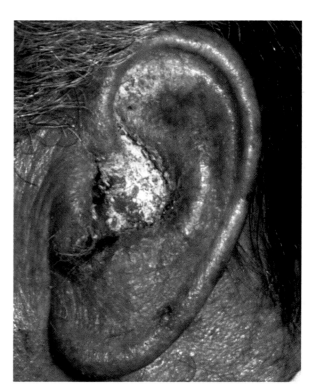

A severe external ear infection. (Photograph by Dr. P. Marazzi. Reproduced by permission of Custom Medical Stock Photo.)

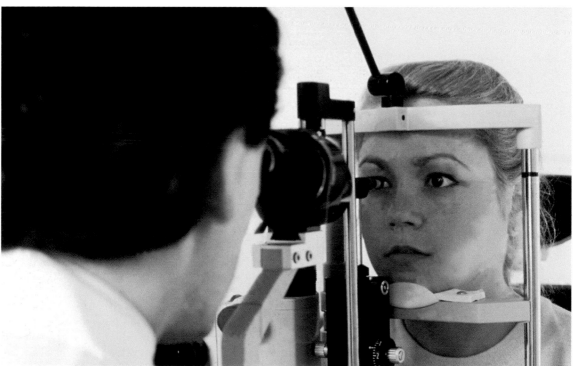

A patient receiving a glaucoma test. (© 1992. Reproduced by permission of Custom Medical Stock Photo.)

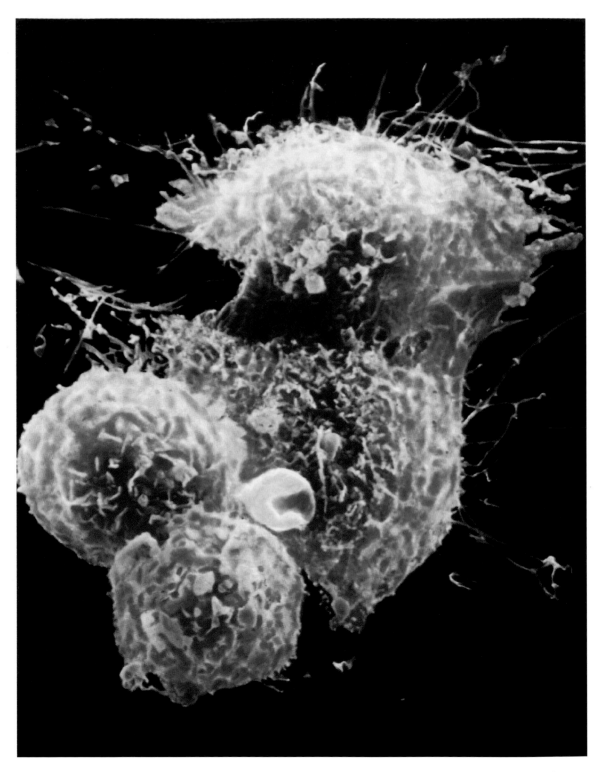

A magnified image of dividing Hodgkin's disease cells. (© 1995 Dr. Andrejs Liepins/Science Photo Library. Reproduced by permission of Custom Medical Stock Photo.)

commonly caused by grass and tree pollen. Pollen is a fine powder by which plants are germinated. A number of weeds can also cause hay fever. These include:

- Ragweed
- Sagebrush
- Lamb's quarters
- Plantain
- Pigweed
- Dock (sorrel)
- Tumbleweed

Perennial hay fever is also caused by a variety of particles found in the air including:

- **Body parts of house mites.** House mites are tiny insects. They can be seen only with the aid of a microscope. They feed on fibers, fur, and skin shed by people who live in the house. When they die, their body parts get into the air.
- **Animal wastes.** Animals constantly shed fur, skin flakes, and dried saliva. Common sources of these materials are pet dogs, cats, and birds. These materials easily get into the air. They cause allergic reactions in many people.
- **Mold spores.** Mold is a fungus that grows in warm, damp places. It lives in basements, bathrooms, air ducts, air conditioners, refrigerator drains, mattresses, and stuffed furniture. Mold reproduces by giving off tiny seed-like particles called spores. These spores are released into the air. They can cause hay fever in many people.

Other possible causes of perennial hay fever include the following:

- Cigarette smoke
- Perfume
- Cosmetics
- Cleansers
- Chemicals used in copy machines
- Industrial chemicals
- Gases given off by construction materials, such as insulation

SYMPTOMS

Common symptoms of hay fever include a tender, itchy, runny nose, accompanied by sneezing and coughing. The sinuses may also begin to swell, causing the eustachian (pronounced you-STAY-shee-un) tube to close up. The eustachian tube connects the inner ear to the throat. The closing of the eustachian tube causes a feeling of stuffiness. Mucus may drip from the sinuses into the throat, causing the throat to become sore. Hay fever may also cause red, itchy, watery eyes. Fatigue and headache are also common.

Hay fever can usually be diagnosed quite easily. Symptoms and a medical history usually indicate the presence of the condition. When symptoms appear in the spring and disappear in the fall, seasonal hay fever is likely to be the cause. Perennial hay fever can often be diagnosed by asking the patient what substances seem to cause his or her symptoms.

Skin tests are often used in diagnosing hay fever. The first step in conducting a skin test is to place a small amount of a suspected allergen on the skin. The doctor then scratches the skin very lightly. The scratch allows the allergen to get into the bloodstream. After a few minutes, the doctor checks the area being tested. A redness and swelling indicate that the patient is allergic to the material being tested. In most cases, twenty or more materials can be tested at one time. The tests are carried out on the patient's back or forearm.

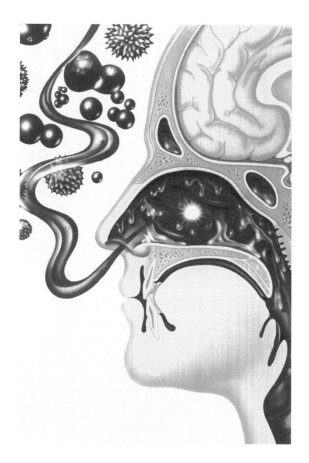

Illustration of excessive mucus production in the nose after inhalation of airborne pollen. (Reproduced by permission of Photo Researchers, Inc.)

TREATMENT

The best treatment for hay fever is to avoid the allergens that cause the condition. For example, people who are allergic to grass should not mow the lawn. It may be difficult to avoid allergens, however. In that case, two other treatments are available: drugs and immunotherapy.

Drugs

Some types of drugs used to treat hay fever include the following:

- **Antihistamines.** Antihistamines block the action of histamine (pronounced HISS-tuh-meen) in the immune system. Histamine is a chemical that causes many of the symptoms of hay fever. Antihistamines can be used after the symptoms of hay fever appear, but they are more effective if used before the symptoms appear. Many older types of antihistamines caused drowsiness. Some newer types do not have this side effect.
- **Decongestants.** Decongestants constrict (shrink) blood vessels. They reduce the loss of fluid from blood vessels that causes many symptoms of hay fever. Decongestants are sold as pills and as nasal (nose) sprays. One dangerous side effect is that they increase blood pressure and heart rate. They should not be taken for more than a few days at a time.

- **Topical corticosteroids.** Topical corticosteroids (pronounced kor-tih-ko-STIHR-oids) reduce inflammation and swelling of tissue. They tend to work more slowly and last longer than other forms of medication. As a result, they should be started before the hay fever season begins.
- **Mast cell stabilizers.** Mast cells are cells produced by the immune system. They are responsible for the early stages of an allergic reaction. Mast cell stabilizers stop the allergic reaction before it gets started. They can also be used before the hay fever season begins. In that case, they reduce the chance that hay fever will develop.

Immunotherapy

Immunotherapy is also known as desensitization or allergy shots. The principle behind immunotherapy is to get the immune system more familiar with an allergen. The procedure consists of a series of injections of the allergen to which the patient is allergic. The first few shots contain a very small amount of the allergen. Over time, the shots contain slightly more al-

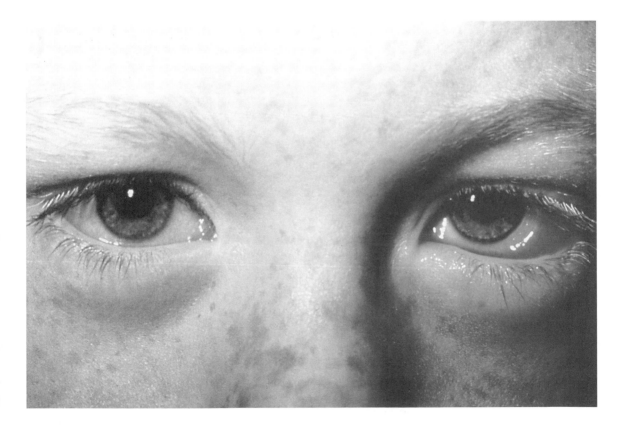

Hay fever can cause red, watery, itchy eyes. (© 1994 NMSB. Reproduced by permission of Custom Medical Stock Photo.)

lergen each time. With each shot, the immune system becomes more familiar with the allergen. It produces a more limited reaction to the material. Eventually, the injections contain as much allergen as a patient is likely to encounter in daily life. At that point, the immune system may no longer react to the allergen.

Immunotherapy may take many weeks, months, or even years to achieve this goal. Sometimes the procedure does not work at all. One serious side effect of immunotherapy is anaphylaxis (pronounced a-neh-feh-LAK-siss). Anaphylaxis is characterized by a sharp drop in blood pressure and difficulty with breathing. A person can go into anaphylactic shock and die very quickly. For this reason, the person giving an allergy shot must watch the patient very closely for any unexpected responses.

Alternative Treatment

Some alternative practitioners believe that hay fever should be treated by strengthening the immune system. They may recommend a more balanced diet and changes in one's lifestyle. Vitamin C is sometimes recommended to reduce inflammation of tissues. Some herbs that are recommended for relief of hay fever symptoms include eyebright, bee pollen, and nettle.

PROGNOSIS

Hay fever can usually be kept under control. By avoiding allergens, taking medications, and using immunotherapy, a person can reduce or eliminate most symptoms. In some cases, allergic reactions become worse over time. In other cases, they improve.

PREVENTION

There are many things a person can do to avoid allergic reactions. Some of the most common recommendations for preventing seasonal hay fever include:

- Stay indoors with windows closed during the morning hours, when pollen levels are highest.
- Keep car windows closed while driving.
- Wear a surgical mask when it is necessary to be outdoors.
- Avoid trees, bushes, flowers, and other plants to which one is allergic.
- Wash clothes and hair after being outside.
- Clean air conditioner filters in the home regularly.
- In severe cases, consider moving to an area with fewer allergens.

To reduce the symptoms of perennial hay fever, one needs to avoid mold spores, house dust, and animal wastes by taking steps such as the following:

- Keep the house dry through ventilation and use of dehumidifiers.
- Keep bathroom floors and walls clean with a disinfectant.
- Clean and disinfect air conditioners and coolers.
- Throw out moldy or mildewed books, shoes, pillows, and furniture.
- Vacuum frequently and change the vacuum bag regularly.
- Clean floors and walls with a damp mop.
- Avoid contact with pets to which one is allergic.
- Wash hands after contact with pets and other animals.
- Keep pets out of the bedroom, and off furniture and other areas where their waste materials may collect.
- Have pets bathed and groomed regularly.

FOR MORE INFORMATION

Books

Jelks, Mary. *Allergy Plants: That Cause Sneezing and Wheezing.* Tampa, FL: World-Wide Publications, 1994.

Novick, N. L. *You Can Do Something about Your Allergies.* New York: Macmillan, 1994.

Sussman, Les. *Relief from Hay Fever and Other Airborne Allergies.* New York: Dell Books, 1992.

Organizations

American Academy of Allergy, Asthma, and Immunology. (800) 822–2762. http://www.aaaai.org.

Asthma and Allergy Foundation of America. 1125 15th Street, NW, Suite 502, Washington, DC 20005. 800–7ASTHMA. http://www.aafa.org/home.html.

National Institute of Allery and Infectious Diseases. Building 31, Room 7A-50, 31 Center Drive, MSC 2520, Bethesda, MD 20892-2520. http://www.niaid.nih.gov.

Web sites

"Allergies." *About.com* [Online] http://allergies.miningco.com (accessed on October 21, 1999).

The On-Line Allergy Center. [Online] http://www.sig.net/~allergy/welcome.html (accessed on October 21, 1999).

HEAD INJURY

DEFINITION

Head injury refers to any damage to the scalp, skull, or brain. There are two general categories of head injuries: closed and penetrating. A closed head injury is one in which the skull is not broken open. For example, a boxer who receives a blow to the head may experience brain damage even though the skull is not damaged. This is a closed head injury. In a penetrating injury, the skull is broken open. For example, a bullet wound to the brain causes damage to the skull as well as to the brain. It is classified as a penetrating head injury. Both closed and penetrating head injuries can cause damage that ranges from mild to very serious. In the most severe cases, head injury can result in death.

DESCRIPTION

Head injuries can take many forms. These include skull fractures (broken bones in the skull), blood clots between the brain and the skull, and damage to the brain itself. Brain damage can occur even if the skull itself is undamaged. The brain may move around inside the skull with enough force to cause bruising and bleeding.

Most people have had some type of head injury at least once in their lives, but these events are usually not serious enough to require hospital care. However, about two million Americans experience serious head injuries every year. Up to 750,000 of these individuals require hospital treatment. Brain injuries are most likely to occur in males between the ages of fifteen and twenty-four. The most common causes of these injuries are car and motorcycle accidents. About 70 percent of all accidental deaths are due to head injuries, as are most disabilities resulting from accidents.

CAUSES AND SYMPTOMS

The most common causes of head injuries are traffic accidents, sports injuries, falls, workplace accidents, assaults, and bullet wounds. The

WORDS TO KNOW

Computed tomography (CT) scan: A diagnostic technique that uses X rays focused on a portion of the body from different directions to obtain a three-dimensional picture of that part of the body.

Computerized axial tomography (CAT) scan: Another name for a computed tomography (CT) scan.

Electroencephalogram (EEG): A record of the electrical impulses produced by the brain's activity as a way of measuring how the brain is working.

Magnetic resonance imaging (MRI): A diagnostic technique for studying the structure of organs and tissues within the body without using radiation of any kind.

Positron emission tomography (PET): A diagnostic technique that uses radioactive materials to study the structure and function of organs and tissues within the body.

head may be damaged both from direct physical injury to the brain and from secondary factors. Secondary factors include lack of oxygen, swelling of the brain, and loss of blood flow to the brain. Both closed and penetrating head injuries can cause tearing of nerve tissue and widespread bleeding or a blood clot in the brain. Swelling may cause the brain to push against the skull, blocking the flow of blood and oxygen to the brain.

Trauma (sudden shock) to the head can cause a concussion (pronounced kun-KUH-shen). A concussion often causes loss of consciousness without visible damage to the skull. In addition to loss of consciousness, initial symptoms of brain injury include:

- Memory loss and confusion
- Vomiting
- Dizziness
- Partial paralysis or numbness
- Shock
- Anxiety

After a head injury, a person may experience a period when his or her brain does not function normally. The person may become confused, have partial memory loss, and lose the ability to learn normally. Other people experience amnesia (memory loss) that may last for a few weeks, months, or even years. As the patient recovers from the head injury, memory normally returns slowly.

A less common aftereffect of head injury is epilepsy (see epilepsy entry). Epilepsy is a seizure disorder characterized by shaking and loss of control over one's muscles. Epilepsy occurs as a result of 2 to 5 percent of all head injuries.

Closed Head Injury

Closed head injury is any head injury in which the skull is not broken open. A common cause of closed head injury is a direct blow to the head. Sudden starts and stops in a motor vehicle may also cause a closed head injury. In such cases, the brain is suddenly thrown with great force against the skull, causing damage to the brain.

Penetrating Head Injury

Penetrating head injuries occur when some object passes through the skull into the brain. The object itself may cause damage to the brain. A bullet wound to the head is an example. Pieces of the skull can also be pushed into the brain by the object. These pieces can damage the brain. An open wound to the brain may also lead to an infection that can cause further brain damage.

Skull Fracture

A skull fracture is an event in which one or more of the bones that make up the skull are broken. Skull fractures are serious accidents and require immediate medical attention. Some skull fractures are visible. Blood and bone fragments may be obvious. In some cases, however, there are no visible signs of a skull fracture. In such cases, other symptoms may indicate the possibility of a skull fracture. These include:

• Blood or clear fluid leaking from the nose or ear
• Pupils in the eyes having unequal sizes
• Bruises or discoloration around the eyes or behind the ears
• Swelling or a dent on any part of the head

Intracranial Hemorrhage

Bleeding inside the skull may accompany a head injury and may cause additional damage to the brain. A blood clot may also form between the brain and the skull. A blood clot is a mass of partly solidified blood that forms in the body. The clot can press against the brain and interrupt the flow of blood and oxygen through the brain. A reduced flow of oxygen prevents the brain from functioning normally.

Bleeding can also occur deep within the brain. Wherever it occurs, bleeding in the brain is a very serious condition. It can lead to unconsciousness and death. The symptoms of bleeding within the brain include:

• Nausea and vomiting
• Headache

COMPUTERIZED AXIAL TOMOGRAPHY

The discovery of X rays in the late 1890s changed the course of medicine. X rays gave doctors a way of seeing into a patient's body. Hard materials, like bone and teeth, show up clearly in an X-ray photograph.

But X-ray photographs have some serious disadvantages. They provide only a two-dimensional ("flat") view. They may not show cuts, breaks, lumps, and other disorders behind a bone or some other object. The problem is similar to trying to find out what the back of a person's head is like by looking at a photograph of his or her face.

In the 1960s, scientists found another way to use X rays that solved this problem. The technique is known as axial tomography. In axial to-mography, X-ray photographs are taken of thin slices of an object. The X-ray camera is aimed at one part of the body, and a photograph taken. Then the camera is moved just slightly, and another photograph is taken. This process is repeated over and over again. Eventually, the researchers has a whole set of photographs of a part of the patient's body.

The problem is that it takes a long time to examine all these photographs and to see how they fit together. The obvious solution to that problem is to let a computer do the work. Today, the X-ray photographs can be fed into a computer, which assembles them into a three-dimensional photograph called a computerized axial tomography (CAT) scan or a computed tomography (CT) scan. The final product provides a much more detailed image of the body part being studied.

- Loss of consciousness
- Pupils in the eyes having unequal sizes
- Listlessness

Postconcussion Syndrome

Mild head injuries usually produce symptoms such as headache, confusion, dizziness, and blurred vision. In some cases, these symptoms may last for a few days or weeks. Up to 60 percent of patients who sustain a head injury experience these symptoms for an even longer period of time. The symptoms can last as long as six months or a year after the injury. This condition is known as postconcussion syndrome.

Postconcussion syndrome is often difficult to diagnose. The symptoms include:

- Headache
- Dizziness
- Mental confusion
- Behavior changes
- Memory loss
- Loss of ability to think clearly
- Depression
- Sudden changes in mood

DIAGNOSIS

Some types of head injuries can be diagnosed based on the symptoms listed above. It is often difficult, however, to know how serious a head injury is. The fact that a person has a headache following a head injury, for example, does not really indicate how serious that injury is.

The extent of a head injury can be determined in a number of ways. The Glasgow Coma Scale is based on a patient's ability to open his or her eyes, give answers to questions, and respond to physical stimuli, such as a doctor's touch. A person can score anywhere from three to fifteen points on this scale. A score of less than eight points on the scale suggests the presence of serious brain damage.

Patients who are suspected of having severe brain damage should be referred to a medical specialist. The specialist will usually recommend a series of tests. The most common of these tests are the computed tomography (CT) scan, magnetic resonance imaging (MRI), positron emission tomography (PET) scan, and electroencephalogram (EEG, pronounced ih-LEK-tro-in-SEH-fuh-lo-gram). These tests provide visual images of the brain and of the electrical activity taking place within the brain. They are often helpful in discovering damage to the brain.

Some forms of head injury are still difficult to diagnose, even with the best available tests. In such cases, the advice of experts in head injuries may be necessary for diagnosis and treatment.

TREATMENT

The first step in treating most forms of head injury is to keep the patient quiet in a darkened room. The patient's head and shoulders should be raised slightly on a pillow or blanket.

The next step in treatment depends on the nature of the injury. In the case of a penetrating wound, for example, surgery may be necessary. In a closed head injury, surgery may also be required to drain blood from the brain or to remove a clot. Surgery may also be needed to repair severe skull fractures.

Hospitalization is often necessary following head injuries. Medical workers will observe a patient to watch for any change in his or her condition. In addition, drugs can be given to prevent seizures. A tube can also be inserted into the brain to drain off excess fluid.

A person with a severe head injury may require long-term treatment. This treatment may be needed to help the person recover mental functions lost as a result of the injury. Long-term treatment can sometimes be conducted in day treatment programs. People with the most severe forms of head injury may need to be cared for in a special institution.

PROGNOSIS

The best hope for recovery from head injury is prompt diagnosis and treatment. However, the long-term prognosis for head injuries is often difficult to predict in the first few hours or days after an injury. In some cases, the prognosis is not known for months or years.

Individuals who experience mild head injuries often recover completely and fairly quickly. Some symptoms, however, may last for up to a year after the accident. These symptoms include headache, dizziness, and an inability to think

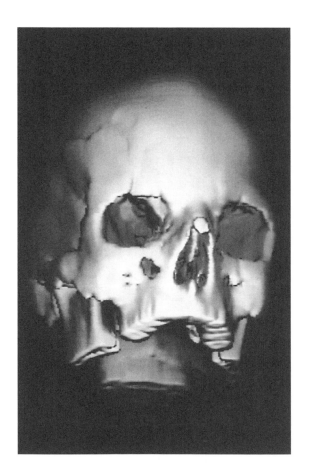

CAT scan of a skull fracture. (Reproduced by permission of Custom Medical Stock Photo)

clearly. These symptoms can obviously affect a person's ability to work and to deal normally with other people.

The prognosis for severe head injuries is not as good. Such injuries can often produce permanent physical or mental disabilities. Epileptic seizures are an example. Recovery from a severe head injury may take up to five years or more. The length of recovery often depends on a number of personal factors, such as a person's age, the length of time the person was unconscious following the injury, the number and location of brain injuries, and the duration of amnesia.

PREVENTION

Severe head injuries can often be prevented by some simple steps. People who take part in contact sports or ride bicycles or motorcycles, for example, should always wear helmets. Seat belts and airbags have prevented many head injuries in car accidents. People who work in dangerous occupations should also wear protective headgear on the job.

FOR MORE INFORMATION

Books

Stoller, Diane. *Coping With Mild Traumatic Brain Injury.* Garden City Park, NY: Avery Publishing Group, 1998.

Weiner, William J. *Neurology for the Non-Neurologist,* 3rd edition. Philadelphia: J. B. Lippincott, 1994.

Organizations

American Epilepsy Society. 638 Prospect Ave., Hartford, CT 06105. (203) 232–4825.

Brain Injury Association. 1776 Massachusetts Ave., NW, Suite 100, Washington, DC 20036. (800) 444–6443.

Head Injury Hotline. PO Box 84151, Seattle, WA 98124. (206) 621–8558.

Head Trauma Support Project, Inc. 2500 Marconi Ave., Suite 203, Sacramento, CA 95821. (916) 482–5770.

National Head Injury Foundation. 333 Turnpike Rd., Southboro, MA 01722. (617) 485–9950.

Web sites

"Ask NOAH About: Spinal Cord and Head Injuries." *NOAH: New York Online Access to Health.* [Online] http://www.noah.cuny.edu/neuro/spinal.html (accessed on October 21, 1999).

HEADACHE

DEFINITION

A headache is a pain in the head. A headache can be caused by some other physical disorder, or it may be a disorder in and of itself.

DESCRIPTION

There are three major types of headaches: tension (or stress), migraine, and cluster. A tension headache is caused by the tightening of muscles in the neck and head. A migraine headache occurs when blood vessels in the brain dilate (swell up). Cluster headaches are characterized by very severe pain.

Tension headaches are probably the most common form of the disorder. Nearly everyone has a tension headache from time to time. Migraine headaches are less common. About 18 percent of American women and 6 percent of American men experience migraine headaches on a relatively regular basis. Cluster headaches are fairly rare. Less than 0.5 percent of Americans experience cluster headaches. Men make up 80 percent of all cluster headache sufferers.

Approximately forty to forty-five million people in the United States suffer headaches on a regular basis over an extended period of time. Headaches have a major impact on society because of missed workdays.

Headaches can also be caused by other kinds of diseases, injuries, and disorders. Headaches of this kind are not discussed in this entry.

WORDS TO KNOW

Abortive: Describes an action that cuts something short or stops it.

Biofeedback: A technique in which a person learns to consciously control the body's response to a stimulus.

Prophylactic: Referring to a treatment that prevents the symptoms of a disorder from developing.

Transcutaneous electrical nerve stimulation: A procedure in which mild electrical currents are used to stimulate nerves in order to prevent the transmission of pain messages in the body.

CAUSES

Brain tissue itself does not feel pain, but other kinds of tissue in and around the brain can feel pain. For example, muscles in the scalp, face, or neck can contract and become painful, and blood vessels in the brain and face can swell, causing pain in the muscles and tissue on the skull.

Tension headaches are thought to be caused when muscles in and around the head contract (tighten up) due often to stress or poor posture. Tension headaches are also triggered by eyestrain, overexertion, loud noises, and other disturbing factors in the environment.

Migraine headaches are thought to occur when blood vessels in the brain dilate. In either case, pressure is exerted on certain tissues that can feel pain. Migraines are often triggered by food items, such as red wine, chocolate, and aged cheeses. For women, hormone changes may also be a cause of migraines. Women may experience migraines at certain times in menstrual cycle, when they are taking oral contraceptives, or after menopause.

Cluster headaches seem to be associated with alcohol and tobacco use. They can also be triggered by tension and by histamines (a compound the body releases as part of an allergic reaction; see allergies entry).

SYMPTOMS

Migraine headaches are intense throbbing headaches that occur on one or both sides of the head. The pain is often accompanied by other symptoms, such as nausea, vomiting, blurred vision, and a high sensitivity to light, sound, and movement.

The usual tension headache is described as a tightening around the head and neck, accompanied by a steady ache that forms a tight band around the forehead. Tension headaches usually affect both sides of the head and usually appear at the front of the head, although they can appear at the top or back of the skull. Tension headaches often begin in the afternoon and can last for several hours. They can occur every day. When this happens it is called a chronic tension headache.

A cluster headache can cause excruciating pain. The headache is usually centered around one eye. It may also cause the eyes to tear and nasal (nose) congestion. A cluster headache usually lasts from fifteen minutes to four hours. It may occur several times in a day.

Cluster headaches are classified as either episodic or chronic. Approximately 80 percent of cluster headaches are episodic, that is, they occur during one to five month periods followed by six to twenty-four month attack-free period. There is no such reprieve for chronic cluster headache sufferers.

DIAGNOSIS

The first step in diagnosing a headache is to find out whether it is related to some other medical problem. For example, people who have experienced a head injury (see head injury entry) may also have headaches. A doctor needs to find out whether the headache is a result of such a condition or is the problem itself.

If the headache is the sole problem, a doctor conducts a physical examination and takes a medical history. He or she may ask how often the headache occurs, where it is located, what factors seem to cause the headache, and what other symptoms may accompany it. The answers to these questions help the doctor classify the headache into one of the three categories listed above.

Nearly everyone has headaches from time to time. Some conditions, however, are warning signs that medical care is necessary. These signs include:

- "Worst headache of my life." This complaint could mean that damage has occurred to a blood vessel in the brain. Immediate medical attention may be required.
- Headache accompanied by a weakness on one side of the body, numbness, loss of vision, or problems with speaking. These symptoms are possible indications of a stroke.
- Headaches that become worse over a period of six months, especially if they occur in the morning. This pattern may suggest the presence of a brain tumor.
- Sudden onset (beginning) of a headache. The presence of a fever along with the headache may indicate a serious brain disorder known as meningitis ("brain fever," pronounced meh-nen-JI-tiss).

To diagnose conditions such as these, a doctor may use a variety of tests, such as a computed tomography (CT) scan or magnetic resonance imaging (MRI). A CT scan is a procedure by which X rays are directed at a patient's body from various angles and the set of photographs thus obtained assembled by a computer program. This procedure is sometimes called a computerized axial tomography (CAT) scan. An MRI is a technique for studying the structure of internal organs by using magnetic waves.

ASPIRIN

Aspirin is one of the oldest drugs known to humans. Ancient people discovered long ago that pain and fever could be controlled by chewing on the bark of the willow tree or by rubbing oil of wintergreen on a sore part of the body. Willow trees and wintergreen both contain a chemical known as salicylic (pronounced SAL-ih-SILL-ik) acid.

Of course, the ancients did not know the chemical composition of willows and wintergreen. It was not until the mid-1800s that chemists gained that knowledge. Then, they became excited about the possible uses of salicylic acid. They thought it might be able to cure many different kinds of diseases. They also believed that it could be used to preserve foods.

They were right about the second point, but wrong about the first. For a time, salicylic acid became popular as a food preservative. But it was soon replaced by other, more effective methods.

Although salicylic acid did not cure disease, it was effective in reducing fever and relieving pain. But it had one serious side effect: It usually upset the stomach. Eventually, researchers found a solution to this problem. They converted salicylic acid into another form, called sodium acetylsalicylate (pronounced uh-SEAT-el-suh-LIS-ih-late). Sodium acetylsalicylate also acts to reduce fever and relieve pain. But it is less harmful to the stomach.

In 1899, the German chemical company, Bayer AG, began making sodium acetylsalicylate commercially. They named the product aspirin. Today, aspirin is probably the most widely used drug in the world.

TREATMENT

There are two kinds of headache treatment, called abortive and prophylactic. Abortive treatment is used with headaches that are already in progress. Prophylactic treatments are used to prevent headaches from occurring.

The most common drugs used to treat tension and migraine headaches are aspirin, acetaminophen (pronounced uh-SEAT-uh-min-uh-fin), ibuprofen (pronounced EYE-byu-pro-fin), or naproxen. Antidepressants and muscle relaxants can also be used to treat tension headaches. Three drugs that have had some success in the treatment of migraines include ergotamine tartrate, sumatriptan, and extra-strength Excedrin (which includes caffeine). Cluster headaches are also treated with ergotamine tartrate (pronounced ur-GOT-uh-meen TAR-trait) and sumatriptan (pronounced SOO-muh-TRIP-tan), as well as with pure oxygen. Prophylactic treatments include prednisone (pronounced PRED-nih-zone), calcium channel blockers, and methysergide (pronounced METH-ih-SIR-jide).

Alternative Treatment

A number of alternative treatments have been recommended for treating and preventing headaches. These include:

- Acupuncture or acupressure
- Biofeedback

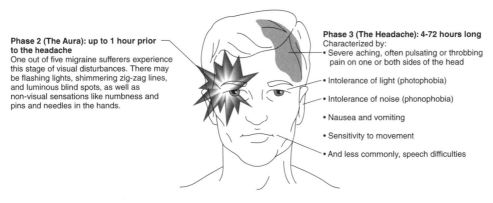

Phase 1 (The Prodrome): up to 24 hours prior to the headache
Roughly half of all migraine sufferers experience this stage, which is characterized by symptoms of heightened or dulled perception, irritability or withdrawal, and food cravings.

Phase 2 (The Aura): up to 1 hour prior to the headache
One out of five migraine sufferers experience this stage of visual disturbances. There may be flashing lights, shimmering zig-zag lines, and luminous blind spots, as well as non-visual sensations like numbness and pins and needles in the hands.

Phase 3 (The Headache): 4-72 hours long
Characterized by:
- Severe aching, often pulsating or throbbing pain on one or both sides of the head
- Intolerance of light (photophobia)
- Intolerance of noise (phonophobia)
- Nausea and vomiting
- Sensitivity to movement
- And less commonly, speech difficulties

Phase 4 (The Postdrome): up to 24 hours after the headache
Most migraine sufferers experience aching muscles and feel tired and drained after the headache, although some few go through a period of euphoria.

The phases of a typical migraine headache. (Illustration by Hans & Cassady, Inc.)

- Chiropractic
- Herbal remedies, such as chamomile, feverfew, valerian, white willow, and skullcap
- Homeopathic remedies
- Hydrotherapy
- Massage
- Magnesium supplements
- Regular physical exercise
- Relaxation techniques, such as meditation and yoga
- Transcutaneous electrical nerve stimulation, a technique that uses mild electrical shocks in an effort to prevent pain signals in the body

PROGNOSIS

As painful as headaches can be, they are not fatal (as long as they are not a symptom of some more serious disease or disorder). Neither do they have harmful long-term effects. Most headaches disappear on their own or are relieved by the treatments mentioned above.

PREVENTION

People can avoid some headaches by avoiding the factors that cause them. For example, one is less likely to develop tension headaches if one avoids stress in everyday life. Headaches caused by food allergies can be prevented by not eating the foods that bring on the headaches. Regular exercise and certain alternative treatments, such as relaxation exercises, may also help prevent some headaches.

FOR MORE INFORMATION

Books

Burks, Susan L., and Fred D. Sheftell. *Managing Your Migraine: A Migraine Sufferer's Practical Guide.* Totowa, NJ: Humana Press, 1994.

Inlander, Charles B. *Headaches: 47 Ways to Stop the Pain.* New York: Walker & Company, 1995.

Robbins, Lawrence D. *Headache Help: A Complete Guide to Understanding Headaches and the Medicines That Relieve Them.* Boston: Houghton Mifflin Company, 1998.

Votava, Andrea. *Coping With Migraines and Other Headaches.* New York: Rosen Publishing Group, 1997.

Organizations

American Council for Headache Education. 19 Mantua Road, Mt. Royal, NJ 08061. (609) 423–0043; (800) 255–2243. http://www.achenet.org.

National Headache Foundation. 428 West St. James Place, Chicago, IL 60614. (773) 388–6399; (800) 843–2256. http://www.headache.org.

Web sites

"Ask NOAH About: Headache." *NOAH: New York Online Access to Health.* [Online] http://www.noah.cuny.edu/headache.headache.html (accessed on October 21, 1999).

HEARING LOSS

DEFINITION

Hearing loss is any reduction in a person's ability to detect sound.

DESCRIPTION

Hearing is a complex process that consists of many steps. It begins when sound waves strike the outside of the ear. Sound waves are vibrations that occur in air. When sound waves hit the ear, they cause tissue in the ear to start vibrating.

The ear consists of three major sections: the external ear, the middle ear, and the inner ear. The external ear acts like a small sound-collecting tube. Sound waves enter the ear and pass down a narrow canal called the auditory canal. At the end of the canal, the sound waves strike a thin membrane called the tympanic (pronounced tim-PA-nik) membrane, or ear drum. They cause the tympanic membrane to begin vibrating.

Just beyond the tympanic membrane is the middle ear. The middle ear contains three bones called ossicles (pronounced AH-sih-kulls). Vibration of the tympanic membrane is passed along to the ossicles. They too begin to vibrate.

WORDS TO KNOW

Audiometer: An instrument for testing a person's hearing.

Auditory canal: A tube that leads from the outside of the ear to the tympanic membrane.

Auditory nerve: A bunch of nerve fibers that carries sound from the inner ear to the brain.

Conductive hearing loss: Hearing loss that occurs in the external or middle ear.

Eustachian tube: A passageway that connects the middle ear with the back of the throat.

Ossicles: A set of tiny bones in the middle ear responsible for transmitting sound vibrations from the outer ear to the inner ear.

Otosclerosis: A disorder in which the bones of the middle ear become joined to each other.

Sensory hearing loss: Hearing loss that occurs in the inner ear, auditory nerve, or brain.

Tympanic membrane: A thin piece of tissue between the external ear and the middle ear.

The ossicles are connected to the inner ear. The inner ear is filled with a clear, watery fluid. As the ossicles vibrate, they create another wave inside the watery fluid in the inner ear. This wave is similar to a water wave on a lake or the ocean.

In the last stage of hearing, the water wave in the inner ear collides with the auditory nerve. The auditory nerve picks up these vibrations and transmits them to the brain. The brain "reads" these vibrations as a sound.

Hearing loss can occur at any stage of this process. For example, sound waves may be blocked as they try to pass down the auditory canal. Or they may not be able to pass through the ossicles in the middle ear. Or they may not be transmitted through the liquid of the middle ear or along the auditory nerve. Finally, the brain may lose its ability to make sense out of the vibrations it receives from the auditory nerve.

Hearing loss is usually defined as being either conductive or sensory hearing loss. Conductive hearing loss is caused by damage to the external or middle ear. Sound vibrations are unable to pass down the auditory canal, across the tympanic membrane, and through the ossicles. Sensory hearing loss occurs in the inner ear and the auditory nerve. Sound waves may reach the inner ear, but they are not transmitted successfully to the brain.

CAUSES AND SYMPTOMS

Some possible causes and symptoms of hearing loss at each of the above stages are as follows:

- **External ear.** The auditory canal may become blocked with ear wax, foreign objects, infection, or a tumor. A tumor is a mass of cells that forms a lump somewhere in the body. This blockage prevents all or some of a group of sound waves from passing down the auditory canal.
- **Middle ear.** The tympanic membrane and ossicles can be damaged by injury or infection. A sharp object inserted into the ear can break the membrane. A blow to the head may damage the membrane or the ossicles. High water pressure caused by a deep-sea dive can also damage the middle ear. Infection of the middle ear may be caused when fluids from the throat pass down the Eustachian (pronounced you-STAY-shee-un) tube into the middle ear. The Eustachian tube connects the middle ear with the back of the throat. A disease called otosclerosis (pronounced oh-toe-skle-RO-suss) can cause the ossicles to bind to each other. When that happens, they are not able to vibrate properly.
- **Inner ear.** The primary cause of sensory hearing loss is exposure to loud noise. By some estimates, more than one million people have hearing problems for this reason. Exposure to loud noise may be caused by listening to loud music or working at a job where loud sounds are produced. Sensory

hearing loss also occurs as a natural part of aging. About a third of the people over the age of sixty-five have partial or complete hearing loss. Infections of the inner ear and brain can

also cause hearing loss. Certain drugs, including some common antibiotics, may damage the inner ear or auditory nerve. Finally, damage to the brain, such as stroke (see stroke entry) or multiple sclerosis (see multiple sclerosis entry), can cause hearing loss.

DIAGNOSIS

Hearing loss can often be diagnosed with a physical examination. A doctor may look directly into a patient's ears to see if any blockage is present, such as an infection or tumor. Another test involves the use of a tuning fork. A tuning fork is a metallic instrument that vibrates when struck. The tuning fork is placed next to the ear or placed against the patient's head. The vibrations it produces result in a musical tone. The patient's responses can help the doctor determine the patient's range of hearing.

Another important tool in the diagnosis of hearing problems is the audiometer (pronounced aw-dee-AH-meh-tur). An audiometer is a device that produces very pure tones of differing pitch and volume (loudness). A patient is provided with earphones connected to the audiometer. He or she is then asked to indicate the level at which various sounds can be heard. The data provided by this test may diagnose the type and severity of a patient's hearing loss. Many other tests are available to diagnose hearing disorders within the inner ear, the auditory nerve, and the brain itself.

TREATMENT

Conductive hearing loss can almost always be restored to some degree, if not completely. Some effective treatments include the following:

• Matter blocking the auditory canal can usually be removed easily.
• Middle ear infections can be treated with antibiotics. If necessary, the middle ear can be drained through the tympanic membrane. The tympanic membrane normally heals quickly after this surgery.
• Damaged tympanic membranes can usually be repaired with a small skin graft.
• Otosclerosis can be repaired surgically. Artificial parts can be substituted for the original ossicles.

Sensory hearing loss presents more serious problems. It often cannot be cured. Fortunately, hearing aids can help restore some of the hearing loss. Hearing aids can be dispensed only with a physician's prescription. They can make hearing at least ten times better.

Hearing problems are common. A number of organizations have been formed to help people with hearing loss. Special language training is available for children with reduced hearing. They may learn both lip reading and sign language.

PROGNOSIS

The prognosis for hearing loss varies widely. The likelihood of improvement depends on the type of hearing problem. Most conductive hearing losses can be cured. Normal hearing can be restored by relatively simple procedures. Sensory hearing loss is more difficult to treat. It can seldom be cured or repaired. Hearing aids can often provide people with near-normal hearing, however.

SENSORY HEARING LOSS OFTEN CANNOT BE CURED.

PREVENTION

Many types of hearing loss can be prevented. Infections of the throat and upper respiratory (breathing) tract should be monitored carefully. These infections can spread to the ears. If the ears do become infected, they should be treated as quickly as possible.

Noise reduction can prevent a large number of hearing problems. People who work in noisy environments, for example, should always wear protective headgear. People who enjoy loud music should use some restraint in listening to their favorite performers. This step alone can prevent thousands of cases of hearing loss each year.

FOR MORE INFORMATION

Books

Carmen, Richard, ed. *Consumer Handbook on Hearing Loss and Hearing Aids: A Bridge to Healing.* Sedona, AZ: Auricle Ink Publishers, 1999.

Pope, Anne. *Hear: Solutions, Skills and Sources For People With Hearing Loss.* London, New York: DK Publishing, 1997.

Turkington, Carol A. *The Hearing Loss Sourcebook: A Complete Guide to Coping With Hearing Loss and Where to Get Help.* New York: Plume, 1997.

Wayner, Donna S. *Hear What You've Been Missing: How to Cope With Hearing Loss: Questions, Answers, Options.* New York: John Wiley & Sons, 1998.

Organizations

Alexander Graham Bell Association for the Deaf. 3417 Volta Place, NW, Washington, DC 20007-2778. (202) 337–5220. http://www.agbell.org.

The League for the Hard of Hearing. 71 West 23rd St., New York, NY 10010-4162. (212) 741–7650. http://www.lhh.org.

Self Help for Hard of Hearing People, Inc. 79 Woodmon Ave., Suite 120C, Bethesda, MD 20814. (301) 675-2248. http://www.shhh.org.

Web sites

Vessel, B., "Deaf Source." [Online] http://home.earthlink.net/~drblood (accessed April 26, 1998).

HEART ATTACK

DEFINITION

A heart attack is caused by the death of, or damage to, part of the heart muscle. Heart attacks usually occur because the supply of blood to the heart muscle is greatly reduced or stopped. A heart attack is also called a myocardial infarction (pronounced my-uh-KAR-dee-al in-FARK-shun).

DESCRIPTION

Heart attack is the leading cause of death in the United States. More than 1.5 million Americans suffer a heart attack each year. About one-third of them die from the heart attack.

The conditions leading to a heart attack often develop over many years. Like all organs in the body, the heart requires a constant supply of blood. It gets that blood from arteries that lead into the heart. In some cases, plaque (pronounced PLAK) may build up on artery walls. Plaque is a collection of cells deposited on the walls of the artery. Over time, the plaque becomes larger and larger. Eventually, it greatly reduces the amount of blood reaching the heart. The plaque can also close off the artery entirely. When that happens, the blood supply to the heart is completely cut off. In such cases, heart cells die and a heart attack occurs.

The prognosis for a heart attack depends greatly on how quickly it is treated. The longer the blood supply is reduced, the more heart muscle cells die.

WORDS TO KNOW

Anticoagulant: Able to prevent a blood clot from forming.

Coronary: Referring to the heart.

Myocardial infarction: The technical term for heart attack.

Plaque: A deposit of fatty material and other substances that forms on the lining of a blood vessel.

Thrombolytic: Capable of dissolving a blood clot.

About one-fifth of all heart attacks are "silent." The patient usually feels no pain. He or she does not realize that a heart attack has occurred. Still, silent heart attacks can cause damage to the heart.

CAUSES

Heart attacks are usually caused by severe coronary artery disease (CAD). CAD is any condition that affects the coronary arteries. The coronary arteries are the blood vessels that supply blood to the heart. Plaque in an artery is a common type of coronary artery disease.

Major Risk Factors

A number of risk factors increase the chance of developing coronary artery disease. Some major risk factors can be changed and others cannot. Among those that cannot be changed are the following:

- **Heredity.** People whose parents have CAD are more likely to develop the condition. African Americans are also at increased risk for CAD.
- **Gender.** Men under the age of sixty are more likely to have heart attacks than women of the same age.
- **Age.** Men over the age of forty-five and women over the age of fifty-five are at higher risk than younger people. People over the age of sixty-five are more likely to die of a heart attack.

Some risk factors that can be changed are:

- **Smoking.** Smokers are more than twice as likely to have a heart attack than nonsmokers. They are 2 to 4 times more likely to die of a heart attack.
- **High cholesterol.** Cholesterol is a material that occurs naturally in all animals, including humans. It has many important biological functions. High levels of cholesterol in the blood, however, may increase the chance that plaque will form in blood vessels. It contributes to the risk of CAD and heart attack.
- **High blood pressure.** High blood pressure (see hypertension entry) makes the heart work harder. Over time, the heart becomes weaker. High blood pressure also increases the risk of stroke, kidney failure, and other types of heart disease.
- **Lack of physical exercise.** Even modest physical activity can be helpful if done regularly.

Contributing Risk Factors

Other conditions may affect the risk of CAD and heart attack. Scientists are not certain how these factors are involved in these conditions, however. The factors are:

- **Diabetes mellitus** (see diabetes mellitus entry). People with diabetes are at much higher risk for heart attack. About 80 percent of all diabetics die of some type of heart or blood vessel disease.

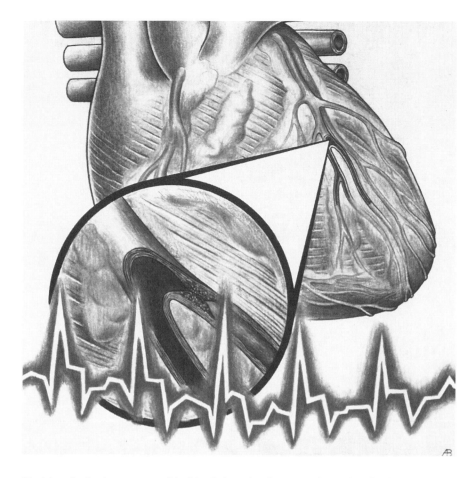

Most heart attacks are caused by blood clots that form on atherosclerotic plaque, which block a coronary artery from supplying oxygen-rich blood to part of the heart, as highlighted in the illustration above. (Illustration by Andrew Bezear, Reed business Publishing. Reproduced by permission of Science Photo Library and Photo Researchers, Inc.)

- **Obesity** (see obesity entry). Excess weight places a strain on the heart. It increases the risk of CAD and heart attack.
- **Stress and anger.** Stress and anger both increase blood pressure and heart rate. Some researchers think that these emotions can contribute to the chance of heart attack.

Many of the above risk factors are related to each other. For example, obesity and stress both contribute to high blood pressure. People with more than one risk factor are even more likely to develop CAD and have a heart attack.

heart attack

More than 60 percent of heart attack patients experience symptoms before the attack actually begins. These symptoms sometimes occur days or weeks ahead of time. Unfortunately, many people do not know the symptoms of heart attack, or they prefer not to recognize those symptoms when they appear. Typical symptoms include:

- Uncomfortable pressure, fullness, squeezing, or pain in the center of the chest. The pain may last for a few minutes, or it may go away and return.
- Pain that spreads to the shoulders, neck, or arms.
- Chest discomfort accompanied by light-headedness, fainting, sweating, nausea, or shortness of breath.

All symptoms do not occur with every heart attack. Symptoms sometimes disappear and then reappear. A person with these symptoms should receive immediate medical attention.

Smokers are more than twice as likely to have a heart attack than nonsmokers and they are 2 to 4 times more likely to die of a heart attack. (© 1998. Reproduced by permission of Custom Medical Stock Photo.)

DIAGNOSIS

People who are familiar with heart attacks can usually diagnose the condition simply by looking at a patient. To confirm the diagnosis, the patient's heart rate and blood pressure may be measured. Both an electrocardiogram (pronounced ih-LEK-tro-KAR-dee-o-gram) and blood tests provide further evidence for a heart attack. An electrocardiogram is a test that measures the electrical function of the heart.

TREATMENT

The first stage in treating a heart attack usually involves steps simply to keep the patient alive. If the patient has stopped breathing, cardiopulmonary resuscitation (CPR; pronounced car-dee-oh-PULL-mon-air-ee ree-sus-i-ta-shun) may be needed. CPR may involve breathing into the patient's mouth or pushing on the chest to restore breathing.

Once a patient has reached the hospital, a number of other emergency treatments may be necessary. For example, defibrillation may be required. Defibrillation (pronounced DEE-fib-ri-lay-shun) is used if the patient's heart is beating in an irregular pattern. An electric shock is applied to the patient's chest. The shock causes the heart to stop beating briefly. The heart then begins to beat again, in a more regular pattern.

A patient may also require oxygen therapy. In oxygen therapy, the patient is allowed to breathe air to which extra oxygen has been added. The extra oxygen makes it easier for the heart to work. Oxygen therapy can reduce the damage done to the heart.

Drug Treatments

A variety of drugs may be given following a heart attack. Some examples of these drugs are:

- **Thrombolytics.** Thrombolytic (pronounced throm-buh-LIH-tik) drugs are chemicals that dissolve blood clots. The most widely used of these drugs is tissue plasminogen activator (tPA). Patients who receive tPA within hours after a heart attack have a greatly increased chance of survival.
- **Anticoagulants.** Anticoagulants are drugs that thin the blood. Blood thinners reduce the chance that new blood clots will form. Aspirin is one of the most common and most effective blood thinners. Two other blood thinners are warfarin and heparin.
- **Pain relief.** Nitroglycerin (pronounced nite-roh-GLIS-er-in) tablets are commonly used to treat pain. In more severe cases, morphine may be needed to control pain.

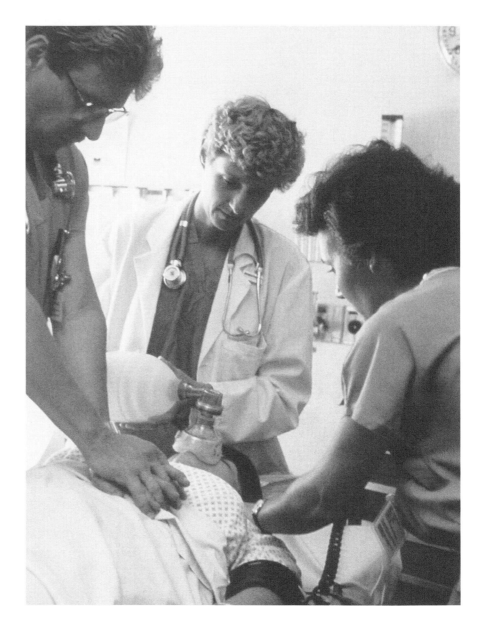

An emergency team giving cardiopulmonary resuscitation (CPR) to a heart attack patient. (© 1992. Reproduced by permission of Custom Medical Stock Photo.)

- **Tranquilizers**. Heart attack patients are often extremely upset. Tranquilizers such as diazepam (pronounced di-AZE-uh-pam, trade name Valium) can help relieve emotional distress.
- **Beta-blockers.** Beta-blockers slow down the heart rate. They give the heart a chance to start healing. They may also prevent the development of an irregular heart beat.

- **Vasodilators.** Vasodilators cause blood vessels to open up. This makes it easier for blood to flow through them and reduces the work the heart has to do.
- **Drugs that control arrhythmia (pronounced uh-RITH-mee-uh).** These drugs help the heart to pump at a regular rate. They reduce the risk that abnormal and potentially fatal irregular heart rhythms may develop.

The key to surviving a heart attack is to open the blood vessels to the heart again. In many cases, thrombolytics and anticoagulants can achieve this goal. When they cannot, surgery may be necessary.

Surgery

Two forms of surgery are often used with heart attack patients. The first is called coronary angioplasty (pronounced AN-jee-o-PLAS-tee). The tool used for coronary angioplasty is a catheter with an empty balloon attached at one end. The catheter is a thin plastic tube that can be inserted into a patient's artery, usually in the thigh or arm. It is then threaded up the artery until it gets to the blocked coronary artery.

At that point, the balloon is inflated. The inflated balloon pushes on the plaque that is blocking the artery and opens up the artery. Blood is able to flow more freely into the heart. The balloon is then deflated, and the catheter removed from the person's body.

Angioplasty is initially successful in about 90 percent of all cases. In about one-third of all cases, the artery narrows again after the procedure. In such cases, the procedure can be repeated.

The second surgical procedure is called bypass surgery. The purpose of bypass surgery is to provide a new pathway for blood to reach the heart. The procedure requires three steps. First, a section of healthy vein is removed from some part of the patient's body, such as a leg or arm. Then a cut is made just below and just above the blockage in the patient's coronary artery. Finally, the healthy vein is attached to the coronary artery. The attached vein provides a new pathway around the blocked section of the artery.

Coronary bypasses are completely successful in about 70 percent of all cases. In another 20 percent of cases, partial relief is obtained. Five years after surgery, the survival rate (the number of patients still alive) for patients who have had a coronary bypass is about 90 percent. It is as high as 80 percent even after ten years.

PROGNOSIS

The aftermath of a heart attack is often severe. Two-thirds of all heart attack patients never recover fully. About one-quarter of all men and nearly

TO REDUCE THE RISK OF HEART ATTACK, GET REGULAR MODERATE EXERCISE THAT LASTS FOR THIRTY MINUTES, FOUR OR MORE TIMES PER WEEK.

one-half of all women who have had heart attacks die within a year. Additional heart attacks are not unusual. About one-quarter of all men and one-third of all women have a second heart attack within six years.

PREVENTION

Some risk factors for heart attack cannot be controlled. There may be hereditary factors that make a person more or less likely to have CAD and a heart attack. However, many risk factors can be managed. Some ways a person can reduce the risk of CAD and heart attack are:

- Eat a healthy diet that includes a variety of foods low in fat, low in cholesterol, and high in fiber. The diet should include plenty of fruits and vegetables, and limited sodium.
- Get regular moderate exercise that lasts for thirty minutes, four or more times per week. Helpful forms of exercise include walking, jogging, cycling, and swimming. Everyday activities, such as active gardening, climbing stairs, and brisk housework, can also help.
- Maintain a proper body weight by watching one's diet and exercising.
- Stop smoking or don't start smoking. People who quit smoking gradually become less at risk for CAD and heart attack.
- Adults should consume only moderate amounts of alcohol. In some adults moderate drinking is not necessarily bad for the body and may even help protect against CAD. Excessive drinking is bad, however, because it raises blood pressure and can produce toxins (poisons) in the body.
- Adopt a more moderate lifestyle that reduces stress and anxiety. This kind of change may contribute to lower blood pressure and reduced risk of CAD and heart attack.
- Take one aspirin tablet per day. Aspirin helps thin the blood and reduce the risk of a blood clot forming.

FOR MORE INFORMATION

Books

American Heart Association. *Guide to Heart Attack Treatment, Recovery, Prevention.* New York: Time Books, 1996.

American Heart Association. *Your Heart: An Owner's Manual.* Englewood Cliffs, NJ: Prentice Hall, 1995.

DeBakey, Michael E., and Antonio M. Grotto, Jr. *The New Living Heart.* Holbrook, MA: Adams Media Corporation, 1997.

McGoon, Michael D. *Mayo Clinic Heart Book*. New York: William Morrow & Company, 1993.

Notelovitz, Morris, and Diana Tonnessen. *The Essential Heart Book for Women*. New York: St. Martin's Press, 1996.

Organizations

American Heart Association. National Center. 7272 Greenville Ave., Dallas, TX 75231-4596. (214) 373–6300. http://www.medsearch.com/pf/profiles/amerh.

National Heart, Lung, and Blood Institute Information Center. PO Box 30105. Bethesda, MD 20824-0105. http://www.nhlbi/nibli.htm.

Web sites

"Ask NOAH About: Heart Disease and Stroke." *NOAH: New York Online Access to Health.* [Online] http://www.noah.cuny.edu/heart_disease/heartdisease.html#H (accessed on October 22, 1999).

HEART MURMUR

DEFINITION

A heart murmur is an abnormal extra sound made when the heart beats. The sound is produced by blood moving through the heart and its valves.

DESCRIPTION

Blood flows from the body into the heart through veins. It moves from one side of the heart (the atria) into the other side of the heart (the ventricles). It then flows out of the heart through arteries. The flow of blood is controlled by muscular flaps called valves. The valves open and close as blood flows through each part of the heart. When the valves between the atria and the ventricles close, they make a "lubb" sound. When the valves between the ventricles and the major arteries close, they make a "dubb" sound. When doctors listen to the heart beat of a healthy person, they hear a "lubb-dubb" sound.

WORDS TO KNOW

Atrium (plural: atria): One of the two upper chambers of the heart.

Echocardiogram: A test that uses sound waves to produce an image of the inside of the heart.

Electrocardiogram: A test that measures the electrical activity of the heart to determine whether it is functioning normally.

Ventricle: One of the two lower chambers of the heart.

A heart murmur is a sound other than the usual "lubb-dubb" sound produced by the heart. It usually lasts longer than a normal heart sound and can be heard between the normal "lubb-dubb" sounds.

Heart murmurs occur in normal hearts. They are especially common among young children. Harmless heart murmurs are known as innocent heart murmurs. Innocent heart murmurs are usually very faint. They come and go in an irregular pattern. They do not pose a health threat to the person in whom they occur.

Other heart murmurs are more dangerous. They are called pathological heart murmurs. One cause of pathological heart murmurs is a damaged heart valve. Pathological heart murmurs may be an indication of a serious heart problem. The sound they make is louder and more continuous than that of an innocent heart murmur. They are sometimes described as a clicking or galloping sound.

CAUSES

Innocent heart murmurs are caused by the normal sound of blood flowing through the heart and its blood vessels. They may also be caused by emotions, such as stress or fear, or by health problems, such as fever or anemia (see anemia entry).

Pathological heart murmurs are usually caused by one of two problems. One of these problems is a defective heart valve. The valve may not close or open completely. When that happens, blood does not flow normally through the heart. Enough blood may not be able to get through the heart, or the blood may back up and go the wrong direction.

The other problem is a hole in the heart. A hole sometimes develops in the wall between the left and right sides of the heart. A hole of this kind may be relatively harmless, or it may cause heart problems that require surgery.

SYMPTOMS

Innocent heart murmurs usually have no symptoms. They have no effect on the way the heart functions. Murmurs caused by defects in the heart do have symptoms. Those symptoms include shortness of breath, dizziness, chest pains, palpitations (a feeling that the heart is beating faster or less regular than normal), and congestion of the lungs.

DIAGNOSIS

Heart murmurs can usually be detected quite easily. A doctor listens to a patient's chest with a stethoscope. Any sounds other than the normal "lubb-dubb" beating of the heart can be heard. If the sounds are faint, they may indicate an innocent heart murmur. An innocent heart murmur usually requires no further treatment.

One exception involves faint heart murmurs that occur in infants and children with other symptoms. Those symptoms in infants include poor appetite, problems with breathing normally, and failure to develop normally. In older children, symptoms include loss of consciousness or inability to take part in normal exercise.

The presence of a loud heart murmur may lead to further tests. A chest X ray, for example, may show the presence of defects in the heart. An electrocardiogram (ECG, pronounced ih-LEK-tro-KAR-dee-o-gram) shows

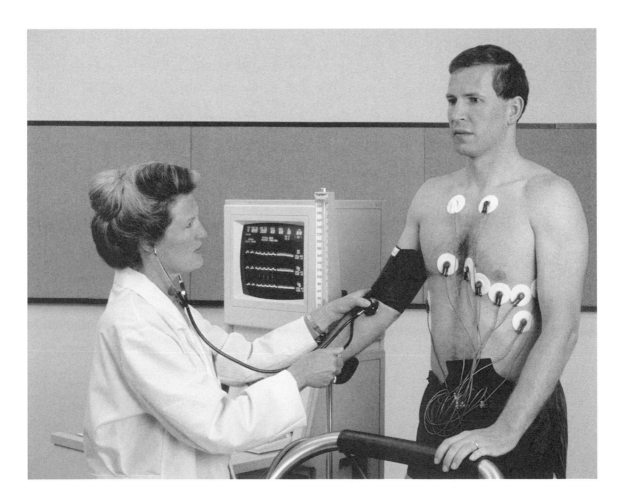

An electrocardiogram records the electrical activity of the heart and can be used to diagnose whether the heart is functioning normally. (© 1989 Jon Feingersh. Reproduced by permission of The Stock Market.)

whether the heart is beating normally. An electrocardiogram is a test in which the electrical activity of the heart is recorded.

An echocardiogram (pronounced ekko-KAR-dee-o-gram) may also be used to diagnose heart murmur. An echocardiogram is a test in which sound waves are sent through the heart. The path taken by the sound waves is recorded. The pattern of reflected sound may show any defects in the heart.

TREATMENT

Innocent heart murmurs require no treatment. Pathological heart murmurs may also require no treatment unless they are serious. In that case, surgery may be required to correct the heart defect such as defective valves or holes in the heart.

PROGNOSIS

Most children with innocent heart murmurs outgrow them by the time they reach adulthood. Severe cases of pathological heart murmurs may require surgery. If surgery is not successful, murmurs may develop into more serious heart problems that, in relatively rare cases, may lead to death.

PREVENTION

There is no known method for preventing heart murmurs.

FOR MORE INFORMATION

Organizations

American Heart Association. National Center. 7272 Greenville Ave., Dallas, TX 75231-4596. (214) 373–6300. http://www.medsearch.com/pf/profiles/amerh.

Web sites

"Heart Murmurs in Infants: Not Always Cause for Alarm." *Mayo Health Oasis.* (February 26, 1998) [Online] http://www.mayohealth.org (accessed on March 4, 1998).

"When Your Child's Doctor Hears a Heart Murmur." *Children's National Medical Center 1998.* [Online] http://www.cnmc.org/heart.htm (accessed on March 6, 1998).

HEAT DISORDERS

DEFINITION

Heat disorders are a group of illnesses caused by prolonged exposure to hot temperatures, restricted fluid intake, or failure of the body's ability to regulate its temperature. The general term used for heat disorders is hyperthermia (pronounced hi-per-THUR-mee-uh). The three most common forms of hyperthermia are heat exhaustion, heat stroke, and heat cramps.

DESCRIPTION

Hyperthermia can cause harm to people of all ages. But its effects are more serious with increasing age. The conditions that cause heat cramps in a teenager may cause a more serious form of hyperthermia—heat exhaustion—in a middle-aged person. Those same conditions may cause even more serious effects in an older person, a form of hyperthermia known as heat stroke.

The human body functions normally only within a very narrow range of temperatures close to 98.6°F (37°C). If the body gets much warmer or much colder than 98.6°F, health problems develop. Raising or lowering the body temperature by only a few degrees can cause death in a short period of time.

The body's temperature control center is in the brain. It senses changes in internal and external temperatures. It determines the changes that must be made to keep body temperature at 98.6°F. It then relays instructions to the body's cells to make these changes.

One method the body uses to cool down is perspiring (sweating). Perspiration is the loss of water from the skin. Body heat provides the energy needed to evaporate water from the skin. The more a person perspires, the cooler the body becomes.

However, excessive perspiration can cause problems. The body may lose too much water. It may become dehydrated. Dehydration can cause a variety of medical problems.

Heat Cramps

Heat cramps are the least serious form of hyperthermia. They are the first sign that the body is having difficulty with increased temperature. Heat cramps are a warning sign that more serious problems may soon develop.

WORDS TO KNOW

Electrolytes: Chemicals that occur naturally in the body and that maintain the proper balance of fluids in the body.

Hyperthermia: The general name for any form of heat disorder.

Heat Exhaustion

Heat exhaustion is more serious than heat cramps. The condition may be caused when a person is exposed to high temperatures for a long period of time. Or the body may become dehydrated, or its temperature regulation system may begin to fail. Heat exhaustion is a common problem among athletes, firefighters, construction and factory workers, and anyone who wears heavy clothing in hot weather.

Heat Stroke

Heat stroke is the most serious form of hyperthermia. The condition can cause death in a short period of time. Heat stoke often results in death. The conditions that lead to heat stroke are the same as those that cause heat exhaustion. However, those conditions cause more serious symptoms in the case of heat stroke.

CAUSES

The primary cause of all types of hyperthermia are prolonged exposure to hot temperatures, restricted fluid intake, or failure of the body's ability to regulate its temperature. The three forms of hyperthermia are caused by progressively greater exposure to heat.

SYMPTOMS

Symptoms for the different types of hyperthermia vary. The longer one is exposed to heat, the more serious the symptoms of hyperthermia become.

Heat Cramps

At relatively warm temperatures, the body begins to perspire. Perspiration results in the loss of water. The body slowly becomes dehydrated. Dehydration leads to heat cramps.

As heat cramps develop, muscle tissue becomes less flexible. It becomes more difficult and more painful to move. Muscles in the legs are most frequently affected. A person may find it difficult to walk or maintain his or her balance. Young children, the elderly, and people with circulation problems are more likely to be affected by heat cramps.

Heat Exhaustion

After hours in a hot environment, perspiration increases and body temperature rises. The skin may appear cool, moist, and pale. Other symptoms of heat exhaustion include headache, nausea, exhaustion, and a general sense of weakness. Before long, dizziness, faintness, and mental confusion develop.

Heat exhaustion is a common problem among athletes, firefighters, construction and factory workers, and anyone who wears heavy clothing in hot weather. (© Richard Hutchings. Reproduced by permission of Photo Researchers, Inc.)

Breathing becomes rapid and shallow. The urine of a person with heat exhaustion is likely to be dark yellow or orange.

Heat Stroke

Under the most extreme conditions, the body's temperature regulation system may begin to fail. The brain is no longer able to send messages to the rest of the body telling it how to cool off. Heat stroke may occur after the body temperature has reached 104°F (40°C). At this point, the patient may become mentally confused and aggressive. He or she may begin to stagger and feel faint.

During heat stroke, a patient's pulse rate may reach 160 to 180 beats per minute. The skin appears to be dry and flushed. There is very little perspiration. At this point, the patient needs immediate medical attention. Without care, he or she may die in a matter of hours.

DIAGNOSIS

Most cases of hyperthermia can be diagnosed easily. The two key factors are the patient's visible symptoms and recent personal history. A tennis player who collapses while playing a game, for example, may be suspected of having hyperthermia. Testing that person's temperature, heart rate, and other vital factors may confirm the diagnosis quickly.

Blood and urine tests can also be used to confirm a diagnosis of hyperthermia. In any form of hyperthermia, the balance of chemicals in blood and urine changes. Laboratory tests can detect these changes and confirm the presence of hyperthermia.

TREATMENT

The first steps in treating any form of hyperthermia include:

• Moving the patient to a cooler location.
• Providing the patient with cool water.
• Giving the patient liquids that contain electrolytes.

Electrolytes are chemicals that occur naturally in the body and that maintain the proper balance of fluids in the body. The usual liquids given a patient are salt water that contains a low concentration of salt, or a sports drink such as Gatorade.

The patient should not be given salt tablets. The concentration of salt in tablets is too high for the body to absorb. Salt tablets can make a case of hyperthermia more serious, rather than improving it.

The above steps are often sufficient to treat most cases of heat cramps and heat exhaustion. Massage of leg muscles can also offer relief from the pain and soreness of heat cramps. Patients with heat exhaustion should be made to lie down with their feet elevated.

Cases of heat stroke require emergency treatment by trained medical personnel. While waiting for this help, some first aid measures can be taken. Ice packs should be placed around the neck, under the arms and knees, and in the groin. Medical treatment may involve intravenous feeding of fluids and electrolytes. Bed rest is often necessary for many days.

PROGNOSIS

Prompt treatment of heat cramps and heat exhaustion is usually successful. Patients recover in a matter of hours or, at most, a day or two. Heat stroke poses more serious problems. Prognosis depends on the patient's age and general health. In the most serious cases, heat stroke can lead to permanent damage to internal organs, and even death.

PREVENTION

The general rules for avoiding any form of hyperthermia are the same. One should avoid strenuous exercise when it is very hot. Wearing light, loose-fitting clothing can also help. An important factor in preventing hyperthermia is consumption of sufficient amounts of liquids. The warmer it becomes and the more active a person is, the greater the body's need for liquids. Caffeine and alcohol should be avoided in hot conditions because they can contribute to dehydration, increasing the risk of hyperthermia. Eating lightly-salted foods can also help replace electrolytes lost during perspiration.

FOR MORE INFORMATION

Books

American Red Cross. *Standard First Aid.* St. Louis, MO: Mosby Year Book, 1993.

Larson, David E., ed. *Mayo Clinic Family Health Book, 2nd edition.* New York: William Morrow, 1996.

Morris, M., M. Walsh, and Shelton G. Walsh. *The Team Physicians Hand Book.* Philadelphia: Hanley & Belfus, 1990.

HEMOPHILIA

DEFINITION

Hemophilia (pronounced hee-muh-FIH-lee-uh) is a genetic disorder that often results in excessive bleeding. The condition can range from mild to severe. In its most serious forms, it can lead to death.

DESCRIPTION

Injury to a blood vessel is a serious problem for the body. Blood may begin to leak out of the injured area. The body has developed a mechanism for protecting itself from this kind of damage. The mechanism involves the formation of a blood clot over the injured area to prevent loss of blood.

Blood clotting is a very complicated process. It involves blood cells known as platelets and at least twenty different chemical compounds. The first step in the clotting process is the formation of a temporary plug. The plug is formed of platelets that stick to the damaged area. The plug is soon covered by a more permanent structure consisting of fibrin (pronounced FI-brin).

Fibrin is tissue that acts like a permanent patch or bandage on the injured area.

The production of fibrin takes place in a series of steps that requires thirteen different chemicals. These chemicals are known as "clotting factors." In order for fibrin to form, all thirteen clotting factors must be present in the blood.

Hemophiliacs (people who have hemophilia) may lack one or more clotting factors, or their bodies may not make enough of a clotting factor, or the clotting factor may not be made correctly. In any one of these cases, the patient's body is not able to make fibrin. An injury to a blood vessel cannot be properly repaired. Blood continues to escape from the damaged blood vessel.

Various types of hemophilia have been discovered. Each type results from problems with a particular clotting factor. Hemophilia A is the most common form of the disorder. It is caused by a defective clotting factor known as factor VIII. Hemophilia A can range from relatively mild to very severe. The severity of the disorder depends on how much factor VIII the patient's body is able to make.

Individuals with more than 5 percent of normal factor VIII have mild hemophilia. They are likely to experience bleeding problems only when having surgery or dental procedures. Individuals with 1 to 5 percent of normal factor VIII have moderate hemophilia. They may experience bleeding problems if they have a minor injury, such as a fall. Individuals with less than 1 percent of normal factor VIII have severe hemophilia. They may begin bleeding for no reason at all. Surgery and dental procedures can be very dangerous. About half of all hemophiliacs have this form of the disorder.

Hemophilia B is caused by a defective clotting factor known as factor IX. This type of hemophilia is also known as Christmas disease. The range of symptoms of hemophilia B is similar to that of hemophilia A.

Hemophilia C is very rare and is much more mild that hemophilia A or B. It is caused by a defective clotting factor known as factor XI.

CAUSES

Hemophilia is a genetic disorder. A genetic disorder is a medical condition in which a person has one or more abnormal genes. Genes are the chemical units that are present in all cells.

WORDS TO KNOW

Chromosome: A structure located inside the nucleus (center) of a cell that carries genetic information.

Clotting factor: One of the chemicals necessary for blood clotting.

Fibrin: A thick material formed over an injured section of blood vessel by the process of blood clotting.

Gene: A chemical unit found in all cells that carries information telling cells what functions they are to perform.

Hemorrhage: Severe, massive bleeding.

Platelet: A type of blood cell involved in the clotting of blood.

They tell cells what functions to perform. For example, everyone has certain genes that tell cells how to make clotting factors. There is one gene for making clotting factor I, one gene for clotting factor II, one gene for clotting factor III, and so on.

Inherited Hemophilia

Sometimes a person inherits a defective gene from a parent. That defective gene carries no instructions, or the wrong instructions, for performing some function. A cell does not know how to make a certain material, such as clotting factor VIII, or it makes the material incorrectly. In such cases, a genetic disorder may develop.

Genes are arranged in cells on long strings known as chromosomes. Under a microscope, chromosomes look like a string of beads, in which genes are the individual beads.

All normal human cells contain twenty-three pairs of chromosomes. Half of the chromosomes come from the father, and half from the mother. One pair of chromosomes is the sex chromosomes. These two chromosomes determine sexual characteristics, along with other characteristics. Two types of sex chromosomes exist: an X chromosome and a Y chromosome. Men have one X and one Y chromosome. Women have two X chromosomes.

The genes for making clotting factors are located on X chromosomes. This means that males are more likely to have hemophilia than females. A female always has two X chromosomes. She may inherit one defective X chromosome, but she will probably not inherit *two* defective X chromosomes. Her normal X chromosome will still carry the correct instructions for making clotting factors.

Males, however, carry only one X chromosome. If the X chromosome a male inherits is defective, he will not have a normal X chromosome to compensate for the defective one. His cells will not receive the correct instructions for making clotting factors.

For this reason, hemophilia is almost entirely a disorder in males. The condition very rarely occurs among women. Even if women carry one defective X chromosome, they will not have the disorder. However, they will have the ability to pass the disorder on to their children. For that reason, a female with just one defective X chromosome is said to be a carrier for the disorder.

Spontaneous Gene Mutation

About 30 percent of all people with hemophilia A or B are the first members of their family to ever have the disease. These individuals have the unfortunate occurrence of a spontaneous mutation. In their early development some random genetic accident caused a defect in their X chromosome. Once

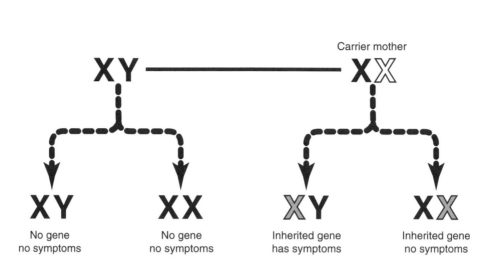

Transmission by a carrier mother

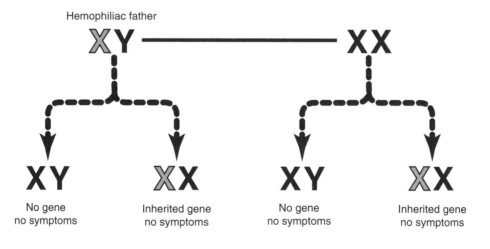

Transmission by a hemophiliac father

a genetic mutation takes place, offspring of the affected person can inherit the newly-created, flawed chromosome.

SYMPTOMS

The primary symptom of hemophilia is bleeding. The amount of bleeding that occurs depends on how serious the patient's condition is. In the most severe cases, bleeding can cause serious health problems, including death.

Severe hemophilia is usually discovered before a child has reached the age of eighteen months. For example, circumcision can result in heavy bleeding. Toddlers with severe hemophilia are at serious risk because they fall frequently. Bleeding may occur in the soft tissue of the arms and legs. This bleeding may cause bruising and noticable lumps, but usually does not require treatment.

As a child becomes more active, bleeding into the muscles may occur. This form of bleeding is more serious and more painful. Muscle bleeds cause pressure on nerves. This pressure can cause pain, numbness, and damage to nerves.

Some of the most serious damage caused by bleeding occurs in joints, especially the knees and elbows. Repeated bleeding can cause scarring of the joints. Joints may become deformed and permanently damaged.

Bleeding in the head can be especially serious. Many people receive blows to the head, but they seldom suffer serious damage. In the case of hemophilia, a blow to the head can cause extensive bleeding in the brain. Since the skull cannot expand, the bleeding causes pressure on delicate brain tissue. Permanent brain damage may occur.

More serious accidents can cause even more extensive bleeding. A hemophiliac who is in a motor vehicle accident, for example, may suffer from massive hemorrhaging (bleeding) that can result in death.

DIAGNOSIS

Abnormal bleeding patterns are usually the first clue that a person has hemophilia. Simple bumps and bruises that result in uncontrolled bleeding are a common early symptom of hemophilia.

OPPOSITE: Hemophilia A and B are both caused by a genetic defect present on the X chromosome. Approximately 70 percent of people with hemophilia A or B inherit the disease. The remaining 30 percent develop the disease due to a spontaneous genetic mutation. (Reproduced by permission of Electronic Illustrators Group)

Diagnosis of hemophilia is confirmed with blood tests. These tests are able to measure how much of various clotting factors are present in the blood and how quickly they work to produce clots. These tests can be used to diagnose the type of hemophilia a person has and the seriousness of the condition.

TREATMENT

Hemophilia can be treated with injections of missing clotting factors. Patients with hemophilia A receive injections of factor VIII, and those with hemophilia B get factor IX.

The frequency of treatment depends on the severity of the disease. People with mild hemophilia may require treatment only when they have been injured. They may also need treatment before surgery or dental work. Patients with more severe forms of the disorder may require regular injections of the missing factor.

The use of injections to treat hemophilia is accompanied by some possible complications. For example, in some cases, the body's immune system begins to make antibodies against factors contained in the injections. Antibodies are chemicals produced by the immune system to protect the body against infection. The immune system may become confused and react as if the injected factors are bacteria, viruses, or other harmful materials.

THE ROYAL DISEASE

In 1837, Queen Victoria ascended to the throne of England. Although she was a much-loved ruler, she left a terrible legacy to her country. She was a carrier for the gene for hemophilia. Although she did not suffer from the disease herself, she passed it on to one of her sons. In addition two of her daughters and three of her granddaughters were also carriers of the gene for hemophilia. Five of Victoria's great-grandsons had the disease.

Queen Victoria's son Leopold, according to the Queen's own accounts, had "been four or five times at death's door" because of the disease. At the age of thirty-one, he fell and hit his head. Doctors could not stop the bleeding, and he died a few days later.

Victoria's descendents eventually passed the genes for hemophilia on to the Spanish and Russ-ian Royal houses. Victoria's daughters Beatrice and Alice both married German princes. They transmitted the gene for hemophilia to their own daughters who married into the Spanish and Russian royal families. It is said that two of Victoria's great-grandsons who grew up in Spain played in a park where all the trees were wrapped with cloth to prevent their being injured.

One of Alice's daughters, Alix, married Nicholas II, son of Alexander III, Czar of Russia. Alix's son, Alexis, also inherited the gene for hemophilia. At the age of three, he was injured and nearly bled to death. Alexis' painful and difficult childhood was a great source of distress to Alix. She was comforted when a man named Grigory Rasputin was able to stop the boy's bleeding. Rasputin was honored by Nicholas and Alix. Rasputin's closeness to the royal family and rumored influence was a contributing factor in the decline of the czarist Russian empire.

Complications may result from the way clotting factors are obtained for injections. In some cases, the clotting factors are obtained from people who have donated blood. The donated blood is usually prepared very carefully in order to obtain pure clotting factors. But sometimes mistakes happen. Harmful substances in donated blood may become part of the preparation given to hemophiliacs.

The worst example of this situation involved blood contaminated with the human immunodeficiency virus (HIV). HIV is the virus that causes AIDS (see AIDS entry). In the early years of the HIV epidemic, people who worked with blood did not know about the virus. They were not aware that blood donated by people with HIV also contained the virus. When that blood was used to produce clotting factors, the virus was part of the preparation given to hemophiliacs. Many hemophiliacs developed AIDS in this way. As of 1999, AIDS was still the leading cause of death among hemophiliacs because of this tragedy. Precautions have been put in place to ensure that contaminated blood is not used. The chance of HIV or other harmful agents being present along with clotting factors is very small.

PROGNOSIS

The future of people with hemophilia is very hard to predict. For one thing, the severity of the condition varies widely, from very mild to very severe. Also, hemophiliacs differ in their degree of activity. The more active a hemophiliac is, the more likely injury is to occur.

PREVENTION

There is only one way to prevent hemophilia. Parents who carry a defective X chromosome may pass that chromosome on to their children. If a male child inherits a defective X chromosome he will develop hemophilia. Adults can be tested to tell if they carry a defective X chromosome. They can use that information to make decisions about having children.

People who already have hemophilia can make decisions as to how best to prevent the worst conditions of their disorder. For example, they can avoid the most strenuous forms of work and exercise that might result in injury and bleeding. They also need to make special preparations when surgery or dental procedures are necessary.

FOR MORE INFORMATION

Organizations

National Hemophilia Foundation. 116 West 32nd Street, 11th Floor, New York, NY 10001. (800) 42–HANDI.

HEMORRHAGIC FEVERS

DEFINITION

Hemorrhagic fevers (pronounced heh-meh-RA-jik) are a group of diseases caused by viruses. They occur throughout the world, but are most common in tropical areas. Early symptoms include muscle aches and fevers. The disease can progress to a more serious condition and, in many cases, can be fatal. A prominent symptom in late stages is hemorrhaging (rapid or heavy bleeding) from body openings and internal organs.

DESCRIPTION

Hemorrhagic fevers are a growing concern throughout the world. They are not new diseases, but they are affecting much larger numbers of people every year.

The viruses that cause hemorrhagic fevers live in a great variety of animals, such as arthropods and mammals. Arthropods are insects, spiders, and other animals with hard external skeletons. These animals are called the natural reservoir for the disease. In many cases, these animals do not become ill when infected by the viruses. They do, however, carry the viruses in their body.

Viruses are transferred from these animals to humans by vectors. A vector is an organism that carries a disease from one animal to another. Mosquitoes are common vectors. When they bite an animal, they suck in some of its blood. If the animal is infected with a virus, the blood also contains that virus. When the vector bites a human, it leaves some of its saliva in the wound. Some of the virus may also be left behind. The human becomes infected with the virus.

Hemorrhagic fevers are often endemic. An endemic disease is one that affects many people in a given area over long periods of time. Dengue fever (pronounced DEN-gay) is an example. It affects about 100 million people annually. Most of these people live in southeast Asia. The area is very crowded. People often live in close contact with each other. The disease is transmitted easily from one person to another. In addition, the mosquito that carries dengue fever thrives in southeast Asia.

Some hemorrhagic fevers are very rare. An example is Marburg hemorrhagic fever. It was

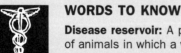

WORDS TO KNOW

Disease reservoir: A population of animals in which a virus lives without causing serious illness among the animals.

Endemic: The widespread occurrence of a disease over a given area that lasts for an extended period of time.

Hemorrhage: Heavy or uncontrollable bleeding.

Ribavirin: A drug used to treat viral infections.

Vector: An animal that transmits an infectious agent, such as a virus, from one animal to another animal.

first discovered in 1967. In the next thirty years after that, fewer than forty people were diagnosed with the disease.

The rate of fatalities (deaths) varies among the different forms of hemorrhagic fever. In the case of dengue fever, the death rate is about 1 to 5 percent. At the other extreme, ebola (pronounced ee-BO-la), an African hemorrhagic fever, kills 50 to 90 percent of those infected.

The onset (beginning) of hemorrhagic fevers may be sudden or gradual. They all have one characteristic in common, however. They all have the potential to result in hemorrhaging. The seriousness of the hemorrhaging also varies. In some cases, it involves no more than tiny pinpoints of bleeding under the skin. In other cases, the patient may bleed extensively from the mouth, nose, and other body openings.

CAUSES AND SYMPTOMS

Many different kinds of hemorrhagic fevers are known. The viruses that cause these diseases are usually found in tropical locations, but some are also found in cooler climates. Typical disease vectors include rodents (mice and rats), ticks, and mosquitoes. The virus can also be passed from person to person through sexual contact or other means.

Filoviruses

Ebola (pronounced ee-BO-la) is the most famous of the filoviruses (pronounced fi-lo-VI-russ-ez). It is endemic to Africa, especially to the Republic of the Congo and to Sudan. Scientists have not discovered the natural reservoir for the filoviruses.

Symptoms of a filovirus infection appear suddenly. They include severe headache, fever, chills, muscle aches, and loss of appetite. These symptoms may be accompanied by nausea, vomiting, diarrhea, and abdominal pain. A person with the infection may become listless and disoriented. Severe bleeding occurs from the stomach and intestines, nose, throat, and vagina. Ebola is fatal in 50 to 90 percent of all cases.

Arenaviruses

Arenavirus (pronounced uh-RE-nuh-virus) infections occur most often in parts of South America and west Africa. In west Africa they cause a disease known as lassa fever. The disease is spread by rodents. The virus is transmitted when humans come in contact with the urine and saliva of rats and mice. Symptoms differ somewhat between South American and west African forms of the disease.

The first symptoms of South American arenavirus infection are fever, muscle ache, weakness, and loss of appetite. Later, patients experience dizziness, headache, back pain, and upset stomach. The face and chest become red, and the gums begin to bleed. In about 30 percent of all cases, hemorrhaging occurs. Bleeding occurs under the skin and in the mucous membranes, the moist tissues that line body openings. In late stages, the nervous system is affected. A person experiences delirium and convulsions and may go into a coma. About 10 to 30 percent of patients die of the disease.

The symptoms of lassa fever are somewhat similar to those of South American infections, but the death rate is usually much lower, about 2 percent.

Flaviviruses

The two best known diseases caused by flaviviruses (pronounced fla-vih-VI-russ-ez) are yellow fever and dengue fever.

Yellow fever occurs in tropical areas of the Americas and Africa. It is transmitted from monkeys to humans by mosquitoes. Some people experience only a mild form of the disease. They may not even realize that they

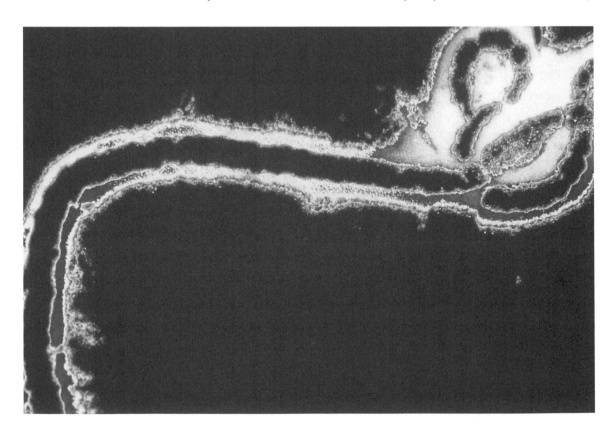

An ebola virus, which causes severe bleeding and is fatal in 50 to 90 percent of cases. (© 1996 CDC/CMPS. Reproduced by permission of Custom Medical Stock Photo.)

have been infected. In more serious cases, a patient experiences fever, weakness, low back pain, muscle pain, nausea, and vomiting. After about a week, these symptoms nearly disappear. Then they come back stronger than before. They develop into delirium (a form of madness), seizures, numbness, and coma. Bleeding occurs under the skin and in the mucous membranes. Blood also appears in stools and vomit.

Bunyaviruses

Bunyaviruses (pronounced BUN-yuh-vi-russ-ez) cause a number of hemorrhagic fevers, including Rift Valley fever and Crimean-Congo hemorrhagic fever. Rift Valley fever occurs in southern Africa and the Nile delta. The disease is transferred from wild and domestic animals to humans by

A city truck in Rio de Janeiro sprays insecticide to fight against an outbreak of dengue fever which is transmitted by mosquitos. (Reproduced by permission of AP/Wide World Photos)

bites of infected animals or through mosquito bites. The death rate is less than 3 percent.

Crimean-Congo hemorrhagic fever is found throughout much of Africa, Asia, and the Middle East. It is found in rabbits, birds, ticks, and domestic animals. Humans contract the disease after being bitten by an infected animal or by infected ticks. Death rates range from 10 to 50 percent. The symptoms of both Rift Valley and Crimean-Congo fevers are similar to those of other hemorrhagic fevers.

DIAGNOSIS

The symptoms of hemorrhagic fevers are similar to those of other diseases. Diagnosis depends on blood tests that show the presence of the virus.

TREATMENT

There are few drugs for the treatment of viral infections. Ribavirin (pronounced RI-buh-vih-rin) is one such drug. It is sometimes used to treat lassa fever and other hemorrhagic fevers. Treatment of these diseases is generally aimed at making patients more comfortable. Patients are often given fluids to replace those lost by vomiting and diarrhea. They may be given antibiotics to protect against other infections. Vitamin K is sometimes given to help stop bleeding. Blood transfusions may also be used to restore blood lost during hemorrhaging.

In many parts of the world, patients with hemorrhagic fevers receive no treatment at all. There are not enough medical or financial resources to treat everyone with the disease. People are left to recover or die on their own.

PROGNOSIS

The prognosis for various forms of hemorrhagic fever vary widely. The death rate for ebola can be as high as 90 percent. For some forms of dengue fever, it can be as low as 1 percent.

Some types of hemorrhagic fever can cause permanent disability. For example, about 10 percent of those who develop Rift Valley fever will suffer eye damage. They may become permanently blind. About 25 percent of patients with South American hemorrhagic fever become permanently deaf.

Proper treatment is very important. It can reduce the death rate dramatically. In some forms of dengue fever, lack of treatment results in a death rate of 40 to 50 percent. With adequate treatment, the death rate drops to less than 2 percent.

PREVENTION

The best way to prevent hemorrhagic fevers is to eliminate the vectors that carry the diseases. For example, efforts have been made to wipe out mosquito or rodent populations in some areas. These efforts are sometimes successful in big cities in developed nations. They are less successful in large rural areas in developing nations. In these cases, the best hope may be personal protection. People should use mosquito netting, insect repellents, and other devices to protect themselves against vectors.

Vaccines have also been developed against some hemorrhagic fevers, including yellow fever, Argentinean hemorrhagic fever, and Crimean-Congo fever. People who plan to travel in areas where these diseases occur should

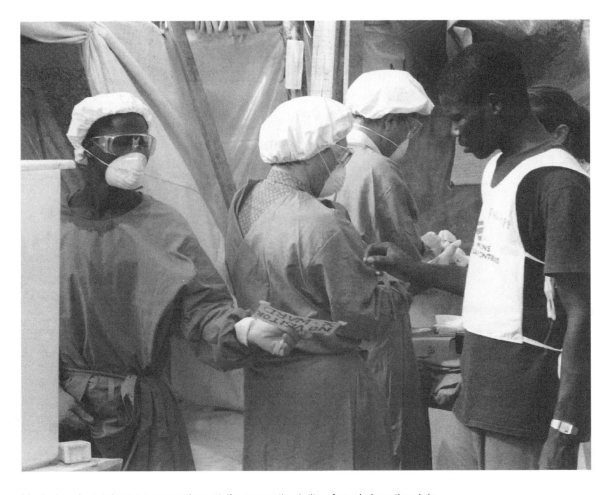

Medical workers take extra precautions at the quarantined site of an ebola outbreak in Gozon, on the Ivory Coast. (Reproduced by permission of AP/Wide World Photos)

be vaccinated against them. The vaccines are costly, however, and many local populations cannot afford them.

FOR MORE INFORMATION

Books

Garrett, Laurie. *The Coming Plague: Newly Emerging Diseases in a World Out of Balance.* New York: Farrar, Strauss, and Giroux, 1994.

Henig, Robin Marantz. *A Dancing Matrix: How Science Confronts Emerging Viruses.* New York: Vintage Books, 1994.

Regis, Edward. *Virus Ground Zero: Stalking the Killer Viruses With the Centers for Disease Control.* New York: Pocket Books, 1996.

Ryan, Frank. *Virus X: Tracking the New Killer Plagues Out of the Present and into the Future.* Boston: Little Brown & Company, 1997.

Periodicals

LeGuenno, Bernard, "Emerging Viruses," *Scientific American* (October 1995): pp. 56+.

Web sites

Outbreak (An on-line information service about emerging diseases) http://www.outbreak.org (accessed October 25, 1999).

National Center for Infectious Diseases. *Viral Hemorrhagic Fever.* http://www.cdc.gov/ncidod/diseases/virlfvr/virlfvr.htm (accessed October 25, 1999).

HEPATITIS

DEFINITION

Hepatitis is an inflammation of the liver. At least six forms of hepatitis are now recognized. They are referred to as hepatitis A, B, C, D, E, and G. They vary considerably in severity. Some forms are acute (sudden and brief) and others are chronic (long-lasting). Some forms have little or no long-lasting effects. Others can become life-threatening diseases.

DESCRIPTION

The liver is one of the most important organs in the body. It regulates the amount of many chemicals that occur in the blood. It removes substances from the blood that are or may become toxic. A toxin is a poison. The liver changes these substances into less harmful forms. It then converts them into a form that will dissolve in water. In this form, the substances are eliminated from the body. If the liver is damaged, toxic substances may build up in the bloodstream. In the worst cases, these substances can cause serious illness and even death.

Most forms of hepatitis are caused by viruses. The viruses have names similar to those of the diseases they cause. Hepatitis A, for example, is caused by the hepatitis A virus (HAV). Hepatitis B is caused by the hepatitis B virus (HBV), and so on.

Hepatitis A and B have been known for many years. At one time they were called infectious and serum hepatitis, respectively. When hepatitis C was first discovered, it was called non-A, non-B hepatitis. It is now known by its simpler name. Hepatitis D, E, and G were discovered during the 1970s, 1980s, and 1990s.

Hepatitis A

Hepatitis A is an acute disorder. An acute disorder is one that comes on suddenly and usually does not last very long. An initial episode of hepatitis A is often followed by a relapse a few weeks later. A relapse is a reoccurrence of the disease. A few people have many relapses.

Children are more likely to contract (catch) hepatitis A than adults, but their symptoms are usually much milder than those of adults.

Among those at highest risk for hepatitis A are the following:

- Children who go to day-care centers.
- Troops living under crowded conditions at military camps or in the field.
- Anyone living in heavily populated and unsanitary conditions.
- Individuals who practice oral-anal sexual contact.
- Tourists visiting an area where hepatitis A is common.

Hepatitis B

Hepatitis B is one of the most common infectious diseases in the world. By some estimates, more than 300 million people worldwide have the disease.

WORDS TO KNOW

Acute: A disorder that comes on suddenly and usually does not last very long.

Antibodies: Chemicals produced by the immune system to destroy invading organisms.

Antigen: Any particles or portion of an organism that can cause an immune response.

Carrier: A person whose body contains the organisms that cause a disease but who does not show symptoms of that disease.

Chronic: A disorder that develops gradually and may last for many years.

Cirrhosis: A liver disorder caused by scarring of liver tissue.

Hemophilia: A disorder characterized by the body's inability to clot blood effectively.

Immune system: A network of organs, tissues, cells, and chemicals designed to protect the body against foreign invaders, such as bacteria and viruses.

Jaundice: A yellowing of the skin, often caused by a disorder of the liver.

Relapse: A reoccurrence of a disease.

Toxin: A poison.

Hepatitis B occurs in both acute and chronic forms. The chronic form is one that develops slowly and remains in the body for a long time. The disease may range from mild to severe. Many people infected with HBV never develop any symptoms. They may not know they have the virus in their bodies, but they are still able to pass the virus on to other people. Such people are said to be carriers of the disease. About 1.5 million Americans are thought to be carriers of HBV.

In its most serious forms, hepatitis B can be a life-threatening disease. The virus causes severe scarring of the liver. The scarring process is called cirrhosis (pronounced suh-RO-suss) of the liver. Cirrhosis damages the liver so badly that it may no longer be able to function normally. It can cause the death of the patient. Cirrhosis can also lead to liver cancer (see cancer entry).

There are three major ways in which hepatitis B can be transmitted. They are:

• During birth, when a mother with hepatitis B passes HBV to her infant.
• Coming into contact with infected blood, as happens when a health worker is stuck with a needle containing infected blood.
• Through sexual contact, especially when such contact results in a tearing of body tissue.

Hepatitis C

Hepatitis C was first identified in 1974. The virus that causes the disease was not found until 1989. The infection is sometimes called "transfusion hepatitis." The name comes from one possible cause of the disease. It may be transmitted along with blood used in blood transfusions. Since the

OTHER FORMS OF HEPATITIS

Two other forms of hepatitis are alcoholic hepatitis and autoimmune hepatitis. Both of these disorders result in damage to the liver. They have symptoms similar to those of hepatitis A, B, C, D, E, and G, but they have different causes.

Alcoholic hepatitis is caused by an excessive consumption of alcohol over a period of time. Alcohol is largely broken down in the liver. The more alcohol a person drinks, the harder the liver has to work. In some cases, the liver can be damaged by processing too much alcohol. The cure for alcoholic hepatitis is simple: the patient must stop drinking. When the liver has less alcohol to deal with, it may return to its normal condition.

Some alcoholics find it difficult to give up drinking. In such cases, they can cause severe damage to their livers. They may develop cirrhosis and/or liver cancer. These diseases are major causes of death among alcoholics.

Autoimmune hepatitis occurs when the body's immune system becomes confused. It begins to attack the cells in its own body the way it attacks foreign invaders. Antibodies released by the immune system may attack the liver and cause inflammation.

Autoimmune hepatitis can be acute or chronic. Unfortunately, there is no way to cure the disease. Some people eventually recover from the condition, while others become so ill that they die.

identification of HCV, tests have been developed to identify the virus. Blood transfusions are no longer a major cause of the disease.

Other ways in which the virus can be transmitted include:

- Through a break in the skin or the inner lining of the mouth or genitals
- From an infected mother to her child
- As a result of sexual intercourse

Hepatitis C can occur in either acute or chronic forms. In its acute form, it is quite mild, but in its chronic form it can be even more dangerous than hepatitis B.

Among those at highest risk for hepatitis C are:

- Health care workers who may come into contact with infected blood
- Intravenous drug users (people who inject drugs directly into their veins)
- Individuals who have their skin pierced with a dirty needle while getting tattooed or pierced
- Hemophiliacs, people with a genetic blood disorder known as hemophilia (see hemophilia entry)
- Kidney dialysis patients who spend time on machines that cleanse their blood for them

Hepatitis D, E, and G are relatively less common. They may occur in conjunction with one of the other forms of hepatitis or on their own.

CAUSES

The exact mechanism by which viruses cause hepatitis is not entirely understood. It appears that the disease is not caused by the virus itself, but by the body's immune system. The immune system is a network of organs, tissues, cells, and chemicals designed to protect the body against foreign invaders, such as bacteria and viruses.

When a foreign invader enters the body, the immune system begins to respond. It produces chemicals designed to kill the invader. These chemicals are called antibodies. The presence of antibodies in the bloodstream may have other effects on the body, including inflammation, swelling, and other symptoms. It appears that the liver becomes inflamed because of the antibodies produced by the immune system, not because of the virus itself.

SYMPTOMS

The symptoms of the various forms of hepatitis are similar. They are caused by damage to the liver. Perhaps the most noticeable symptom is jaundice. Jaundice causes a yellowing of the skin. Other symptoms associated

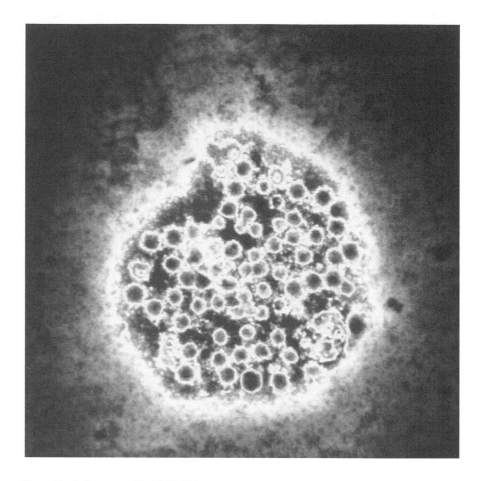

Hepatitis A virus magnified 225,000 times. (© 1990. Reproduced by permission of Custom Medical Stock.)

with hepatitis include fatigue, general achiness, nausea, mild fever, and loss of appetite. As infection spreads in the liver, the organ becomes enlarged. It may cause pain in the abdomen.

In the case of acute hepatitis, these symptoms tend to disappear within a few months. In a very small percentage of cases, symptoms may become worse. In less than 1 percent of cases, the patient's liver may fail completely. Patients then stand only a 50–50 chance of surviving the disease.

In cases where symptoms last for at least six months, the patient is said to have chronic hepatitis. Symptoms may continue to get worse. But the worst damage that occurs is cirrhosis of the liver. Cirrhosis leads to liver cancer in somewhat less than 10 percent of all cases.

Many people who have been infected with a hepatitis virus show no symptoms at all. In the case of hepatitis B, that number may be as high as 50 percent. Up to three-quarters of all children with hepatitis A never have symptoms of the infection. Although these individuals have no symptoms, they are still carriers of the disease. They can pass the virus on to other individuals.

DIAGNOSIS

The appearance of jaundice is often the first step in diagnosing hepatitis. The change in color of one's skin is so pronounced that most patients seek medical advice when they have that experience.

Confirmation of this diagnosis can be easily obtained with a blood test. A sample of the patient's blood is drawn (taken). The sample is then tested for the presence of viral antigens or viral antibodies. A viral antigen is a part of the virus that causes the body's immune system to react. A viral antibody is the chemical produced by the immune system to destroy the virus. Blood tests for either viral antigens or viral antibodies—or both—are available for all forms of viral hepatitis.

TREATMENT

There is no cure for hepatitis. The only approach of value is for patients to get as much bed rest as possible. They should continue to eat and drink as much as possible, but alcoholic drinks should be avoided.

PROGNOSIS

The prognosis for various forms of hepatitis varies considerably. Most patients with hepatitis A recover completely within a few months. They become immune to HAV and will not contract the disease again. Up to three-quarters of all Americans over the age of fifty have been exposed to HAV.

About 90 percent of patients with hepatitis B will also recover completely. Among the remaining 10 percent, however, serious complications are likely to develop. These complications include cirrhosis of the liver and liver cancer. About 2 percent of all patients with hepatitis B become chronically ill with the disease.

The prognosis for patients with hepatitis C is slightly less promising. About 15 percent will develop cirrhosis of the liver or liver cancer. Many more are likely to develop chronic hepatitis or some other liver-related disorder.

PREVENTION

Vaccines have now been developed for two forms of hepatitis, A and B. These vaccines are recommended for individuals who may be at risk for one

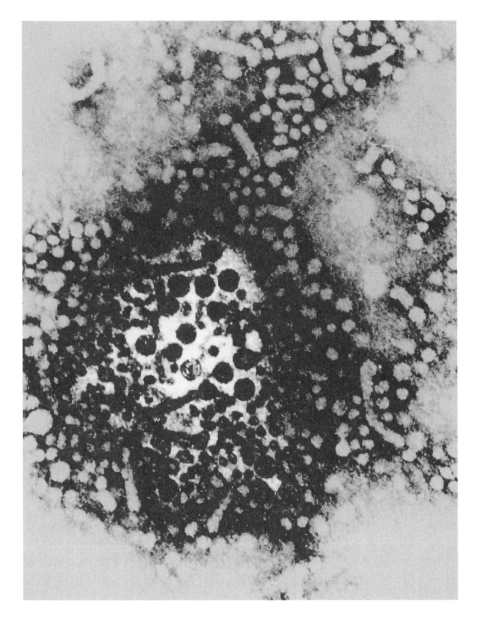

Magnified image of a hepatitis B virus. (© 1994. Reproduced by permission of Custom Medical Stock.)

of these diseases. For example, health care workers and those who plan to travel to areas where hepatitis is common should be vaccinated.

Injections are also available for those who have already been exposed to hepatitis A or B. These injections can be very effective if they are given fairly soon after the exposure has occurred.

Hepatitis infections can also be prevented by following a number of lifestyle suggestions, including:

- Wash hands often, especially after using the toilet or coming into contact with another person's blood.
- Intravenous drug users should not share needles with each other.
- Personal items that can damage the skin, such as razors, nail files, and scissors, should not be shared.
- Condoms should be used during vaginal, anal, and oral sex.
- Travelers in undeveloped areas should boil water and thoroughly wash any fresh fruits or vegetables before eating them.

FOR MORE INFORMATION

Books

Everson, Gregory T. and Hedy Weinberg. *Living with Hepatitis C: Survivor's Guide.* New York: Hatherleigh Press, 1998.

Rosenthal, M. Sara. *The Gastrointestinal Sourcebook.* Los Angeles: Lowell House, 1997.

Roybal, Beth Ann Petro. *Hepatitis C: A Personal Guide to Good Health.* Berkeley, CA: Ulysses Press, 1997.

Silverstein, Alvin, Virginia Silverstein, and Robert Silverstein. *Hepatitis.* Hillside, NJ: Enslow Publishers, Inc., 1994.

Organizations

American Liver Foundation. 1425 Pompton Ave., Cedar Grove, NJ 07009. (800) 223–0179. http://sadieo.ucsf.edu/alf/alffinal/homepagealf.html.

Hepatitis B Foundation. 101 Greenwood Ave., Suite 570, Jenkitown, PA 19046. (214) 884–8786. http://www.hepb.org.

Web sites

HepNet: The Hepatitis Information Network. [Online] http://www.hepnet.com (accessed on February 2, 1998).

King, J. W. *Bug Bytes.* [Online] http://www.ccm.lsumc.edu/bugbytes (accessed on October 25, 1999).

HERNIA

DEFINITION

Hernia is a general term for a bulge or protrusion of an organ through a part of the body in which it is usually contained.

DESCRIPTION

There are many different kinds of hernias. The most familiar are those that occur in the abdomen. In this type of hernia, a part of the intestines protrudes (sticks out) through the wall of the abdomen. An abdominal hernia can occur in different areas. The name given to the hernia depends on the location in which it occurs. Some examples of abdominal hernias are the following:

- An inguinal (pronounced IN-gwin-null) hernia appears in the groin. It may come and go depending on various factors, such as the amount of physical activity. Inguinal hernias account for 80 percent of all hernias. They are more common in men.
- Femoral (pronounced FEH-muh-rull) hernias are similar to inguinal hernias, but they occur lower in the body. They are more common in women, and commonly occur during pregnancy.
- A ventral hernia is also called an incisional hernia. The name reflects the fact that it often occurs at the location of an old surgical scar (incision). A ventral hernia is caused by the stretching of scar tissue. It occurs most commonly in pregnant women and people who are obese (excessively overweight, see obesity entry).
- An umbilical hernia occurs at the navel. Umbilical hernias are common among infants. They occur when the naval area does not close up properly after birth. Some umbilical hernias clear up by themselves within the first year.
- A hiatal (pronounced hi-ATE-ul) hernia is different from other abdominal hernias. It cannot be seen from outside the body. In a hiatal hernia, the stomach bulges upward into the diaphragm. The diaphragm is a muscle that separates the chest from the abdomen. Hiatal hernias are more common in women than in men.

CAUSES

Most hernias develop at weak spots in the abdominal wall. The weakness may be present at birth, or it may develop later in life for a variety of reasons. Any unusual pressure on the abdomen can cause a hernia to develop. Some examples of the causes of hernias are:

- Heavy lifting
- Unusually severe coughing
- Pregnancy
- Obesity or sudden and excessive weight loss
- Aging
- Previous surgical procedures

SYMPTOMS

A person can sometimes feel a hernia as it develops. There may be tenderness or a slight burning sensation in the area where the hernia is developing. Sometimes a person can push the hernia back into place. In other cases, the hernia may just disappear by itself. In still other cases, the hernia cannot be pushed back into place easily.

About half of the people with hiatal hernias have no symptoms. Those who do have symptoms are likely to experience heartburn. Heartburn is caused when stomach acid is pushed back into the esophagus (pronounced ee-SAH-fuh-guss). The esophagus is the tube that leads from the windpipe to the stomach. Heartburn may also be accompanied by chest pain. These symptoms are worse when a person is lying down.

DIAGNOSIS

Hernias are fairly easy to diagnose. A doctor can usually feel the hernia simply by touching it. The doctor may ask the patient to cough. The extra pressure caused by coughing will make the hernia stick out even more, making it even easier to feel.

A hiatal hernia is more difficult to diagnose. The first clue often comes from symptoms described by the patient, such as heartburn and chest pain after eating. A barium swallow can also be used to diagnose a hiatal hernia. A barium swallow is a procedure in which a patient swallows a chalky white substance containing barium. An X ray is then taken of the patient's digestive system. A hiatal hernia shows up as a protrusion into the diaphragm.

Hiatal hernias can also be diagnosed by endoscopy (pronounced en-DOS-kuh-pee). Endoscopy is a procedure in which a small tube is inserted through the mouth, then into the esophagus and stomach to allow the doctor to see the hernia. A hiatal hernia can actually be seen by this method.

TREATMENT

Once an abdominal hernia occurs, it tends to increase in size. Some patients with an abdominal hernia decide not to seek treatment right away. They may try to keep the hernia un-

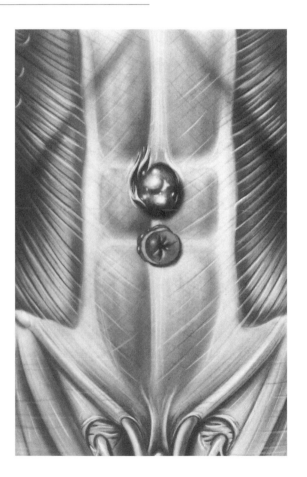

Illustration of an abdominal hernia. In this type of hernia a part of the intestines sticks out through the wall of the abdomen. (Illustration by John Bavosi. Reproduced by permission of the National Audubon Society Collection/Photo Researchers, Inc.)

der control with a truss. A truss is a support garment worn like a belt. It helps keep the hernia from protruding. People with hernias must avoid strenuous activity, such as heavy lifting or straining themselves.

Constant pain, nausea, and vomiting are signs that the hernia has become worse. The patient may notice that the hernia can no longer be pushed back into place. In such cases, medical help should be sought. Surgery will probably be necessary.

The surgical treatment for hernia is relatively simple. The hernia is pushed back into the abdominal cavity. The muscle lying on top of the hernia is then sewed back into place. If necessary, additional support may be added to keep the hernia in place.

If a hernia is not treated, severe complications can result. Part of the intestine can become trapped outside the muscles of the abdomen. A blockage in the intestine may develop. In the worst cases, this blockage can cut off the blood supply to the intestine. Part of the intestine may actually die.

A hiatal hernia is treated differently. Surgery is recommended only as a last resort. Instead, changes in the patient's lifestyle are recommended. Some of these changes are:

• Avoiding lying down after meals
• Avoiding spicy or acidic foods, alcohol, and tobacco
• Eating small, frequent, bland meals
• Eating a high-fiber diet

Several medications can also help relieve the symptoms of a hiatal hernia. For example, antacids are used to neutralize stomach acid and decrease heartburn. Drugs are also available to reduce the amount of stomach acid produced. A third option is a group of drugs that makes the muscles around the esophagus work more efficiently. The stomach empties faster and there is less chance of heartburn.

Alternative Treatment

Alternative practitioners often recommend changes similar to those listed above. In the case of a hiatal hernia, they may also suggest the use of visceral manipulation. Visceral manipulation is a method for returning the stomach to its proper position. Natural products are sometimes recommended for hiatal hernias too. For example, the natural product called deglycyrrhizinated licorice is thought to help reduce the effects of stomach acid.

PROGNOSIS

Abdominal hernias usually do not reoccur in children. They do reappear, however, in about 10 percent of adults. Surgery is considered the only cure. The prognosis will be excellent if the patient does not seek medical help too late.

Hiatal hernias are treated successfully with medication and changes in diet about 85 percent of the time. The prognosis remains good even if surgery is required to repair the hernia.

PREVENTION

Some hernias can be prevented by following some simple rules, such as:

- Maintain a reasonable weight.
- Avoid heavy lifting.
- Follow a program of moderate exercise.

FOR MORE INFORMATION

Books

Delvin, David. *Coping with a Hernia.* Sterling, VA: Capital Books Inc., 1998.

HERPES INFECTIONS

DEFINITION

Herpes infections are a group of diseases caused by a herpes virus. There are eight different herpes viruses that can infect humans. Two of these, herpes simplex type 1 and herpes simplex type 2, occur commonly. They cause cold sores and genital herpes.

DESCRIPTION

Cold sores are a very common health problem. More than 60 percent of Americans have had a cold sore. Nearly 25 percent of these individuals have repeated outbreaks of cold sores. Cold sores are also known as fever blisters or oral herpes. They are usually caused by herpes simplex virus 1 (HSV1).

Most people are first infected with HSV1 before the age of ten. Once the virus enters the body, it remains there for life. Cold sores are painful blis-

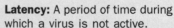

WORDS TO KNOW

Latency: A period of time during which a virus is not active.

Prodrome: A period of time during which certain symptoms signal the beginning of a disease.

Ulcer: An open wound in the skin or mucous membrane that is usually sore and painful.

ters filled with fluid. They usually occur on the lips. By contrast, canker sores usually occur on the tongue, inside the cheeks, or elsewhere inside the mouth.

Genital herpes are also painful blisters filled with fluid. They are caused by a close relative of HSV1, herpes simplex virus 2 (HSV2). A common rule of thumb is that HSV1 causes infections above the waist and HSV2 causes infections below the waist. But that rule is not completely true. Either virus can cause infections above or below the waist. Still, the rule is a good general guideline as to where each virus is most likely to be active.

Viruses that enter the body often go through a latency period. A latency period is a stage during which the virus goes into hiding. It can be found in cells, but it is not active. There are no external symptoms that the virus is in the body.

At some point, however, the virus becomes active again. Any number of factors can cause reactivation of the virus. Physical or emotional shock is a common cause. When the virus becomes active again, symptoms of the infection reappear.

This pattern explains why cold sores and genital herpes commonly appear and then disappear. Each new appearance does not mean a new infection. It means that the virus has emerged from its latency period and become active again.

CAUSES

Both HSV1 and HSV2 are transmitted directly between people. Cold sores are spread, for example, when an uninfected person touches an infected person. A common means of transmission is by kissing. The greatest risk for spreading the virus occurs when blisters are present on the lips. But it can also be spread when there are no blisters.

Genital herpes is spread only through sexual contact. When an uninfected person comes into contact with the blisters on another person's body, the virus may be transmitted. Genital herpes is spread between genital areas in most cases, but it can also be spread to the mouth during oral sex.

SYMPTOMS

Not everyone who is infected with the herpes virus will develop symptoms. Among those who do, the symptoms first appear within two to

NEONATAL HERPES

Pregnant women with genital herpes can pass the infection to their newborn babies. The babies are infected as they pass through the birth canal. The infection that occurs in babies is known as neonatal herpes. About 1 in 3,000 to 5,000 babies born each year in the United States will develop neonatal herpes. The infection can be avoided by having the baby delivered by cesarean section. A cesarean section is a procedure in which an incision (cut) is made in the stomach wall. The baby is then removed through the incision. Babies born with herpes can become very ill and die from the disease.

twenty days of infection. Symptoms that develop after the original infection are generally severer than those that appear in later episodes of the disease.

The first stage of infection often involves a set of symptoms called a prodrome. The prodrome is a warning sign that an infection has begun to develop in the body. Some symptoms of a herpes prodrome include pain, burning, itching, or tingling at the site where the blisters will form. The prodrome lasts anywhere from a few hours to a few days.

Following the prodrome, the characteristic herpes blisters begin to appear. Cold sore blisters first appear in the form of small red bumps that quickly fill with fluid. The blisters are very painful. They may either burst and form a scab or dry up and form a scab. The skin heals without scarring within six to ten days.

The appearance of genital herpes is somewhat different. The blisters formed in the genital area also begin as small red bumps that fill with liquid. In dry areas, the blisters form a scab and heal within two to three weeks. In moist areas, the blisters usually break and form painful ulcers before healing. New blisters may form over a period of a week or longer. They may then join to form very large ulcers (open sores). The pain usually disappears after about two weeks. The blisters and ulcers heal without scarring in three to four weeks.

Both forms of herpes tend to recur on a regular basis. In the case of cold sores, most people experience fewer than two outbreaks each year. This pattern varies considerably, however. Some people never have a second episode of cold sores, while others have many such episodes. Those who do have further outbreaks usually get blisters in the same area each time. They also tend to be triggered by the same factors, such as stress or exposure to sun.

Genital herpes tends to recur more often than cold sores. About 40 percent of persons infected with HSV2 will experience six or more outbreaks per year. The vast majority of patients with genital herpes will have at least one outbreak every year. Reoccurrences of HSV2 infections tend to be less severe than the initial outbreak. Patients usually have fewer blisters and less pain. The time between outbreak and healing may also get shorter with each outbreak.

DIAGNOSIS

Cold sores and genital herpes both have a very distinctive appearance. Simple observation of a patient's symptoms often provides a strong indication of the problem. However, the symp-

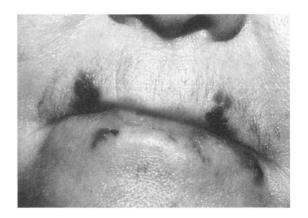

Cold sores are usually caused by the herpes simplex virus 1. (Reproduced by permission of Custom Medical Stock Photo)

toms of the two diseases are somewhat similar to those of other infections. Cold sores, for example, look something like a bacterial infection known as impetigo. There may also be some confusion between cold sores in the mouth and canker sores.

A variety of diseases cause sores in the genital area also. Some examples include syphilis, chancroid, herpes zoster (another infection caused by the herpes virus), and inflammatory bowel disease. In some cases, it is difficult to distinguish the blisters and ulcers caused by genital herpes and sores produced by other diseases.

To confirm a diagnosis, a doctor can do a culture of cells taken from the infected area by wiping a clean cotton swab over the infected area. The material collected on the swab is then kept in a warm, moist environment for a few days. The organisms responsible for the infection can be identified when examined under a microscope.

TREATMENT

There is no cure for herpes virus infections. However, there are antiviral drugs that can relieve some symptoms of these infections. Antiviral drugs interfere with the growth of viruses. They work best when used as early in an infection as possible. For the best results, treatment should begin during the prodrome stage of infection. Antiviral drugs may also prevent future outbreaks of cold sores or genital herpes.

The preferred antiviral for treatment of herpes infections is acyclovir (trade name Zovirax). The drug is most effective when injected directly into the bloodstream or taken orally (by mouth). It can also be used as a lotion and applied directly to sores, but it is less effective when used this way.

Treatments are also available to relieve the symptoms of herpes infections. Patients with cold sores should avoid salty foods, citrus foods, and other foods that irritate the sores. The sores can be washed once or twice a day with warm, soapy water. Over-the-counter medications that contain the chemical phenol can provide some relief too. Blistex Medicated Lip Ointment is an example of this kind of medication. Aspirin, acetaminophen, or ibuprofen can also be used to relieve the pain of cold sores. Children, however, should not take aspirin as it can cause Reye's syndrome (see Reye's syndrome entry).

There are several things a patient can do to reduce the pain of genital sores. Wearing loose-fitting clothing and cotton underwear is helpful. Soaking in a tub of warm water and using a blow-dryer set on the cool setting to dry the infected area may help. Putting an ice pack on the infected area for 10 minutes may also help relieve pain. A zinc sulfate ointment may help heal sores. Applying a baking soda compress to sores may be soothing.

Alternative Treatment

Some people believe that a contributing factor in herpes infections is an imbalance in amino acids. Amino acids are the building blocks from which proteins are made. The two amino acids thought to be involved in a herpes infection are lysine and arginine. Based on this theory, some practitioners recommend a diet rich in lysine to prevent the reoccurrence of cold sores. Foods rich in lysine include most vegetables, legumes (peas and beans), fish, turkey, and chicken.

Herbalists recommend a variety of herbs to protect against herpes infections. Echinacea and garlic are thought to strengthen the immune system. Members of the red algae family are believed to be effective in treating HSV1 and HSV2 infections. Some ointments and salves that may relieve the pain of herpes include zinc sulfate, lithium succinate, licorice, lemon balm, and peppermint.

Stress is thought to be one of the factors that bring on an attack of herpes. Some methods for relieving stress include acupressure, massage, meditation, yoga, tai chi, and hypnotherapy.

PROGNOSIS

There is no cure for any type of herpes infection. Most such infections are painful and sometimes embarrassing. However, they generally get better on their own without any permanent scarring or damage to the body. In many cases, infections become less frequent and severe as a person grows older.

In relatively rare cases, both types of infection can have more serious complications. For example, the spread of HSV1 to the eyes can cause damage, which may impair vision. The spread of HSV2 to the cervix, urinary system, anal opening, and nervous system can produce more dangerous infections of these areas.

PREVENTION

The only way to prevent a herpes infection is by avoiding contact with an infected person. While good advice, that policy may be difficult to follow. Many infected people do not know that they carry the virus. Or they may not be concerned because the virus is in a latent stage. In the case of genital herpes, some people may choose not to tell their sexual partners that they are infected.

Having a man use a condom during sexual intercourse can provide partial protection against genital herpes. The condom reduces, but does not eliminate, the chance of spreading HSV2.

A number of suggestions have been made for reducing the risk of having a reoccurrence of oral herpes. These include:

• Avoid exposure to the sun, which appears to trigger outbreaks of oral herpes.
• Avoid touching cold sores, since doing so may spread the virus to other parts of the face or body.
• Wash hands thoroughly and frequently, so that an infected person is less likely to transfer HSV1 to other persons.
• Avoid physical contact with other people when one has an active infection.
• Wear gloves when applying ointment to a child's sore.
• Be especially careful in handling young babies by not kissing their eyes or mouth if you are infected.
• Monitor children with cold sores so that they do not transmit the virus to other children by way of toys.
• Maintain good general health to reduce the risk of contracting a cold or the flu, which are known to bring on cold sores.

See also: Sexually transmitted diseases.

FOR MORE INFORMATION

Books

Ebel, Charles. *Managing Herpes: How to Live and Love with a Chronic STD*. Research Triangle Park, NC: American Social Health Association, 1998.

Harknett, Philippa. *Herpes Simplex: The Self-Help Guide to Managing the Herpes Virus*. London: Thorsons Publications, 1995.

Sacks, Stephen L. *The Truth about Herpes*. Seattle, WA: Gordon Soules Book Publishers, 1997.

Periodicals

Kott, Andrea. "The Common Cold Sore." *Parents* (November 1997): pp. 101–05.

Web sites

JAMA Women's Health Information Center. [Online] http://www.ama-assn.org/special/std/std.htm (accessed on April 8, 1998).

Mayo Health Oasis. [Online] http://www.mayohealth.org (accessed on March 3, 1998).

HODGKIN'S DISEASE

DEFINITION

Hodgkin's disease is a cancer of the lymphatic (pronounced lim-FAT-ic) system. The lymphatic system consists of blood vessels, tissues, and other structures that carry lymph (pronounced limf) through the body. Lymph is a bloodlike fluid that carries substances from cells to blood vessels.

A variety of cancers can affect lymph tissue. These cancers are called lymphomas. Hodgkin's disease is one kind of lymphoma. It is also called Hodgkin's lymphoma. The cause of Hodgkin's disease is unknown. Many experts believe that genetic and environmental factors work together to cause the disease.

DESCRIPTION

Hodgkin's lymphoma can occur at any age. It is most common, however, in people between the ages of fifteen and thirty-four and after the age of sixty. An understanding of the lymphatic system is necessary in order to understand the nature of Hodgkin's lymphoma.

The Lymphatic System

Lymph is usually a clear, colorless liquid that forms in the space between cells throughout the body. It consists of waste products from those cells.

Lymph is drained into tiny vessels, like blood vessels. These vessels form a network of tubes that eventually leads to large veins at the base of the neck and inside the abdomen. At various points in this network, lymph passes through small lumps of tissue known as lymph nodes.

Lymph nodes contain special kinds of cells that act as filters. These cells remove foreign substances, such as viruses, bacteria, and cancer cells, from lymph. For this reason, they are part of the body's immune system, protecting it from infection.

One kind of cell found in lymph is a white blood cell called a lymphocyte. The role of lymphocytes is to identify foreign bodies in lymph and to help eliminate those materials from the lymph.

WORDS TO KNOW

Biopsy: The removal of a small sample of tissue and its examination under a microscope for the purpose of diagnosing a disease.

Chemotherapy: Treatment of a disease with certain chemicals or drugs that destroy cancer cells.

Radiotherapy: Treatment of a disease using some form of radiation, such as X rays.

Cancer of the Lymph System

Cancer is a condition in which cells grow out of control (see cancer entry). Cancer can appear in any part of the lymph system. Cells within a lymph node, for example, may begin to grow rapidly. They may take on unusual shapes and begin to spread throughout the body. Cancers that affect any part of the lymph system are known as lymphomas.

CAUSES

Hodgkin's lymphoma usually begins in a lymph node. The node enlarges and may or may not become painful. The cancer typically moves from one lymph node to another nearby lymph node. Eventually, cancer cells can be carried to other organs in the body, including the spleen, liver, and bone marrow.

SYMPTOMS

Some of the early symptoms of Hodgkin's lymphoma include fever, weight loss, heavy sweating at night, and itching. Some patients report that drinking alcoholic beverages may cause pain in the infected area.

As lymph nodes swell, they may push on other nearby structures. This pressure may also cause pain and other kinds of discomfort. For example, nerves may be pinched, causing pain and loss of muscular control. Pressure on the ureters, the tubes that carry urine from the kidneys to the bladder, can cause kidney failure. Pressure on veins in the face, neck, and legs can reduce blood flow and cause swelling in those areas. Pressure on the spinal cord can cause paralysis of the legs. Pressure on the upper respiratory (breathing) system can cause wheezing and shortness of breath. Abnormal tissue growth in the liver can cause an accumulation of toxins (poisons), resulting in jaundice. Jaundice is a yellowish discoloration of the skin and whites of the eyes. It is a common sign of liver disease.

As Hodgkin's disease worsens, the lymphatic system becomes less effective in fighting off infections. Patients with the disease are more likely to develop infections caused by bacteria, viruses, and other types of germs.

DIAGNOSIS

Diagnosis involves two steps. First, the doctor must identify Hodgkin's disease as the cause of the patient's symptoms. Second, the doctor must determine how far the disease has progressed.

Hodgkin's disease is usually diagnosed by means of a biopsy. A biopsy is a process in which a small sample of tissue is removed from the infected part

Magnified image of dividing Hodgkin's disease cells. (© 1995 Dr. Andrejs Liepins/Science Photo Library. Reproduced by permission of Custom Medical Stock Photo.)

of the patient's body. In the case of Hodgkin's disease, the biopsy is usually done on a lymph node. The sample is then examined under a microscope. The presence of certain characteristic types of cells is evidence of a lymphoma.

Additional procedures are necessary to see how far the disease has spread. For example, a bone marrow biopsy may be conducted to see if the disease has spread to this part of the body. A computed tomography (CT) scan may be ordered to see if the disease has spread to the abdomen, chest, pelvis, and other parts of the body. A CT scan is a procedure by which X rays are directed at a patient's body from various angles and the set of photographs thus obtained assembled by a computer program. This procedure is sometimes called a computerized axial tomography (CAT) scan. A lymphangiogram can also be performed. A lymphangiogram is similar to an X ray of the lymphatic system. It indicates the parts of the system that have become cancerous.

Finding out how far the disease has spread is important because it determines the kind of treatment the patient should have. Most treatments have serious side effects. A doctor wants to use only enough of a treatment to kill the lymphoma, not enough to do other serious damage to the body.

Hodgkin's disease has the highest cure rate of any type of cancer. Unfortunately, the treatments are extremely painful. Billy Best (above) ran away from home in 1995 rather than endure the treatments. (Reproduced by permission of AP/Wide World Photos)

TREATMENT

Two forms of treatment are used with Hodgkin's disease: chemotherapy and radiotherapy. Chemotherapy involves the use of drugs to kill cancer cells. Radiotherapy uses X rays or other forms of radiation to achieve the same result. Both methods of treatment work quite well with Hodgkin's lymphoma.

Unfortunately, both treatments also have unpleasant side effects. Chemotherapy can result in nausea, vomiting, hair loss, and an increased risk for infections. Radiotherapy can cause sore throat, difficulty in swallowing, diarrhea, and changes in growth patterns for children. Both forms of treatment, especially when they are used together, can cause sterility. Sterility is the loss of the ability to have children. Heart and lung damage are also possible side effects when the two treatments are used together.

One of the most serious problems in the treatment of Hodgkin's disease is the possibility of a secondary cancer. A secondary cancer is a new cancer that occurs elsewhere in the body after the Hodgkin's lymphoma has been cured. Secondary cancers can occur in blood, bone, the thyroid, or other parts of the body.

PROGNOSIS

The cure rate for Hodgkin's disease is among the highest for any form of cancer. Treatments seem to work best with children. About 75 percent of children treated for Hodgkin's disease are still alive twenty years after the original diagnosis. For adults with the most serious forms of the disease, the cure rate is still as high as 50 percent.

PREVENTION

There is no know method of preventing Hodgkin's disease.

FOR MORE INFORMATION

Books

Dollinger, Malin, et al. *Everyone's Guide to Cancer Therapy.* Kansas City, MO: Andrews McKeel Publishing, 1997.

Murphy, Gerald P., et al. *Informed Decisions.* New York: Viking Press, 1997.

Periodicals

Stoval, Ellen. "A Cancer Survivor Discusses Her Experiences." *Washington Post* (February 14, 1995): pp. WH15+.

Organizations

The Lymphoma Research Foundation of America, Inc. 8800 Venice Boulevard, Suite 207, Los Angeles, CA 90034. (310) 204–7040. http://www.lymphoma.org.

Web sites

"Ask NOAH About: Cancer." *NOAH: New York Online Access to Health.* [Online] http://www.noah.cuny.edu/cancer/cantypes.html#H (accessed on October 25, 1999).

HYPERTENSION

DEFINITION

Hypertension is the medical name for high blood pressure.

DESCRIPTION

The circulatory system is the network of organs and blood vessels through which blood travels in the body. Blood is pumped out of the heart into blood vessels known as arteries. After passing through the body, blood returns to the heart by way of blood vessels known as veins.

As blood flows through arteries and veins, it pushes on their walls. Blood pressure is defined as the force exerted by blood inside arteries.

Blood does not flow steadily through the circulatory system. At one moment, the heart muscle squeezes blood out of the heart into the arteries. At this point, the blood pressure is high because of the force exerted by the heart. At the next moment, the heart muscle relaxes to let fresh blood into the heart. At this point, the blood pressure is lower because of reduced force by the heart muscle.

The two stages of high and low blood pressure have special names. The highest pressure reached by blood in the arteries is called the systolic pressure. The lowest pressure reached by blood in the arteries is known as the diastolic pressure.

WORDS TO KNOW

Arteries: Blood vessels that carry blood from the heart to organs and tissues of the body.

Arteriosclerosis: Hardening and thickening of artery walls.

Diastolic blood pressure: Blood pressure exerted by the heart when it is resting between beats.

Sphygmomanometer: An instrument used to measure blood pressure.

Systolic blood pressure: Blood pressure exerted by the heart when it contracts (beats).

Vasodilator: Any drug that causes a blood vessel to relax.

When a doctor or nurse takes a person's blood pressure, he or she records two readings: the systolic (highest) and the diastolic (lowest) pressure. For example, a patient's blood pressure might be recorded as 140/80, which is read as "140 over 80." That reading means that the patient's highest blood pressure is 140 and the lowest blood pressure is 80.

The numbers 140 and 80 are measured in units called "millimeters of mercury" or "mm Hg." This unit is commonly used by scientists to measure pressure.

The American Heart Association considers blood pressure less than 140 and greater than 90 to be normal for adults. A person whose diastolic pressure is less than 90 is said to have low blood pressure. Someone with a systolic pressure of more than 140 is said to have high blood pressure—or hypertension.

Hypertension is a serious problem because people with the condition have a higher risk for heart disease and other medical problems than people with normal blood pressure. If left untreated, hypertension can lead to a number of medical conditions, including:

• Arteriosclerosis
• Heart attack (see heart attack entry)
• Stroke (see stroke entry)
• Enlarged heart
• Kidney damage

Arteriosclerosis is also called hardening of the arteries. The arteries are normally flexible. They expand and contract to adjust to the flow of blood through them. High blood pressure can cause artery walls to become thick and tough. The arteries themselves may become narrower. Blood cannot flow as easily through them.

When that happens, certain substances in the blood can begin to build up inside the arteries. These substances make the openings even narrower. Eventually, an artery may close completely. When that happens, blood can no longer flow through the circulatory system. A blocked artery can result in a heart attack or a stroke.

Hypertension can also damage the heart itself because the heart has to work harder to push blood through the circulatory system. It grows larger to keep up with this job. If the heart becomes too large, it may no longer be able to pump enough blood through the body. The heart may fail.

Kidneys can also be damaged by hypertension. The kidneys filter waste products from the blood. If blood vessels to the kidneys become clogged, fewer wastes are removed from the blood. The kidneys may fail and wastes may build up in the blood. About 25 percent of the people who are treated for failed kidneys have hypertension.

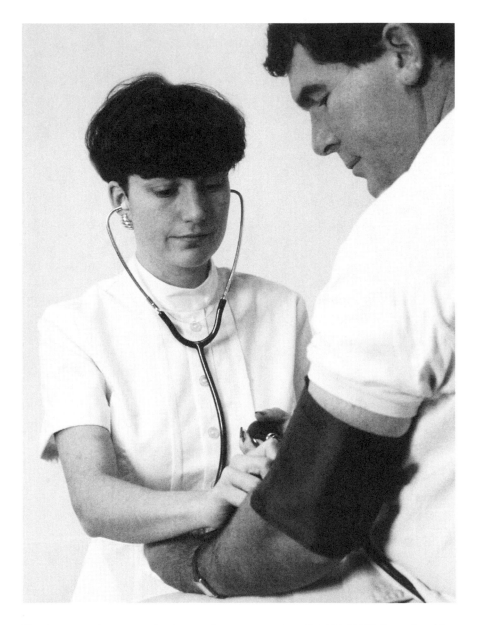

Blood pressure is measured using a sphygmomanometer. (© 1994 CMSP. Reproduced by permission of Custom Medical Stock Photo.)

CAUSES

High blood pressure can be caused by certain events in a person's life. For example, strenuous physical activity or stress can cause blood pressure to rise. However, high blood pressure is usually temporary in such cases.

When the activity ceases or the stress goes away, the blood pressure returns to normal. This form of high blood pressure is not regarded as a form of hypertension.

True hypertension exists only when a person has high blood pressure readings on a number of different occasions. If a doctor suspects hypertension, he or she will take a number of blood pressure readings over a period of weeks. If those readings are consistently high, the patient may have hypertension.

The cause of hypertension in 90 to 95 percent of all cases is not known. One important factor may be heredity. People who have family members with hypertension are more likely to develop the condition than people whose family members have no hypertension. Hypertension with no known cause is called primary hypertension.

Hypertension can also be caused by a variety of medical conditions. For example, people with kidney disorders may develop hypertension. The kidneys regulate the balance of water and salt in the body. If the kidneys do not function normally, the amount of salt and water in the body may increase. This increase can cause high blood pressure.

Other conditions that can cause hypertension include blood vessel diseases, disorders of the thyroid or other glands, alcoholism (see alcoholism entry), pregnancy, and the use of certain prescription drugs. Hypertension caused by some other medical problem is known as secondary hypertension.

Certain factors are known to increase a person's risk for hypertension. These factors include:

• Age over sixty
• Male sex
• Heredity
• Sensitivity to table salt
• Obesity (see obesity entry)
• Inactive lifestyle
• Heavy alcohol consumption
• Use of oral contraceptives (birth control pills)

SYMPTOMS

Hypertension is a major health problem, especially because it has no symptoms. Many people have hypertension without knowing it. In the United States, about fifty million people age six and older have high blood pressure. Hypertension is more common in men than women and in people over the age of sixty-five than in younger persons.

hypertension

Because hypertension does not produce symptoms it is important to have regular checkups. Taking a person's blood pressure is simple and painless. A doctor or nurse uses an instrument called a sphygmomanometer. A sphygmomanometer (pronounced SFIG-moh-muh-nahm-et-er) consists of a cloth-covered rubber cuff and a pressure valve. The cuff is wrapped around the patient's arm, and air is pumped into the cuff. As the air is slowly released, the doctor or nurse listens through a stethoscope to the sound of the blood rushing through the artery. He or she reads the pressure at which he or she hears distinctive heart sounds (the "lubb" and "dubb" made when a heart beats). These readings provide the patient's systolic and diastolic blood pressures.

There is no single point at which a person is said to have hypertension. Instead, certain levels of the condition are set depending on the person's blood pressure. These levels are as follows:

- Normal blood pressure: In the range 130/85
- High normal: In the ranges 130–140/85–90
- Mild hypertension: In the ranges 140–160/90–100
- Moderate hypertension: In the ranges 160–180/100–110
- Severe hypertension: In the ranges 180–210/110–120
- Very severe hypertension: Higher than 210/120

MEASURING BLOOD PRESSURE

Blood exerts pressure. Anyone who has ever cut an artery knows that fact. When that happens, blood gushes out of the artery with surprising force. That fact was first discovered by the English physician William Harvey (1578–1657) in the 1600s.

No one actually tried to measure blood pressure, however, until nearly a century later. Then, the English clergyman and physiologist Stephen Hales devised the first blood pressure measuring device. He cut open the blood vessel in various animals and inserted a metal pipe into the vessel. He then connected the pipe to a long glass tube. Blood was pushed out of the vessel into the glass tube. The blood rose to different levels in the tube for different animals.

It took another century for physicians to find a way to take blood pressure without actually cutting into a blood vessel. In 1876, the German physician Samuel Siegried von Basch (1837–1905) invented the first sphygmomanometer (pronounced SFIG-moh-muh-nahm-et-er). That tongue-twisting name describes the type of blood pressure measuring device used today. It consists of a rubber tube placed around the patient's upper arm. Air is pumped into the tube. Pressure from the air briefly cuts off the flow of blood in the patient's arm.

As the air is released from the tube, the medical worker listens to the patient's arm through a stethoscope. As blood starts flowing in the arm again, the sound produced by systolic pressure can be heard. A few moments later, the sound produced by the diastolic pressure can be heard. The worker notes the amount of pressure observed in a gauge on the arm band at each sound. These two pressures make up the patient's blood pressure reading.

Patients with higher-than-normal blood pressure may then be given other tests. These include:

- **Medical and family histories.** These help a doctor find out if the patient has risk factors in his or her family. If hypertension is common in the family, the patient is likely to be at higher risk for the condition.
- **Physical examination.** Sometimes other health problems may be discovered during a physical examination that explain the patient's high blood pressure.
- **Examination of the blood vessels in the eyes.** High blood pressure may cause blood vessels in the eyes to become thick or narrow. Bleeding in the eyes may also be visible.
- **Chest X ray.** This is used to check for an enlarged heart, other heart disorders, and lung disease.
- **Electrocardiograph (ECG).** This test measures the electrical activity of the heart. It can determine whether the heart muscle is functioning normally.
- **Blood and urine tests.** These help determine the general health of the patient.

TREATMENT

There is no cure for primary hypertension, but blood pressure can almost always be reduced with the correct treatment. The goal of this treatment is to prevent the complications of hypertension.

In cases of secondary hypertension, one approach is to treat the medical condition that causes hypertension. Efforts may be made at the same time to reduce the patient's blood pressure.

A program designed to reduce blood pressure usually has three parts: changes in diet, a plan of regular exercise, and antihypertensive medications. Some changes in lifestyle that can reduce blood pressure include the following:

- Reducing salt intake
- Reducing fat intake
- Losing weight
- Getting regular exercise
- Quitting smoking
- Reducing alcohol consumption
- Learning how to manage stress

For patients with mild or moderate hypertension, these steps may be enough to bring their

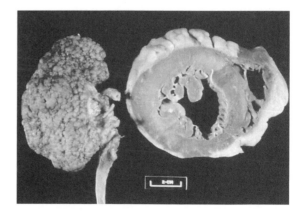

The effects of hypertension on the heart and kidney. Hypertension has caused atrophy and scarring of the kidney (left) and left ventricular hypertrophy in the sectioned heart (right). (Photograph by Dr. E. Walker. Reproduced by permission of Photo Researchers, Inc.)

blood pressure into the normal or high normal range. For patients with more serious hypertension, medications may be prescribed. A variety of medications are available for the treatment of hypertension. They fall into the following categories:

- Diuretics help the kidneys eliminate excess salt and water. The loss of fluid from the kidneys causes arteries to expand and blood pressure to become lower.
- Beta-blockers cause the heart to beat more slowly and with less force.
- Calcium channel blockers help relax muscle cells, reducing the force with which they pump blood.
- Angiotensin converting enzyme (ACE) inhibitors are chemicals that prevent blood vessels from tightening up. As a result, the pressure exerted by blood in the blood vessels is reduced.
- Alpha-blockers act on the nervous system, causing arteries to expand and reduce the pressure exerted by the heart on blood flow.
- Vasodilators are chemicals that act directly on arteries, causing them to relax (dilate) so that blood can move more easily through them.
- Nervous system antagonists and agonists act on the nerves that control the size of arteries. They cause arteries to open and allow blood to flow through them more easily.

PROGNOSIS

There is no cure for hypertension, but it can be controlled by changes in one's lifestyle and the use of medications. The major goal of treatment is to avoid the most serious complications of hypertension, such as heart disease and strokes.

PREVENTION

Some risk factors of hypertension cannot be eliminated. For example, a person may inherit a tendency for the disorder. But many risk factors can be prevented or reduced. Some of the most important changes a person can make in his or her life to prevent hypertension include the following:

- Reduce salt intake.
- Reduce fat intake.
- Lose weight.
- Get regular exercise.
- Quit smoking.
- Reduce alcohol consumption.
- Learn how to manage stress.

FOR MORE INFORMATION

Books

Murray, Michael T. *Heart Disease and High Blood Pressure: How You Can Benefit from Diet, Vitamins, Minerals, Herbs, Exercise, and Other Natural Methods.* Rocklin, CA: Prima Publishing, 1997.

Pickering, Thomas. *Good News About High Blood Pressure: Everything You Need to Know to Take Control of Hypertension—And Your Life.* New York: Simon and Schuster, 1996.

Texas Heart Institute. *Heart Owner's Handbook.* New York: John Wiley and Sons, 1996.

Wood, Stephen, and George Wood. *Conquering High Blood Pressure: The Complete Guide to Managing Hypertension.* New York: Insight Books, 1997.

Organizations

American Heart Association. 7272 Greenview Ave., Dallas, TX 75231-4596. (800) AHS–USA1. http://www.amhrt.org.

National Heart, Lung, and Blood Institute. Information Center. PO Box 30105, Bethesda, MD 20824–0105. (301) 251–1222.

Web sites

"Ask NOAH About: Heart Disease and Stroke." *NOAH: New York Online Access to Health.* [Online] http://www.noah.cuny.edu/heart_disease/heartdisease.html#H. (accessed on October 25, 1999).

HYPOGLYCEMIA

DEFINITION

Hypoglycemia (pronounced HI-po-gli-seem-ee-ah) means low blood sugar. The main fuel used by cells to produce energy is a type of sugar called glucose. Glucose is carried to cells in the bloodstream. In that form, glucose is often referred to as "blood sugar." Cells need a minimum amount of glucose to function properly. When there is not enough glucose in the blood to meet those needs, the condition known as hypoglycemia develops.

DESCRIPTION

An important part of the human diet is carbohydrates—sugars and starches. Carbohydrates are changed in the digestive system to glucose. The bloodstream carries glucose to cells. Cells use glucose to produce the energy needed for walking, talking, and just staying alive.

In some cases, people do not get enough glucose in their regular diet. Or they get enough glucose, but their body does not use it properly. In such cases, the person develops hypoglycemia. Hypoglycemia can develop in several ways.

Drug-induced Hypoglycemia

Hypoglycemia occurs frequently among diabetics (see diabetes mellitus entry). Diabetics are people whose bodies cannot use glucose properly. Their bodies either cannot manufacture or cannot use a compound known as insulin. Insulin (pronounced IN-soo-lin) is needed to convert glucose into a form that cells can use.

Diabetics whose bodies don't manufacture insulin control their disorder by taking insulin shots. Diabetics whose bodies don't recognize insulin can adjust their diet to deal with the condition. Missing a meal or taking too much insulin can cause hypoglycemia. This can cause a severe reaction known as "insulin shock."

Idiopathic Or Reactive Hypoglycemia

Idiopathic hypoglycemia occurs most commonly after a person has eaten. The cause for this type of hypoglycemia is not known. It may occur when an organ, such as the liver or pancreas, is not functioning properly. However, the condition is not related to diabetes.

Idiopathic hypoglycemia also occurs among people who have negative reactions to certain foods and drugs. For example, some children have a negative reaction to aspirin that can cause hypoglycemia. Other children have a negative reaction to natural fruit sugar (fructose) that can produce hypoglycemia.

Fasting Hypoglycemia

Strenuous exercise or going without food for long periods of time may also cause hypoglycemia. This form of hypoglycemia is called fasting hypoglycemia.

Other factors can also cause hypoglycemia, including:

- Pregnancy
- A weakened immune system
- A poorly balanced diet that contains too much sugar
- Prolonged use of certain drugs, including antibiotics

WORDS TO KNOW

Diabetes: A disorder in which the body's cells are unable to use glucose properly in order to make energy.

Glucose: A simple sugar used by cells to make energy.

Insulin: A hormone needed by cells to convert glucose to energy.

Metabolism: A series of chemical reactions by which cells convert glucose to energy.

- Chronic (ongoing) physical or mental stress
- An irregular heartbeat
- Allergies (see allergies entry)
- Breast cancer (see breast cancer entry)
- Surgery in the upper gastrointestinal (digestive) tract

CAUSES

The carbohydrates we eat are changed into glucose in the digestive system. The glucose passes into the bloodstream and is carried to cells, where it is used to make energy.

Under normal conditions, blood contains just the right amount of glucose. Cells receive all the glucose they need to function properly. But sometimes, blood contains too much or too little glucose. These conditions are called hyperglycemia ("hyper" means "too much") and hypoglycemia ("hypo" means "too little"). Cells either get more glucose than they can use or do not get enough to function normally.

These conditions are caused by two factors. First, a person may eat a diet that provides too much or too little glucose to the body. For example, people who eat a lot of sugar may develop hypoglycemia.

IDIOPATHIC HYPOGLYCEMIA ALSO OCCURS AMONG PEOPLE WHO HAVE NEGATIVE REACTIONS TO CERTAIN FOODS AND DRUGS.

Second, the cells in a person's body may lack the ability to use glucose normally. The person may have inherited the defect from his or her parents. Or something may have happened in the person's life to cause the defect. In either case, the person's blood contains too much or too little glucose. In the latter case, hypoglycemia results.

There is some debate about the nature of idiopathic hypoglycemia. The condition is being diagnosed much less frequently than it was a few decades ago. Some doctors think the condition is caused by other medical problems and is not a disorder in and of itself. Others think that idiopathic hypoglycemia is actually an early stage of diabetes.

SYMPTOMS

Symptoms differ somewhat depending on the type of hypoglycemia that occurs. In the case of drug-induced hypoglycemia, the symptoms may resemble those of extreme shock. They include:

- Cold, pale skin
- Numbness around the mouth
- Anxiety
- Palpitations (irregular heartbeat)

- Emotional outbursts
- Hand tremors (shaking)
- Mental confusion
- Dilated (enlarged) pupils
- Sweating
- Fainting

Idiopathic hypoglycemia is often characterized by milder symptoms, such as:

- Extreme tiredness
- Loss of alertness
- Loss of muscular strength and coordination
- Headache
- Double vision
- Staggering or inability to walk
- A craving for salt or sweets
- Allergies
- Ringing in the ears
- Inflammation of the skin
- Pain in the neck and shoulders
- Memory problems
- Excessive sweating

DIAGNOSIS

Hypoglycemia can be difficult to diagnose. Its symptoms may change over time. Patients seldom have all or even most of the symptoms listed above. Also, the symptoms of hypoglycemia are similar to those seen in other disorders.

The first step in diagnosis, therefore, is to rule out other possible causes for a patient's symptoms. Even then, the patient may have two or more problems at the same time, only one of which is hypoglycemia.

Drug-induced Hypoglycemia

Patients with drug-induced hypoglycemia have already been diagnosed with a blood-sugar problem. They may already be taking insulin to control their disorder. Or they may be aware of the need for following a certain diet. These patients can usually diagnose their own episodes of hypoglycemia. They can carry with them a simple machine known as a glucometer. They can take a small sample of their blood and test it in the glucometer. If their blood glucose level is too low, the patient can raise it by eating a small amount of sugar.

Idiopathic Hypoglycemia

A standard test for idiopathic hypoglycemia is called an extended oral glucose tolerance test. The patient is instructed to fast (not eat any food) overnight. The patient then drinks a solution of glucose in water. His or her blood is then tested every hour for five to six hours. The results of this test indicate the patient's ability to metabolize glucose.

HYPOGLYCEMICS SHOULD AVOID SIMPLE SUGARS, ALCOHOL, FATS, AND FRUIT JUICE.

TREATMENT

The fastest treatment for hypoglycemia is to have the patient eat some sugar. A piece of candy or some fruit juice will usually raise blood sugar quickly. Special glucose tablets or injections (shots) of glucose can also be used.

Long-term treatment of hypoglycemia requires changes in a person's diet. The usual recommendation is for a person to eat small but frequent meals throughout the day. They should avoid simple sugars, alcohol, fats, and fruit juice.

Alternative Treatment

Some homeopathic practitioners believe that hypoglycemia may be caused by a number of factors. They recommend a variety of treatments that may include acupuncture and herbal remedies. One suggested drink is made by boiling gentian (an herb) in water. Some practitioners also recommend adding chromium to the diet. Chromium is thought by some practitioners to help stabilize blood-sugar levels. Chromium is found in whole-grain breads and cereals, cheeses, molasses, lean meats, and brewer's yeast.

PROGNOSIS

All forms of hypoglycemia can usually be controlled by following a well-planned diet. In addition, diabetics can often control drug-induced episodes of hypoglycemia by monitoring their blood glucose levels.

PREVENTION

Methods of prevention vary depending on the cause of the hypoglycemia.

Drug-induced Hypoglycemia

The first step in preventing drug-induced hypoglycemia is to maintain a proper diet. Diabetics may also find it necessary to monitor their blood-sugar levels on a regular basis. Low blood-sugar levels indicate that a person should immediately eat candy or some other sweet snack. Insulin pumps are also effective in maintaining the proper level of blood sugar. These pumps can be implanted under the skin and programmed to continuously release the correct amount of insulin.

Idiopathic Hypoglycemia

Idiopathic hypoglycemia can usually be controlled by learning and following certain dietary rules. These rules include the following:

- Avoid overeating.
- Never skip breakfast.
- Include protein in all meals and snacks.
- Limit intake of fats, refined sugar, and processed foods.
- Become familiar with the sugar content in different kinds of vegetables and grain products.
- Keep a food diary that can be used to predict which foods produce the symptoms of hypoglycemia.
- Eat a regular but limited amount of fresh fruits.
- Follow a diet that is high in fiber.

FOR MORE INFORMATION

Books

Budd, Martin. *Low Blood Sugar: Coping With Low Blood Sugar.* London: Thorsons Publications, 1998.

Eades, Michael R., and Mary Dan. *Protein Power.* New York: Bantam Books, 1995.

Krimmel, Patricia, and Edward Krimmel. *The Low Blood Sugar Handbook.* Bryn Mawr, PA: Franklin Publishers, 1992.

Ruggiero, Roberta. *The Do's and Dont's of Low Blood Sugar.* Hollywood, FL: Frederick Fell Publishers, 1988.

Organizations

Hypoglycemia Association, Inc. 1808 New Hampshire Ave., P.O. Box 165, Ashton, MD 20861–0165.

National Hypoglycemia Association, Inc. PO Box 120, Ridgewood, NJ 07451. (201) 670–1189.

HYPOTHERMIA

DEFINITION

Hypothermia (pronounced hi-po-ther-mee-ah) occurs when the body temperature falls below 95°F (35°C). The condition is often fatal.

DESCRIPTION

People who live in cold climates are obviously at risk for hypothermia. They may be stranded out of doors overnight without protection from the cold. Their body temperatures may drop so low that they develop hypothermia. Eventually, they may freeze to death.

Hypothermia also occurs in more moderate climates during cold weather. The problem is more likely to occur among elderly and homeless people. Elderly people may not remember to keep their homes heated properly. Or they may be too poor to pay their heating bills. Their homes may remain at a constant temperature of 50° to 65°F (10° to 17°C). A continuous exposure to this temperature can cause hypothermia.

Homeless people may have to spend most of their lives out of doors. In cold weather, their body temperatures may drop to dangerously low levels. Official records indicate that nearly twelve thousand homeless people died of hypothermia between 1979 and 1994. However, these numbers are probably not accurate. Many deaths of homeless people from hypothermia probably go unreported.

Males, non-whites, and alcoholics are at high risk for hypothermia. These groups make up a large fraction of the homeless population.

CAUSES

The human body functions normally over a very narrow range of temperatures. If body temperature goes higher than about 100°F (38°C) or lower than about 97°F (36°C), problems develop. The chemical changes that take place in cells begin to occur either too rapidly or too slowly. At low temperatures, those chemical changes may slow down so much that the body ceases to function entirely. That condition is known as hypothermia.

WORDS TO KNOW

Electrocardiogram: A test used to determine the electrical activity of the heart to see if it is functioning normally.

Frostbite: A medical condition in which some part of the body has become frozen.

Malnutrition: A condition in which a person is not eating enough of the right kinds of foods.

Stroke: A serious medical condition caused by a loss of blood flow to the brain.

Thyroid: An organ that controls a number of important bodily functions.

Hypothermia is divided into two types: primary and secondary. Primary hypothermia occurs when the body's heat-balancing mechanisms are working properly but the body is subjected to extremely cold conditions. For example, a person might fall into an icy lake. The conditions are so cold that hypothermia develops in spite of the otherwise healthy body.

In secondary hypothermia, the body's heat-balancing mechanisms are not working properly. Hypothermia may develop even if a person is exposed to even mildly cold conditions. Some conditions that can cause secondary hypothermia are stroke (see stroke entry), diabetes (see diabetes mellitus entry), malnutrition, bacterial infection, thyroid condition, spinal cord injury (see spinal cord injury entry), and the use of certain medications and other substances. Alcohol is one such substance. It can interfere with portions of the heat-balancing system. A person may not recognize when he or she is becoming dangerously cooled.

Secondary hypothermia is often a threat to the elderly. They are likely to be on medications or suffering from some medical condition that can cause secondary hypothermia. Elderly people sometimes keep their homes cool to save money on heating costs. They may develop hypothermia even if the temperature is no colder than 60°F (15.5°C).

SYMPTOMS

The signs and symptoms of hypothermia follow a typical course. Though the body temperature at which they occur vary from person to person depending on age, health, and other factors.

Some of the first signs of hypothermia may be lack of coordination, cold and pale skin, and intense shivering. As body temperature begins to fall, speech becomes slurred, muscles go rigid, vision problems develop, and the patient becomes disoriented.

At body temperatures below 90°F (32°C), heart rate, respiratory (breathing) rate, and blood pressure fall. Eventually the patient loses consciousness and may appear to be dead. At even very low temperatures, however, a person may survive for several hours. They can sometimes be successfully revived.

DIAGNOSIS

The situation in which a person is found is often an important clue to diagnosis. Someone pulled from a lake in the middle of winter, for example, is likely to be suffering from hypothermia. Pulse, blood pressure, temperature, and respiration should be checked immediately and monitored. Oral (mouth) temperatures are often not accurate at cold temperatures. Instead, the temperature is taken at some other part of the body, such as in the ear or rectum.

A doctor might use an electrocardiogram (ECG; pronounced ih-LEK-tro-car-DEE-uh-gram; it measure electrical activity of the heart to make sure it is functioning normally) to get information on the functioning of the patient's heart. Blood and urine tests may also be ordered to see how well body functions are operating.

TREATMENT

A person with hypothermia requires immediate medical attention. First aid for such patients is not as obvious as it may seem, however. For example, rubbing the patient's skin or giving him or her a drink of alcohol can be dangerous. Also, the patient should be checked for signs of frostbite (see frostbite entry). Attempting to warm a frostbitten area can be very dangerous.

The first step is to move the patient to a warm, dry location. Gentle handling is necessary to void disturbing the heart. Giving the patient a warm drink can be helpful if he or she can swallow.

Once a patient has reached the hospital, the warming procedure depends on the seriousness of the patient's condition. The stage of hypothermia is defined by the patient's body temperature. The three stages of hypothermia and the temperatures at which they occur are as follows:

- Mild hypothermia: 90° to 95°F (32° to 35°C)
- Moderate hypothermia: 86° to 90°F (30° to 32°C)
- Severe hypothermia: less than 86°F (30°C)

Mild hypothermia is treated with passive rewarming. That is, the patient's body is allowed to come back to its normal temperature on its own. Wet clothing is removed and the patient is covered with blankets and placed in a warm room.

Moderate hypothermia is first treated with active rewarming. That is, the patient is wrapped in an electric heating blanket or placed in a warm bath. As his or her temperature begins to rise, these aids are removed. The body is allowed to return to its normal temperature on its own.

Severe hypothermia usually requires internal rewarming. Some method is needed to start warming the patient's internal organs and tissues. For example, patients may be provided with warm oxygen to breathe. Or they may be given warm fluids to drink. In extreme cases, a procedure known as a cardiopulmonary bypass may be used. In this procedure, a tube is inserted into the patient's blood vessels. Blood is directed out of the body and through an external machine. The external machine warms up the blood. The blood is then returned to the body. This treatment is not available in all hospitals.

PROGNOSIS

People who experience mild or moderate hypothermia usually enjoy a complete recovery. The prognosis for people who experience severe hypothermia is less certain. Recovery depends on a number of factors, such as the person's own body chemistry and how soon treatment was provided.

PREVENTION

Hypothermia can be prevented by following some simple rules. First, people who have to spend time outdoors in cold weather should wear adequate clothing. Head covering is especially important since 30 to 50 percent of body heat is lost through the head. Clothing should also be kept as dry as possible. Water absorbs heat faster than air, so wet clothes cause body temperature to drop quickly. Alcoholic beverages should be avoided also. Alcohol causes blood vessels to expand, causing the body to lose heat faster.

For a number of reasons, hypothermia is a special problem among elderly people. They may be subject to a variety of medical problems that make them more sensitive to cold temperatures. The medications they take may also make them more subject to hypothermia. Elderly people sometimes forget to take necessary precautions against chills, such as keeping the house warm enough and getting adequate meals.

Friends and neighbors can play an important role in preventing the elderly from developing hypothermia. They can check up on older relatives and friends to make sure that they continue to take necessary precautions against hypothermia.

The best method for preventing hypothermia is to wear appropriate clothing in cold temperatures. (© Jeff Greenberg. Reproduced by permission of Photo Researchers, Inc.)

FOR MORE INFORMATION

Forgey, William W. *The Basic Essentials of Hypothermia.* Guilford, CT: Globe, Pequot Press, 1999.

Hall, Christine B. *Cold Can Kill: Hypothermia.* University of Alaska Sea Grant, 1994.

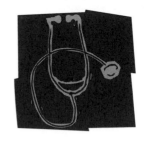

Where to Learn More

BOOKS

Abel, Ernest L. *America's 25 Top Killers*. Hillside, NJ: Enslow, 1991.

American Heart Association. *Living Well, Staying Well*. New York: American Heart Association and American Cancer Association, 1996.

Atkinson, David R., and Debbie Atkinson. *Hope Springs Eternal: Surviving a Chronic Disease*. Virginia Beach, VA: Are Press, 1999.

Bellenir, Karen, and Peter D. Dresser, eds. *Contagious and Non-contagious Infectious Diseases Sourcebook*. Detroit: Omnigraphics, Inc., 1996.

The Burton Goldberg Group. *Alternative Medicine: The Definitive Guide*. Puyallup, WA: Future Medicine Publishing, 1993.

Ciesielski, Paula F. *Major Chronic Diseases*. Guilford, CT: The Dushkin Publishing Group, 1992.

Daly, Stephen, ed. *Everything You Need to Know about Medical Treatments*. Springhouse, PA: Springhouse Corp., 1996.

Darling, David. *The Health Revolution: Surgery and Medicine in the Twenty-first Century*. Parsippany, NJ: Dillon Press, 1996.

Graham, Ian. *Fighting Disease*. Austin, TX: Raintree Steck-Vaughn, 1995.

Horn, Robert, III. *How Will They Know If I'm Dead? Transcending Disability and Terminal Illness*. Boca Raton, FL: Saint Lucie Press, 1996.

Hyde, Margaret O., and Elizabeth H. Forsyth, M.D. *The Disease Book: A Kid's Guide*. New York: Walker and Company, 1997.

Isler, Charlotte, R.N., and Alwyn T. Cohall, M.D. *The Watts Teen Health Dictionary*. New York: Franklin Watts, 1996.

The Johns Hopkins Medical Handbook: The 100 Major Medical Disorders of People over the Age of 50. *New York: Rebus, Inc., 1995.*

Long, James W. *The Essential Guide to Chronic Illness*. New York: Harper Perennial, 1997.

Roman, Peter. *Can You Get Warts from Touching Toads? Ask Dr. Pete*. New York: Julian Messner, 1986.

Shaw, Michael, ed. *Everything You Need to Know about Diseases*. Springhouse, PA: Springhouse Corp., 1996.

Stoffman, Phyllis. *The Family Guide to Preventing and Treating 100 Infectious Illnesses*. New York: John Wiley & Sons, 1995.

Weil, A. *Natural Health, Natural Medicine: A Comprehensive Manual for Wellness and Self-Care*. Boston: Houghton Mifflin, 1995.

WEB SITES

Centers for Disease Control and Prevention. http://www.cdc.gov

The Children's Health Center. http://www.mediconsult.com/mc/mcsite.nsf/conditionnav/kids~sectionintroduction

Healthfinder®. http://www.healthfinder.gov

InteliHealth: Home to Johns Hopkins Health Information. http://www.intelihealth.com

Mayo Clinic Health Oasis. http://mayohealth.org

National Institutes of Health. http://www.nih.gov

NOAH: New York Online Access to Health. http://www.noah.cuny.edu

WHO/OMS: World Health Organization. http://www.who.int

U.S. National Library of Medicine: Health Information. http://nlm.nih.gov/hinfo.html

ORGANIZATIONS

Centers for Disease Control and Prevention. 1600 Clifton Rd., NE, Atlanta, GA 30333. (404)639–3311. http://www.cdc.gov

National Institutes of Health (NIH). Bethesda, MD 20892. (301)496–1776. http:www.nih.gov

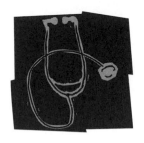

Index

Italic type indictes volume numbers; **boldface** type indicates entries and their page numbers; (ill.) indicates illustrations.